Home Networking
THE MISSING MANUAL

Scott Lowe

POGUE PRESS™
O'REILLY®

Beijing · Cambridge · Farnham · Köln · Paris · Sebastopol · Taipei · Tokyo

Home Networking: The Missing Manual
by Scott Lowe

Copyright © 2005 O'Reilly Media, Inc. All rights reserved.
Printed in the United States of America.

Published by O'Reilly Media, Inc., 1005 Gravenstein Highway North, Sebastopol, CA 95472.

O'Reilly books may be purchased for educational, business, or sales promotional use. Online editions are also available for most titles (*safari.oreilly.com*). For more information, contact our corporate/institutional sales department: (800) 998-9938 or *corporate@oreilly.com*.

Editor:	Peter Meyers
Production Editor:	Jamie Peppard
Cover Designer:	Ellie Volckhausen
Interior Designer:	David Futato

Printing History:

July 2005:	First Edition.

Nutshell Handbook, the Nutshell Handbook logo, and the O'Reilly logo are registered trademarks of O'Reilly Media, Inc. *Home Networking: The Missing Manual*, The Missing Manual logo, Pogue Press, the Pogue Press logo, and "The book that should have been in the box" are trademarks of O'Reilly Media, Inc.

The images on page 2 appear courtesy of Linksys.

Many of the designations used by manufacturers and sellers to distinguish their products are claimed as trademarks. Where those designations appear in this book, and O'Reilly Media, Inc. was aware of a trademark claim, the designations have been printed in caps or initial caps.

While every precaution has been taken in the preparation of this book, the publisher and author assume no responsibility for errors or omissions, or for damages resulting from the use of the information contained herein.

 This book uses RepKover™, a durable and flexible lay-flat binding.

ISBN: 0-596-00558-X
[M]

Table of Contents

The Missing Credits

About the Author

 Scott Lowe is a technology professional by day and a writer by night. With 11 years of professional technology experience under his belt, Scott has also written more than 250 technology related articles for CNET's *TechRepublic* (*www.techrepublic.com*). By day, Scott is the IT Director for Elmira College, a private liberal arts college smack in the Finger Lakes region of beautiful upstate New York. Fortunately for him, his staff is awesome and makes his job quite enjoyable.

When not working or writing, Scott spends as much time as possible with his family: his wife, Amy, his son, Ryan, and his daughter, Isabella, as well as the family's 12 cats. For more about Scott, head to *www.slowe.com*.

About the Creative Team

Peter Meyers (editor) is an editor at O'Reilly Media, where he works on the Missing Manual series. He lives with his wife and cat in New York City. Email: *peter.meyers@gmail.com*.

J.D. Biersdorfer (editor) is the author of *iPod & iTunes: The Missing Manual* and writes the weekly technology Q&A column in *The New York Times*. She has a degree in theater from Indiana University and was last seen on Broadway hailing a cab. E-mail: *jdbiersdorfer@mac.com*.

Greg Dickerson (tech reviewer) is a systems administrator at O'Reilly. During his time at O'Reilly he has helped tech review several titles and was the QA lead for O'Reilly's Deluxe CD Bookshelf's product line.

Chris Stone (tech reviewer) is a senior systems administrator (the Mac guy) at O'Reilly Media, Inc. He's contributed to *Mac OS X: The Missing Manual, Panther Edition* published by Pogue Press/O'Reilly, and is co-author of *Mac OS X Panther in a Nutshell,* also published by O'Reilly.

Jamie Peppard (production editor) has worked in a variety of technology-related publishing roles.

Linley Dolby (copy editor) spent several years in the production department at O'Reilly before moving to Martha's Vineyard to pursue a freelance career. She now helps whip technical books into shape for several companies, including O'Reilly and Pogue Press. Email: *linley@gremlinley.com*.

Rose Cassano (cover illustration) has worked as an independent designer and illustrator for twenty years. Assignments have ranged from the nonprofit sector to corporate clientele. She lives in beautiful Southern Oregon, grateful for the miracles of modern technology that make working there a reality. Email: *cassano@uci.net*. Web: *www.rosecassano.com*.

Acknowledgements

The entire success of this book, my other writing, and with life in general, lies squarely in the lap of my wife, Amy, who I was fortunate to find and marry, and with whom I share the role of "parent" to two beautiful children (Ryan and Isabella), both born while this book was being written. Special thanks go also to my former employer, the National Association of Attorneys General, and my current employer, Elmira College, for their flexibility while I undertook this endeavor.

The Missing Manual Series

Missing Manuals are witty, superbly written guides to computer products that don't come with printed manuals (which is just about all of them). Each book features a handcrafted index; cross-references to specific page numbers (not just "see Chapter 14"); and RepKover, a detached-spine binding that lets the book lie perfectly flat without the assistance of weights or cinder blocks.

Recent and upcoming titles include:

Mac OS X: The Missing Manual (Panther and Tiger editions) by David Pogue

Excel: The Missing Manual by Matthew MacDonald

iPhoto 5: The Missing Manual by David Pogue

iLife '05: The Missing Manual by David Pogue

GarageBand: The Missing Manual by David Pogue

iMovie 5 & iDVD: The Missing Manual by David Pogue

Google: The Missing Manual by Sarah Milstein and Rael Dornfest

Switching to the Mac: The Missing Manual by David Pogue

Mac OS X Power Hound, Panther Edition by Rob Griffiths

Dreamweaver MX 2004: The Missing Manual by David Sawyer McFarland

Office X for Macintosh: The Missing Manual by Nan Barber, Tonya Engst, and David Reynolds

Office 2004 for Macintosh: The Missing Manual by Mark H. Walker and Franklin Tessler

AppleWorks 6: The Missing Manual by Jim Elferdink and David Reynolds

Windows XP Home Edition: The Missing Manual by David Pogue

Windows XP Pro: The Missing Manual by David Pogue, Craig Zacker, and Linda Zacker

Applescript: The Missing Manual by Adam Goldstein

Photoshop Elements 3: The Missing Manual by Barbara Brundage

QuickBooks 2005: The Missing Manual by Bonnie Biafore

eBay: The Missing Manual by Nancy Conner

FrontPage: The Missing Manual by Jessica Mantaro

Introduction

A decade ago, the Internet took off, thanks to a number of happy coincidences: PCs were cheaper and easier to use than ever; computer scientists developed an easy way to share information over the Internet (the Web); and some guy figured out how the Web could be used to help trade his girlfriend's Pez dispensers (eBay). The rest, as they say, is history.

Home networking today is undergoing similar growth, albeit on a slightly smaller scale. Thanks to computer prices dropping even further (many homes now have multiple PCs), operating systems that have built-in networking capabilities (true for both Windows and the Mac OS), and a growing number of devices such as printers, stereos, and game consoles that are ready to network, more and more people are coming to the tantalizing, yet potentially hair-pulling conclusion: "Hey, maybe it's time for me to set up a home network."

The next step usually involves a quick peek at the Sunday paper's networking gear ads or a visit to the local electronics store. Exit enthusiasm, enter fear. Not only are the gadgets confusingly and intimidatingly named (802.11g Wireless Cable/DSL Router with Built-in 4-port Switch, anyone?), there are precious few people in the world who understand how this stuff works *and* who are capable of explaining what mainstream civilians need in their homes.

That's where *Home Networking: The Missing Manual* comes in. Using clear, jargon-free language, this book helps you understand what kind of gear you need for your home network, how to set things up, and how to use that network once it's up and running.

What Can You Do with a Home Network?

Most people first think about setting up a network so that everyone at home can get online at the same time. And given the rapidly falling prices of networking gear today—an inexpensive basic network can be put together for less than 50 dollars—that's a worthwhile reason to get connected. But Internet connection sharing is only the first among many things you'll learn how to do once you've laid down your links:

- **Go wireless.** Networking's been possible for years, but only recently has it gone wireless (or *WiFi*, as you've probably heard it called). Chapter 3 shows you how easy it is to get unplugged.

- **Extend your network to the far corners of your house.** You don't need to live in a mansion to run into one of the most basic challenges known to networking-kind: how to extend your network into those hard-to-reach corners of your home. Learn how WiFi (Chapter 3) and the powerlines (Chapter 4) currently running through your walls can help solve the problem.

- **Share your files.** Gone are the days when moving a file from one computer to another meant carting it around on a disk. With a home network, you can zap anything—Word documents, MP3 files, digital photos, and so on—across your network (Chapters 5, 6, and 7 show you how). And you can do it all in a way that's quite a bit easier than that ol' "Honey, can you email to my computer the 84 photos we took last weekend?"

- **Print across the network.** Having multiple computers doesn't mean you also need to have multiple printers. Home networks make it easy to set up your printers so that everyone—Mac and PC fans alike—can use any printer attached to any computer (Chapters 5, 6, and 7).

- **Share storage space.** Once you've gotten the hang of digital photography, MP3-collecting, or PowerPoint production, it doesn't take long to to run out of room on your computer. Networks are a great way to take advantage of unused space on all the computers in your home (Chapter 8).

- **Protecting your files.** Sharing's great, but that doesn't necessarily mean everyone in the house should have access to all of each other's files. Fortunately, both Windows machines and Macs give you the tools to limit who gets to see what (Chapters 5 and 6).

- **Communicate between PCs and Macs.** Thanks to some major strides on the part of both Microsoft and Apple, mixed operating system networking has never been easier (Chapter 7).

Note: Got an older version of Windows or the Mac OS? No problem. In addition to Windows XP and Mac OS X, this book covers Windows 95, 98, Me, and 2000, as well as Mac OS 9.

- **Hook up your game consoles to the network.** Sure, video games are fun, but you can get bored playing against your system. Plug your Xbox or PlayStation2 into your home network, and soon you'll be fighting the good fight with millions of people around the world (Chapter 8).

- **Display digital pictures on your TV.** Your digital photo collection doesn't have to suffer the fate of its ancestors: confined to shoeboxes and rarely opened albums. With not much effort, you can use your network to premier all your photos on your television (Chapter 8).

- **Play your PC's music on your stereo.** Bored by your computer's creaky little built-in speakers? Ready to use your stereo to listen to all those Aretha Franklin tunes you've got stored on your PC? Your home network is ready and willing (Chapter 8).

- **Tap into your network when you're on the road.** Or tap into your office network while you're at home. Either way, once you've got a network, these kinds of remote access chores are possible (Chapter 9).

About This Book

This book is broken down into two main parts: Part One covers planning, buying, and setting up your network. The four chapters in this part help you decide what kind of network makes sense for your home; how to pick out the right gear; and how to get everything plugged in and running. By the end of Part One, all the computers in your home can tap into and share a nice, juicy Internet connection.

Part Two covers the things you can actually *do* on your network once it's working, including exchanging files between computers, connecting your PCs to your stereo, and tapping into your network when you're on the road. Here's a quick rundown of what you'll find in each chapter.

Note: Throughout this book you'll see that the setup instructions mention high-speed Internet connections (like cable modem service or DSL), rather than plain old dial-up links. Does that mean that if you've got a dial-up Internet connection you can't use this book? No, but frankly many of the scenarios described in this book will be painfully slow if you try to carry them out with a dial-up connection. So home networking works for everybody, but it's a lot more fun if you've got a fast Internet connection.

Part One

Chapter 1 introduces you to the major types of home networks in use today: wired, wireless, and wired through your electrical system. You'll learn the pros and cons of each network type so you can pick the one that's right for you and your home.

After reading Chapter 1, if you decide you're ready for a traditional wired Ethernet network (the kind with those thick plastic cables that you probably have in your office), you can go right to Chapter 2, which tells you everything you need to know about setting up an Ethernet network.

Want to minimize the cables in your life and have the freedom to roam the house surfing the Web as you follow your toddler around? You may have heard of *WiFi* (short for "Wireless Fidelity"), the networking technology that beams your data around the house over radio waves instead of through plastic-coated cables. There are several types of WiFi to choose from, and Chapter 3 explains what they are so you can decide which version makes sense for you. The chapter also includes a section on wireless-network security so you can learn how to protect your network airspace from those who may try to horn in.

Like the notion of wireless but have trouble connecting the network down to the basement office? As explained in Chapter 4, *Powerline* devices can convert your home's electrical system into a data network. Powerline is an up-and-coming technology that you may not have heard much about. You'll learn how Powerline works and what you'll need to get plugged in.

Part Two

Once you've installed your home network, Part Two helps you put the network to work. In Chapter 5, you'll learn how to share files, folders, and printers among computers running all modern versions of the Windows operating system.

If you have a house full of Macintosh machines, Chapter 6 is for you. It shows you how to configure your Mac OS X computers, as well as those running the older version of Apple's operating system: good ol' Mac OS 9.

It's a cross-platform world out there, though, and if you happen to have a mix of Windows PCs and Macs in your house, Chapter 7 shows you how to get the two systems talking to each other.

Chapter 8 is where the real fun begins—if you consider streaming music around the house, playing network video games, and putting your digital photos on the big screen fun. And because we all have to leave the house sometimes, Chapter 9 tells you how to connect to your home network when you're on the road.

About → These → Arrows

Throughout this book, and throughout the Missing Manual series, you'll find sentences like this: "Open the Start → My Computer → Local Disk (C:) → Windows folder." That's shorthand for a much longer instruction that directs you to open three nested icons in sequence, like this: "Click the Start menu to open it. Click My Computer in the Start menu. Inside the My Computer window is a disk icon labeled Local Disk (C:); double-click it to open it. Inside *that* window is yet another icon called Windows. Double-click to open it, too."

Similarly, this kind of arrow shorthand helps to simplify the business of choosing commands in menus, as shown in Figure P-1.

About MissingManuals.com

At the *www.missingmanuals.com* Web site, you'll find articles, tips, and updates to the book. In fact, you're invited and encouraged to submit such corrections and updates yourself. In an effort to keep the book as up-to-date and accurate as possible, each time we print more copies of this book, we'll make any confirmed corrections you've suggested. We'll also note such changes on the Web site, so that you can mark important corrections into your own copy of the book, if you like. (Click the book's name and then click the Errata link to see the changes.)

In the meantime, we'd love to hear your own suggestions for new books in the Missing Manual line. There's a place for that on the Web site, too, as well as a place to sign up for free email notification of new titles in the series.

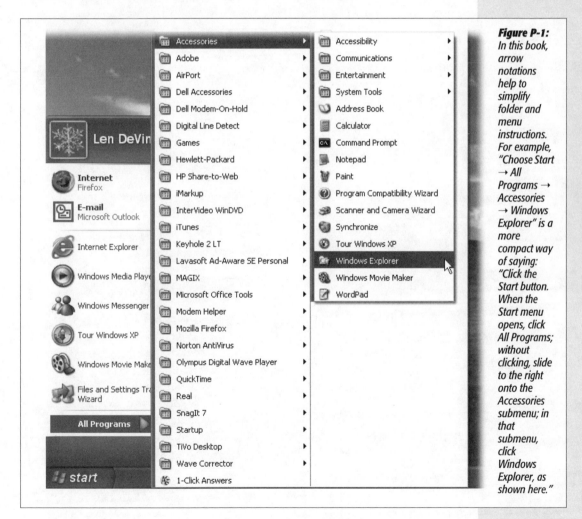

Figure P-1:
In this book, arrow notations help to simplify folder and menu instructions. For example, "Choose Start → All Programs → Accessories → Windows Explorer" is a more compact way of saying: "Click the Start button. When the Start menu opens, click All Programs; without clicking, slide to the right onto the Accessories submenu; in that submenu, click Windows Explorer, as shown here."

Safari Enabled

 When you see a Safari® Enabled icon on the cover of your favorite technology book, that means the book is available online through the O'Reilly Network Safari Bookshelf.

Safari offers a solution that's better than eBooks. It's a virtual library that lets you easily search thousands of top tech books, cut and paste code samples, download chapters, and find quick answers when you need the most accurate, current information. Try it free at *http://safari.oreilly.com*.

Part One:
Setting Up Your
Network

1

Planning Your Home Network

Sure, there are a heck of a lot of products in the networking aisle down at Big Giant Computer Store, but don't be overwhelmed. Planning a home network is a lot like picking the types of telephones you need when you're moving into a new home: you can choose between old-fashioned landlines and snazzy wireless cellphones, corded and cordless handsets, speakerphones and headsets. Nowadays, you can even get walkie-talkie features or the ability to make calls over the Internet. But, thankfully, in order to choose from this smorgasbord of options, you don't need to know *anything* about the phone system's underlying technology. You do, however, need to understand some telephone basics, like the fact that you don't need to have a phone jack in every room if you're going to go the cordless phone route.

Home networks are a lot like phones in that you don't need to understand the gory details of how computers talk to each other—but you do need to know what equipment makes sense for your situation. For example, if you want to be able to surf the Web while sitting next to your pool, wireless networking—also known as *WiFi*—will save you from running 30 feet of ugly cable out your back door. But if you've got only two desktop computers in your home office, a small wired network is probably your best bet. This chapter explains the main components of a home network, a few variations on the theme, and how to decide what's best for *you*.

Home Networking Hardware

To set up a home network, you need three things (beside computers, electricity, and a little bit of moxie):

- **A router.** This device distributes your cable or DSL (digital subscriber line) Internet connection to the computers on your network. It's like the clerk at the train station giving everyone on your network a ticket to ride. Figure 1-1 shows a picture of both a wired and wireless router. .

Figure 1-1:
Whether they're wired (top) or wireless (bottom), your network's router keeps the traffic moving along your network and divvies up that high-speed cable or DSL connection, distributing it from your Internet service provider to all the computers connected to your home network.

Routers designed for wired networks typically have jacks on the back so that they can connect (via network cables) to a modem and all the PCs that are on the network. Wireless routers, on the other hand, have jacks to hook up to your broadband modem and maybe one other network device. But wireless routers use invisible radio waves to connect to PCs that are within range.

You connect the router to your cable or DSL modem with a cable, and, depending on the kind of equipment you choose, you connect your individual computers to the router either with cables or using wireless technology.

Note: It's *possible* to set up a home network that doesn't use a router and simply links all your computers to each other to share files. But since one of the biggest reasons to set up a home network is to share a high-speed broadband connection among several computers, the heart of most home networks is the router.

• **Cables or wireless signals.** Whether they're colorful strands of plastic-coated cable (Figure 1-2) or invisible radio waves (not shown, because invisible doesn't photograph so well), these are ways you connect your computers to the network.

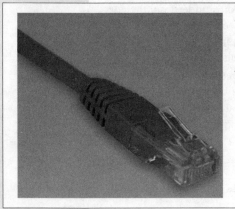

Figure 1-2:
Computer network cable is available in varying lengths and many festive colors from most computer stores. You need one cable for every computer you want to connect to your network. You should also make sure the cable is long enough to reach the router. Chapter 2 tells you everything you need to know about picking out the right type of cable.

- **Network adapters.** This term is really just a fancy name for the jack on the back (or side) of your computer where you'll plug in your cables or exchange wireless signals. You need one of these doodads on all the computers and devices (such as a printer) that you want to add to your network.

Way back in the 1990s, having a computer with a network jack already installed was a rare, beautiful, and expensive thing. These days, network jacks (and sometimes even wireless network adapters) typically come standard on new machines. In fact, you'd be hard pressed today to find *any* computer for sale without a wired network adapter, which is also known as an *Ethernet connection* or *Ethernet port.* Wireless network adapters—usually called *WiFi cards*—are increasingly standard on laptops, and you can add them to any computer (page 42).

There are three kinds of network adapters, as shown in Figure 1-3, each of which connects to a computer in a different way:

- A *Peripheral Component Interconnect (or PCI) card* plugs into the *motherboard* (a circuit board inside the computer). The card endows your computer with a connection jack that peeks outside the PC's case.

- A *USB adapter* plugs into the USB port on any kind of computer and parks itself on the outside of your machine. (See the box "Catching the Universal Serial Bus" on page 7.)

- A *PC card* plugs into a special slot on laptops.

Figure 1-3:
Network adapters for the computer come in all shapes and sizes.

Top: This PCI card plugs into a slot inside the computer and provides one Ethernet jack for connecting a network cable. (You need to open up your computer's case to install one of these.)

Middle: PC cards work with laptop computers. The card plugs right into the PCMCIA slot and supplies an Ethernet jack for a wired network connection. (You can also get similar-looking cards to use with a wireless network.)

Bottom: This USB adapter plugs into the computer's USB port and saves you the trouble of wrestling the machine apart to install a network card. USB adapters can be quite convenient but require the full-time use of one of your computer's USB ports.

Note: If your computer doesn't have a network adapter at all or if you want to install a wireless adapter, take a stroll to page 20.

As if the term "network adapter" weren't geeky enough, the electronics industry also calls these devices *network cards, Network Interface Cards* (or *NIC*), and *Ethernet adapters,* to name a few possibilities—all adding to the swirling mess of nerd words now inside your head. Despite the intimidating names, they're all just jacks for your network cables or receiving points for wireless signals.

That's it. You just need three basic pieces of hardware to build a rollicking network to make everyone in the house incredibly happy. "Okay," you say to yourself. "'Three pieces of hardware' sounds pretty easy."

But what about software?

UP TO SPEED

Making Sense of Routers

A router's main job is to function as the switchboard of your home network, delivering an Internet connection to all the computers in your home and, in turn, relaying any requests these computers make to other computers, either inside the network or out on the Internet. But there are other things a router *can* do.

Like telephone switchboards of old, most of today's routers come equipped with a bunch of connection ports, so plenty of computers can join the network party. But this is possible only because the majority of routers also do the work of another device, known as a *switch*. A switch works like the power strips that people plug into an electrical outlet: it adds a handful of *ports,* or openings, to the router.

The only reason you'd need to buy a separate switch is if you were about to run out of ports on your router: plug a switch into the last remaining port and—presto!—you've got as many new ports as your switch contains.

But what if you want to go wireless? You still need a router but, in addition to ports you can plug computers into, you

need an *access point,* a device that broadcasts a router's Internet signal and makes it available to WiFi-ready computers. As with switches, many manufacturers are putting access-point capability right into their routers.

Finally, a router can have a broadband modem built right in. Such a combo device is usually called a *gateway* or *residential gateway.* Most people get their modems from their Internet service provider, but if you want to cut down on the number of devices stacking up under your desk, consider getting one of these.

In the end, it may be most helpful to think of all these router-type devices like the combo fax/printer machines that weigh down the shelves of most electronics stores today: their basic mission is to print stuff out. But since there are other paper-handling type duties that are similar to printing (such as faxing and copying), manufacturers offer up these all-in-one machines. The same thing is happening in the world of home networking: you definitely need a router, but it's not hard to find one that will also handle other chores.

Home Networking Software

Good news: the software that lets your computers hop onto a network is already part of your operating system! You don't need any other complicated software, just maybe a little program called a *driver,* which is a piece of code that comes with your networking hardware and lets it talk to your computer's operating system.

POWER USERS' CLINIC

Catching the Universal Serial Bus

Many people think that popping off the top of the computer case and installing a network card inside the machine is the only way to get a computer on the Internet. But if the thought of poking around your PC's innards makes you queasy, there's another way to make the connection: the *Universal Serial Bus,* otherwise known as the *USB.*

USB jacks have been standard on PC and Macintosh hardware since the late 1990s. Not only can they connect everything from scanners and printers to external hard drives and force-feedback gaming joysticks, they can also hook you to the network without forcing you to take apart your computer.

As mentioned on page 5, a USB network adapter is all you need. You just pop the adapter into one of your available USB ports, install the software that comes with it, and insert an Ethernet cable into the other end of the adapter.

In a pinch, you can even link a couple PCs together and make a mini-network by stringing a special USB cable called a *USB-to-USB adapter* or a *USB bridge.* This can be helpful if you don't have a network set up yet but want to copy three gigabytes of digital photos from one computer to the other.

USB is available in two versions, USB 1.1 and the newer USB 2.0, which is much faster, and especially useful when you hook things like iPods to your computer, because you can quickly copy over 20 gigabytes of music files. Most new computers these days have the USB 2.0 ports, but all USB connections use the same flat, rectangular connector, so you can still use a slower USB 1.1 device in a USB 2.0 port.

Hundreds of devices use a USB connection, and products for USB wireless networking are also available. If the world of USB (and everything you can plug into it) intrigues you, check out the official USB home page at *www.usb.org* for info on how to do cool stuff with what's available now, and also what's coming up next.

As far as networks are concerned, all operating systems are created equal. Your network can play host to computers running just about any operating system out there—Windows, Macintosh, Linux, DOS, you name it. But like the pigs in *Animal Farm,* some operating systems are more equal than others.

Sleek and modern, Windows XP and Mac OS X are particularly good for home networkers, because they're both designed to run multiple *accounts* and they're compatible with all WiFi equipment. (The term "accounts" here has nothing to do with banking; computer systems like Windows XP and Mac OS X allow each person using the machine to create his own *user account* with a separate name, password, settings, and files, for both security and aesthetic reasons. Chapters 5 and 6

---

tell you everything you need to know about accounts.) If your computers are running older versions of Windows or the Mac OS, you can still, of course, join the network party, but you'll have a little more setup work to do. Throughout this book, you'll find specific tips and instructions relevant to *all* flavors of Windows and the Mac OS.

POWER USERS' CLINIC

Hardcore Hardware: Firewalls and VPNs

Every network needs a router, network adapters, and cabling or wireless signals. But some people need extra protection for their network—either to keep the bad guys out or to provide secure access back to the network's goodies from on the road. A *firewall* lets you batten down the virtual hatches by keeping unwanted Internet fiends off your home network and from tippy-toeing through the personal data on your PC.

If you travel frequently and want to tap into your network back home, consider a *Virtual Private Network,* also known as a *VPN.* The VPN wraps all the incoming and outgoing network traffic within an encrypted container, sort of like those pneumatic tubes that safely carry your paycheck and deposit slip to the teller at the bank's drive-up window.

Firewall

If you live in a townhouse or condominium, you probably have a fortified wall called a *firewall* between you and your neighbor to prevent the spread of fire. Corporate networks use hardware and software of the same name designed to prevent hackers (the fire) from gaining access to the corporate network (the townhouse) via the Internet (the hacker's evil townhouse next door).

With the increasing use of residential high-speed Internet connections, home computers are becoming a favorite target for hackers. Even worse, with the "always on" nature of broadband connections, your unprotected computers and your network are at risk even when you're not using the Internet.

By virtue of the fact that they come between your home network and the Internet, most basic routers help protect your network from outsiders. However, some advanced routers include full firewall capability. While a standard router simply forwards appropriate information to and from the Internet, one with a firewall is like a big burly bouncer, keeping intruders out of your personal club. Rather than just forwarding information, the firewall actually verifies that the information being passed on is safe for consumption. A firewall-enabled router won't forward any information from the Internet that you don't specifically request.

Routers with built-in firewalls will be clearly labeled, so keep an eye out if you think you'll want this extra security for your home network.

VPN router

If you're setting up a small network at your business and want to enable folks outside the office, such as traveling sales people or telecommuters, to access your network's resources (like the company sales calendar, personal email, or other files), you may want to consider setting up a VPN.

A VPN provides a secure "tunnel" into your network so that your data can travel without being spied on by little weasel eyes along the way.

Many routers come with VPN capability, which is useful for two reasons. First, it lets you allow designated colleagues to securely connect to your network. Second, you can generally configure the VPN-equipped router to permanently connect to a remote network, which means all of the computers on your own home network can seamlessly use the stuff over there on that far-away network.

Note: If you're an all-Microsoft house (using Windows XP, Windows 98, Windows ME, or Windows 2000), you'll find Windows specifics in Chapter 5. Mac mavens will be interested in Chapter 6. And if you've got computers running a mix of Windows and Mac OS X, Chapter 7 walks you through this sort of cross-platform setup.

But before you dash off to Computer Cathedral to buy your network's goods, you first need to decide whether you need a network that's wired, wireless, or both. That's what the rest of this chapter will help you figure out.

UP TO SPEED

A Bit about Bits

A bit isn't a huge amount of food; it's a unit of measure that gauges a network's speed. Specifically, it represents the amount of information transmitted each second over a network. Engineers rate networks and modems by the amount of data they can transfer per second and use the abbreviations *Mbps* and *Kbps,* which stand for "megabits per second" and "kilobits per second," respectively. 1,024 kilobits equals one megabit, if you're keeping score at home.

A bit itself is a small chunk of data, eight of which add up to a *byte*. But while amounts of data are measured in *megabytes,* data-transfer speeds (like the time it takes to copy a

10-megabyte file from one computer to another over a network) are measured in *megabits.*

You may not care about data-transfer speeds until you have to sit there and wait for some monster file to download. To give you an idea of the importance of data speeds, consider the average time it takes to transfer a 10-megabyte file (about the size of two songs) over the Internet using an old 56 Kbps dial-up modem versus a 1.5 Mbps DSL line. While the dial-up modem takes 23 minutes and 8 seconds to transfer the file, the high-speed DSL modem takes a mere 50 seconds to complete the transfer.

Wired Networks

While you may have heard lots about wireless networking, *wired* networks are often the easiest to set up, the cheapest to buy, and the most stable to maintain. Wired networks come in two main flavors:

• **Ethernet** uses cables that look like fat telephone wires. Ethernet is by far the most common type of network in use today because it's fast, cheap, and reliable. *How fast?* It runs anywhere from 10 to 1,000 *megabits per second* (see the box "A Bit about Bits" for detailed information about these data speeds, but for now, just imagine that at 10 Mbps, you could transfer the entire contents of a 40-gigabyte iPod in about 9 hours across your network; with a 1,000 Mbps connection, you'd be done in under 6 minutes). Practically every piece of home-networking equipment in existence includes Ethernet ports. Even wireless networking equipment includes Ethernet capabilities so that you can easily connect it to a wired network. This standardization is particularly important because it makes it a lot easier to mix and match networking technology.

Note: The speed of your Ethernet network depends on your hardware. 100 Mbps is the most common speed today, and 1,000 Mbps, (also called *Gigabit Ethernet*), is gaining popularity. 10 Mbps is going the way of the vinyl record.

The only downside to Ethernet is that if you want to connect computers in more than one room, or if you want the freedom to use your laptop on the sofa or in bed, you have to run unsightly cables to every computer in every room you want to connect to your network. Chapter 2 covers Ethernet in detail.

• **Powerline,** which is also called **HomePlug**, uses your existing electrical lines to carry your network's data. This type of network is even easier to set up than Ethernet, because you don't need to buy and run cables from room to room. To set up a Powerline network you need just a few Powerline adapters (Figure 1-4), which easily connect your computers and your router to your electrical wiring, and come equipped with either Ethernet or USB connections.

The great thing about Powerline networking (unless you live in a yurt or an old New York City apartment) is that you probably have electrical outlets in every room, which makes it easy to extend your network throughout your home.

On the downside, Powerline networks are not as fast as most Ethernet networks. They run at 14 Mbps—still nearly 10 times faster than most broadband Internet connections (see the box on page 12 that explains the difference between your Internet connection speed and your network's internal speed). In addition, Powerline adapters must be plugged directly into the wall, so you can't use an extension cord or most power strips. If all this sounds workable, check out Chapter 4, which covers Powerline networking in detail.

Figure 1-4:
The blocky Powerline Ethernet adapter makes hooking your computer to the network as easy as plugging in a hair dryer. Just plug the adapter into a nearby power outlet and plug one end of a network cable into the jack on the bottom. Connect the other end of the cable to the Ethernet port on your computer, and you'll be surfing the Web in no time.

Wireless Networks

Wired networks have lots of advantages, but they can require enough wiring to reach Mars—and they keep you chained to your nearest network connection. Enter wireless networking, which uses radio signals instead of cables to transmit data. It can be a handy alternative to having your desk chair get tangled in a mass of Ethernet cable spaghetti, and it lets you roam as far as your signals reach, like out under the shade of a tree on a nice summer day. In addition, if you have a laptop that's ready for wireless, you can hop online at an ever-growing number of places—known as *WiFi zones* or *hot spots*—that broadcast Internet signals, like airports, public parks, and trendy coffee shops.

Note: Engineers, when not making up complicated names for things, develop wireless networking technology according to a series of rules. An international association–the Institute of Electrical and Electronics Engineers, known as IEEE (pronounced "eye triple E")–creates those rules, or *standards,* which specify how wireless devices work: what part of the radio spectrum they use and how they talk to each other. "WiFi" refers to the predominant family of wireless standards.

To set up a wireless network, you need a *wireless router* or *base station* (the term Apple prefers), which broadcasts your network traffic (including your Internet connection), over the airwaves. Depending on the type of wireless technology inside, wireless routers usually beam their signals over an area of about 50 to 150 square feet. Any computer with a wireless network adapter (page 42) can join the network. Figure 1-5 shows you how it works.

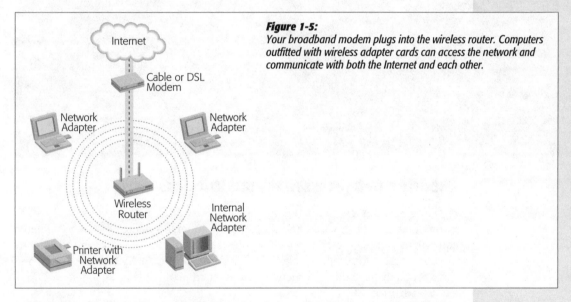

Figure 1-5:
Your broadband modem plugs into the wireless router. Computers outfitted with wireless adapter cards can access the network and communicate with both the Internet and each other.

While WiFi offers terrific convenience, it does have a few disadvantages. It's not as fast as old, wired Ethernet; 54 Mbps is the current speed limit. Configuring the system can be tricky (but Chapter 3 is here to guide you through the process). And interference from other devices that use radio waves, such as cordless phones and microwave ovens, can drag down and diminish the stability of your network.

In fact, radio waves from your *neighbors'* wireless networks can interfere with your system. And physical objects or barriers like pipes or thick walls can also degrade your signal. Finally, while no network is airtight, wireless networks can be especially susceptible to hackers if you don't set up some safeguards. (Page 52 tells you how to dig the virtual moat and pull up the digital drawbridge around Castle Wireless Network)

UP TO SPEED

Up to Speed?

Most people have "the need, the need for speed," but when it comes to home networking, there are two different aspects of speed to clock.

First, there's the speed of your Internet connection. If you have broadband cable or DSL service, your connection speed probably tops out at around 1.5 megabits per second (see that box way back yonder on page 9 if this megabit stuff isn't ringing a bell). Think of this as your *outside* connection, because it's the link between your personal network and the vast world out there on the Internet.

But then there's also the speed of your internal network *inside* the house. This is the rate at which you can transfer files such as Word documents, songs, and movies between the computers connected to your home network.

The internal network speed depends on what type of networking technology you use—and it can run anywhere from 11 Mbps to 1,000 Mbps. (Both wired and wireless networks come in different varieties, all of which have different speeds.)

But regardless of the type of network you choose, you can surf the Web and send email only at the speed of your broadband connection.

If you intend to use your network only for common online tasks like surfing the Web and sending email, then all the available network technologies will meet your needs because they're faster than the Internet connection you already have. But if you want to use your network to stream Hulk-size movie and music files to your wireless home-entertainment center, your internal network speed becomes much more important.

The one rare exception is if you happen to be among the lucky few with a super-speedy Internet connection, such as a T-3 line or a fiber-optic link, which offer speeds from as fast as your typical cable modem to as fast as NASA's super-computers. In these cases, make sure you pick a networking technology that isn't *slower* than your Internet connection.

Choosing Between Wired and Wireless

Deciding between a wired network, a wireless network, or a *hybrid* network—that is, one that uses both wired and wireless components—depends on what type of equipment you plan to connect, how you want to use the network, and the layout of your house. (After all, people living in glamorous, Donald Trump–sized mansions probably have different network needs than people living in 300-square-foot studio apartments.)

It may be obvious to you right off the bat that your house calls for an all-wired or pure wireless network. For instance, if you just moved into a spiffy new condo with Ethernet cabling built into every room and all your computers are desktop models, WiFi may be a waste of money and radio signals. Or, if you're just going to connect a couple of computers that happen to be in the same room, an Ethernet network will work just fine and is quite easy to string up. On the other hand, if you have a killer outdoor deck, and you want to use your laptop to surf the Web while soaking up the rays, WiFi may be your sunniest option.

But if you're not sure whether to go wired or wireless, don't worry: you can experiment and build your network over time. You may even find that a combination of wired and wireless technologies works best for you. For instance, you may discover through trial and plenty of error that the wireless router in your top-floor home office won't reach the kitchen on the ground floor. The solution? Extend your network with Ethernet cables or Powerline, and off you go, browsing those food sites on the Web for the perfect side-dish recipe while you whip up the main course.

To help you figure out what's best for you, this table compares the network types:

	Ethernet	Powerline (HomePlug)	WiFi
Speed	10, 100, or 1,000 Mbps (100 is typical).	Up to 14 Mbps currently. A new standard increases this speed to a much higher level but is not yet available.	Anywhere from 11 to 54 Mbps.
Ease of installation	Single rooms: piece o' cake. Multiple rooms: a bear unless cabling is installed during home construction.	An exercise in simplicity.	Simple. Requires only setting up the router and possibly installing network adapters.
Cabling	Specialized—not found in most houses, but easy to buy in stores.	Electrical cable—multiple jacks in every room of the house. Uses either USB or Ethernet to connect to computer.	Wireless = no wires.
Security	Very secure.	Very secure.	Runs the gamut from somewhat secure all the way down to "more open than Denny's after an all-night party."
How does its future look?	Excellent.	Good.	Excellent.
Cost	Low.	High.	Medium–high.

The next three chapters tell you what you need to know to actually set up a network. If you've decided that you'd like to start with an Ethernet network, head to Chapter 2. If pure wireless is your desire, leaf over to Chapter 3. And if Powerline is most likely to meet your needs, Chapter 4 is the place to go. Each chapter also includes information about setting up hybrid networks.

Creating a Wired Network the Ethernet Way

It may sound like some sort of anesthesia, but Ethernet is the most popular networking technology in the world today. Linking computers together with colorful cables is not a brand-new technology, either. Ethernet was invented back in the early 1970s in that happy bell-bottomed era of macramé vests and early Elton John. Created by Bob Metcalfe at Xerox's Palo Alto Research Center, Ethernet offered a way to let everyone in the building use the first laser printer ever invented—which Xerox PARC also happened to have. (Some things never change: people on computer networks have been trying to make do with one shared printer ever since.) But over the decades, Ethernet has gotten faster, sturdier, and more powerful and remains an excellent choice for a network.

Note: Unless your house is pre-wired for Ethernet, with conveniently placed network jacks in each room, you probably won't want to use Ethernet to string together PCs spread across the far corners of your home. Wiring the innards of a whole house is a bit more than most people are willing to undertake, and stringing Ethernet cable down hallways can get old quickly. Therefore, the examples in this chapter assume that your computers are fairly close to one another—for example, clustered in a home office, or in neighboring rooms within reach of a 30-foot cable.

In this chapter, you'll learn about the hardware that makes Ethernet zoom, and you'll get step-by-step instructions for setting up your very own home Ethernet network. As you get started, it's a good thing to remember that you're not limited to just one type of network technology. For example, there might come a time when you want to add a wireless wing to your Ethernet network. Here and in the next few chapters, you'll find sections on mixing and matching different types of networks. By the end of *this* chapter, all your computers will be linked using Ethernet and will be able to use the Internet.

Ethernet Hardware

Every network needs three basic things:

- **A router** (page 3)
- **Network adapters for the computers**
- **A way to get from A to B** (either cables or radio signals over the airwaves)

This section tells you what you need when you're ready to whip up an Ethernet network. For help picking out the specific devices you need, look for the shopping lists in each section to recap what you should buy and how much you can expect to spend.

The Router

As your network traffic cop and the last stop between all the linked computers inside your house and the rough-and-tumble world of the Internet outside, a reliable Ethernet-ready router is tool number one in your network.

When you're wandering the aisles at Big Giant Computer Store looking for your router, you'll probably be bombarded with boxes bearing confusing terms such as "Cable/DSL Router with 4-port Ethernet Switch." You might see something about "10/100 Ethernet" or "Ethernet/Fast Ethernet" on the box, too.

You'll learn more about switches in a moment, but for now, just know you want your router to have a switch, because switches let a whole bunch of computers plug into the router. (See the box "Making Sense of Routers" on page 6 for a synopsis of the various types of routers you'll see in stores these days.)

Phrases like "10/100" or "Ethernet/Fast Ethernet" describe a router's network speed. The older version of Ethernet, called plain ol' *Ethernet,* has a top speed of 10 megabits per second (enough to, say, beam 600 pages of plain text per second from one computer to another). The newer, speedier, and all-around better version of Ethernet is called *Fast Ethernet.* It has a top speed of 100 megabits per second and can blast through 6,000 pages of plain text per second.

Tip: You don't need to waste any brain cells thinking about those speed distinctions. When you buy a router with a built-in Ethernet switch these days, it'll support both 10 Mbps and 100 Mbps Ethernet.

On the back of the router/switch, you'll see several ports that look like telephone jacks that have been working out at the gym. These wide-style jacks are designed for a plug called an *RJ-45 connector,* shown in Figure 2-1 which is exactly what you'll find on the end of an Ethernet cable.

Note: The prefix "RJ" stands for *Registered Jack,* a designation indicating the plug's official status with the Federal Communications Commission. In comparison, your telephone's smaller wall connector plug also enjoys membership in the Registered Jack club, but it joined up earlier: it's the eleventh one in the series and is called an *RJ-11 connector.*

Standalone switches

A standalone switch is a box the size of a hardcover novel; it lets multiple computers plug into your home network. A standalone switch works exactly like a router with a built-in switch, but the standalone switch doesn't have full router powers, like the ability to connect multiple computers to a single Internet connection. A switch's sole purpose in life is to add more connection ports to a router. Professional geeks sometimes use standalone switches for connecting hordes of devices or a whole business unit's worth of PCs.

Figure 2-1:
Ethernet cables have RJ-45 connectors on both ends so you can connect your computer's network card to your router.

For home networkers, a separate switch isn't usually necessary since router/switch combos generally have enough ports for your needs. But when your octuplets get laptops or your parents move into your house, you might need to add a separate switch to provide additional network connections. In that case, you'll plug your switch into your router. You'll need cables, as you may have suspected, to make this connection. You'll learn all about cables in the next section.

Like routers, switches come in a wide variety of models. You can get a switch with anywhere from 4 to 24 ports (if you have a *really* large family or perhaps a small business), as well as switches that can run at different data-transfer speeds. Almost any switch you buy today runs at speeds of up to 100 Mbps. However, some of the newest switches on the market are capable of an even faster technology called *Gigabit Ethernet* (page 10) that runs at an astounding speed of 1,000 Mbps.

If all you're doing is connecting a bunch of computers to a network so they can share your Internet connection, plunking down the cash for a gigabit switch is a waste of perfectly good money, because you're still going to be hog-tied by the speed of your Internet connection, which is almost always going to get smoked by the speed of your internal network (see "Up to Speed" on page 12 for a refresher on the difference).

Gigabit switches are a great idea, though, if you want to do a lot of stuff *between* connected computers, like streaming a DVD-quality movie over the network or blasting aliens in a round of multiplayer gaming. So if the thought of playing Quake and Doom with a buddy over your home network sounds appealing, check out the items on the standalone switch shopping list in the next section.

For most people, the best option is a 10/100 Ethernet switch built into a router. It'll be fast and robust enough to support your networking needs for a very long time.

Ethernet router and switch shopping list

As of this writing, the popular Netgear RP614 router with a built-in firewall (page 8) and four Ethernet ports (which you'll see in a supporting role, later in this chapter) costs about $45.

Routers from other popular networking companies (such as Linksys, Belkin, and D-Link, to name a few) cost about the same, but prices vary if you want additional ports or features such as wireless capability (see Chapter 3 for more about the wonderful world of wireless).

If you need to plug a switch into your router, expect to spend $60 to $70 for a good 8-port standalone switch. Stick with well-reviewed hardware brands when you buy your equipment. (The electronics section of Amazon.com is never short of opinions, and many computer magazines also offer reviews of consumer products.) If you want to save a few bucks, you can get a no-name cheapo chunk of hardware, but it may be more trouble than the money you save, considering the lousy documentation, the minimal tech support, and the unreliable performance you're likely to get.

UP TO SPEED

Truth or Advertising?

One trick that some hardware vendors like to use is the old "double your speed for the same price!" marketing ploy.

When you're shopping for switches, you may notice some product packaging that boasts that the switch can run at speeds of up to *200 Mbps*, instead of the standard 100 Mbps. This claim is a touch misleading, because Fast Ethernet is Fast Ethernet is Fast Ethernet, and it doesn't *go* faster than 100 Mbps.

So, are these switch makers lying to you? Well, not exactly.

What they're saying is that your Ethernet network can run at speeds of 100 Mbps…in *both* directions.

The speed is 100 Mbps from the switch to the computer and it's also 100 Mbps going back in the other direction. The companies add up those two numbers and tell you that their equipment is rated for 200 Mbps. So while the promise of 200 Mbps might sound appealing, the reality of it is a matter of how you do the math. All 10/100 Ethernet switches on shelves these days can do the same thing.

Network Adapters

An Ethernet network adapter (page 6) is the component on each computer that lets it communicate with your network's router. You'll also sometimes hear these referred to as *Ethernet cards*. If you've got an Ethernet card *inside* your machine, then you'll also have a jack to plug in a network cable on the *outside* of the computer, usually on the back. If you have an *external* network adapter, like a PC card or a USB network adapter, the jack for your network cable is right on the end of the device.

Fortunately, network adapters are also about the easiest and the cheapest piece of the networking puzzle to get, because most new Windows PCs and all Macintosh computers come with Ethernet adapters already installed when you buy them. To make the machine work on your network, all you have to do is plug one end of a cable into the Ethernet port and plug the other end of the cable into a router.

If you're not sure if your computer has an internal Ethernet adapter, turn the machine around and take a look at the back where all of the ports and connectors (and probably big dust bunnies) hang out. Again, look for the distinctive RJ-45 port that looks just like the jacks on your router. If you'd like a visual aid, take a look at Figure 2-2.

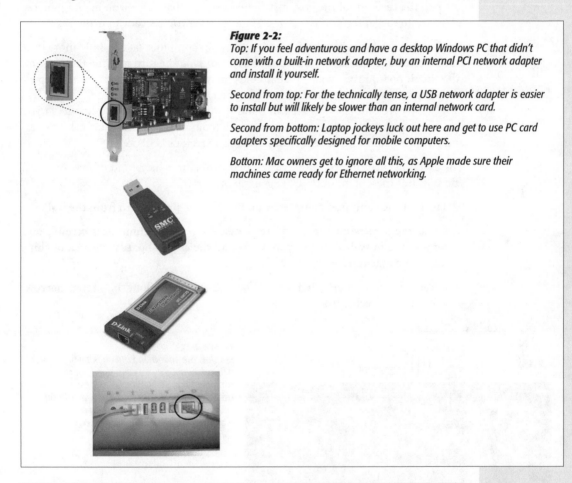

Figure 2-2:
Top: If you feel adventurous and have a desktop Windows PC that didn't come with a built-in network adapter, buy an internal PCI network adapter and install it yourself.

Second from top: For the technically tense, a USB network adapter is easier to install but will likely be slower than an internal network card.

Second from bottom: Laptop jockeys luck out here and get to use PC card adapters specifically designed for mobile computers.

Bottom: Mac owners get to ignore all this, as Apple made sure their machines came ready for Ethernet networking.

Note: When scrabbling around looking for an RJ-45 port on your computer, don't mistake the machine's dial-up RJ-11 telephone modem jack for an Ethernet adapter. The two jacks look decidedly similar, but the Ethernet RJ-45 port is slightly wider. Most computers these days put an icon of a telephone next to the modem jack to help distinguish it from its networking cousin.

If your computer didn't come with an Ethernet adapter, don't worry. You can usually pick one up for less than $50 at your local computer store or on the Internet. As mentioned on page 4 in the previous chapter, network adapters come in three basic varieties: *PCI adapters* for desktop computers, *USB adapters* for any kind of computer with a USB port, and *PC Card adapters* for laptops. If your computer doesn't have a network adapter, you'll have to install one, which the next section explains.

Installing a Network Adapter Card

Laptop owners and those who can opt for a USB network adapter have it the easiest: just pop the card out of the box, install any software that came with it, and plug the adapter into the laptop's card slot or USB port. Then you're ready to network.

Adding an Ethernet network adapter to a desktop computer takes a little more time and involves opening up the machine so you can plug the card into the *motherboard* (the circuit board inside your PC that holds many of its vital organs). For some people, this procedure is very exciting, but for others, it can be terrifying to see what lurks inside. If you're on the fence, keep in mind that the Ethernet card is going to let you communicate more quickly with your network (compared to a USB network adapter) and gives you the added benefit of not hogging a precious USB port.

The exact installation procedure varies, depending on what brand of network card you buy, but these steps outline the general process:

1. **Turn off the computer completely and unplug its power cord from the wall.**

2. **Undo the screws on the computer's case (if your machine uses screws) and remove the outside cover so you can see all the circuit boards, wires, and chips inside the machine.**

3. **Locate the computer's PCI slots (Figure 2-3), which look like long, narrow, white-plastic rectangles.**

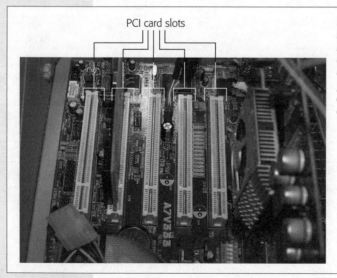

PCI card slots

Figure 2-3:
PCI slots are your friends. In addition to network adapters, you can extend your computer's capabilities by filling these slots with cards such as a TV tuner card to watch TV on your PC, or a FireWire card so you can connect a digital video camera directly to your computer.

4. Choose a PCI slot and remove the thin metal strip that covers the narrow opening in the back of the computer's case. You need to remove this strip so the RJ-45 jack on the network adapter will be visible on the back of the computer once you install the card.

   Save the screw holding the strip in place and set it aside for a minute.

5. Without touching any of its metal parts, gently take the network card out of the antistatic plastic bag it came in and carefully snap it into the empty PCI slot. The RJ-45 jack should be showing on the back of the computer.

6. Use the screw from step 4 and secure the card to the back wall of the computer.

7. Replace the computer's outside case, reconnect its power cord, and start it up.

Some network adapter cards may require you to install software before they'll work, but most cards these days are so-called *Plug-and-Play* models that work right out of the box, allowing you to *plug* them in and go off to *play* without wrestling with software issues.

Network adapter shopping list

Before you buy a network adapter, make sure your computer doesn't already have one built in. Keep in mind that there are three types of network adapters: use PCI adapters in desktop computers, PC Card adapters in laptops, and USB adapters in any computer with USB ports.

You can find Ethernet network adapters for around the following prices in most computer stores:

- **PCI adapter:** $25 to $30
- **PC Card adapter:** $35 to $40
- **USB adapter:** $30 to $40

Ethernet Cables

Okay, class, let's review. You've learned about Ethernet-enabled routers, which can share an Internet connection while providing a jack for every computer on the network to plug into. You've also learned that computers themselves need to have some sort of a network adapter installed so they can communicate with the router. The last key component in a wired Ethernet network is (drum roll, please!) the wire. Yes, you need cables to connect router to computer.

An *Ethernet cable* looks similar to a telephone cable but it's a little thicker and rounder. As with each of the device's connectors, the two cables are not interchangeable.

When you buy Ethernet cables, visions of the hurricane-rating scale may come to mind, since the most common cable types are labeled according to how they're rated: Category 5, Category 5e, or Category 6. While these ratings may make meteorologists a tad nervous, they're just an industry-standard way to identify different types of network cable (see the following box, "The Label on the Cable"). If you have a choice, stick with Category 6 cables, because they're the best quality of the bunch and are less prone to problems like interference, but both Category 5 and 5e should work fine, too.

POWER USERS' CLINIC

The Label on the Cable

When it comes to network cables, the term "Category" refers to part of a standardized rating system developed by the Electronic Industry Alliance and the Telecommunications Industry Alliance.

As with other products, standardized ratings agreed upon by manufacturers are a good thing, because they guarantee that all similarly rated products perform the same functions.

So the Category 6 cable you buy at Best Buy works the same as the Category 6 cable you buy at CompUSA. And what happened to Categories 1 through 4? Alas, they've been mostly tossed in the junk drawer of computer history and, as outdated standards, aren't suitable for today's Ethernet networks.

Ethernet cable shopping list

Your Ethernet network won't go very fast without cables connecting it all together. Pricing depends on the length of cable you buy. Most big chain computer stores sell 10-foot Ethernet cables for $25 to $35, which is pretty expensive. Smaller, independent computer stores, or places like Radio Shack, usually have better prices. You can find a perfectly fine cable for $5 to $7. The Web, as always, is often a good place to find bargains, and some sites sell 10-foot Ethernet cables for less than $3.

This is one area in which you can save a whole lot of money by shopping around. Just make sure you buy Category 5e or Category 6 Ethernet cables when possible, and your network should zoom with joy.

Tip: When it comes to cables, you can do two things up front to save yourself some hassle later on. First, but some extra cables and stash them away; they're bound to come in handy during network emergencies like the new beagle puppy who's decided to munch on your network for a snack.

Second, when you're buying cables, choose lengths longer than what you actually think you need. Distances can be hard to judge when you have to wend cables around furniture, plus the extra length gives you some room to move if you rearrange the room.

A Basic Network Setup

If you're reading this book, the chances are fairly good that you have a computer or two at home and want to figure out how you can link them together so you can do things like use a single printer or share a high-speed Internet connection.

For most people with a regular cable or DSL modem and a couple of computers, a basic network is pretty straightforward to set up. Here's the Cliffs Notes version: you take the network cable out of your modem (the one that *used to* plug directly into a single PC) and plug it into the modem port on your new router. You make sure each computer you want to connect has an Ethernet network adapter installed or attached. Then you take one network cable for every computer and plug one end into an available port on the back of the router and the other end into the computer's Ethernet port. Then you turn everything on and have a race to see who can be the first one on the new network to order a pizza online.

Note: Let's say you're not the average Josephine and you arrive at the network setup dance wearing a slightly different dress. For example, say you've been assigned (or requested) a *static IP address*. A static IP address is an Internet address for your computer that never changes; some folks get them when they want to run their own Web server. If you have a static IP address, you will probably have to take a couple extra steps in your network setup adventure.

Similarly, some Internet providers force their subscribers to use an older connection method called *PPPoE* (which stands for the long and windy name *Point-to-Point Protocol over Ethernet*) to get online. You'll also probably have a few extra steps to perform. Both the static IP folks and the PPPoE people need to follow the numbered steps below and then move on to "Manually Configuring Your Router" on page 26.

In the example described here and shown in Figure 2-4, our Model Home has two computers in the same room—say, the spare bedroom upstairs that Mr. and Mrs. Model are using as a home office until they have little Models scampering around. They've got a nice PC running Windows XP Home Edition, a gleaming Macintosh running Mac OS X 10.3 (also known as Panther), and a Netgear RP614 router. Of course, these are fake people and *you* might be running different operating systems, or have an additional computer to jack in, or some other slight variation.

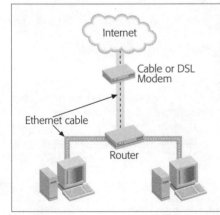

Figure 2-4:
Your mission, should you choose to accept it, is to connect your networking hardware to your computers as shown. The broadband modem connects to the router, and then each computer on the network plugs into the router. Your Internet connection gets fed into the router, which then shares it with all the connected computers.

The cool thing about networking in the 21st century is that whichever company you buy your Ethernet gear or your computers from, the setup has become a pretty uniform process. The smart engineers that created Ethernet, and the related gadgets and software that make use of it, designed things so your network works no matter which manufacturer's products you use—as long as you properly connect all the parts.

So your devices might vary from the equipment used in this example. Heck, the Netgear RP614—a router with a four-port Ethernet switch built-in—might not even be available by the time you read this paragraph. It doesn't really matter all that much. Even though routers come in all shapes and sizes, they all perform the same basic function.

The bottom line is that by the time you finish with the steps outlined below, all your computers should be able to connect to the Internet. And when you're bored with browsing the Web and catching up on email, flip on ahead to Part 2 of this book to learn how to get your computers to share files and other documents with each other over your new home network.

The basic steps for installing a network in a single room or rooms within a cable's reach of your router and modem go like this (*a-one* and *a-two*...):

1. **Buy your networking equipment: router, adapter, and cables.**

   While you're at the computer store, don't forget to pick up enough Ethernet cables to connect all your computers plus any other devices you want to put on the network (like a printer). Most routers come with only a single Ethernet cable.

Tip: If your particular router doesn't include an Ethernet switch and you have multiple computers, consider getting a router with the switch built-in. It's just easier that way.

---

2. **Install the network adapters in each computer.**

   If you've got Macs in the mix, they're born ready for Ethernet action, but you may have to check your Windows machines and install adapters if necessary (page 20). Once you're done with this step, turn your computers off.

3. **Unpack the router.**

   Free your new router from its cardboard confinement and find a place for it near your broadband modem. The two devices are going to connect to each other, so they need to be no farther away than the length of the Ethernet cable you're using to connect them. Make sure there's an electrical outlet within reach, too.

4. **Connect your network cables.**

   Plug one end of an Ethernet cable into the RJ-45 jack on one of your computers and plug the other end into one of the numbered ports on the back of the router. Repeat this step for every computer you want to put on your network. Push the Ethernet cable's RJ-45 connector into each jack until you hear it click. It doesn't hurt to push gently on it to make sure the connection is secure.

Note: Don't yank on an Ethernet cable if you ever want to unplug it, or you may break the connector. Remove the cable from the jack by pressing down the tab on the top of the RJ-45 connector while pulling the cable out.

Finally, connect your DSL or cable modem's Ethernet cable to the port marked *WAN* or *Modem* on the router. The port might also be called *Internet* or *Cable/ DSL*. (WAN stands for Wide Area Network and is a term used to describe networks that connect to one another across vast geographic boundaries. Your personal network here is called a *LAN*, or Local Area Network.)

5. **Plug the router into the electrical outlet.**

   Most routers don't have separate power switches and will power on as soon as you plug the unit into the wall.

6. **Turn on the computers.**

   Every version of Windows and the Mac OS that have been on the market in the past decade have the ability to automatically get the Internet access settings they need from the router. The router turns around and automatically gets *its* information from your Internet service provider. (How does the router do this? A little trick called *Dynamic Host Configuration Protocol,* or DHCP. See the following box if you want to know more.) Once you turn on the computers, you should be able to open up a Web browser and start surfing.

POWER USERS' CLINIC

DHCP: The Host with the Most

Just being able to plug in a network cable to your computer and get out on the Internet without having to wade through screens full of configuration boxes is a thing of beauty and great joy.

It's all possible due to a little network service that hands out Internet Protocol addresses (a series of identification numbers that every computer connected to the Net must have) faster than a waitress slinging hash at your favorite diner. This protocol, Dynamic Host Configuration Protocol (DHCP), was designed for large networks so that the poor system administrators wouldn't have to manually keep track of tens of thousands of IP addresses strewn about their organizations.

These addresses, with memorable names like 66.98.244.52, can be a pain to remember, and companies are usually assigned hundreds of them (by their Internet service provider) so the company's computers can get online.

But with a DHCP server, all these IP addresses can be loaded up and automatically dispensed when a computer requests one, leaving the system administrators more time to figure out the important stuff like what snacks to bring to tonight's D&D game (*just kidding, system administrators!*).

Most Internet service providers use DHCP servers to assign IP addresses to customers unless a static IP address is requested.

That's it. Plug and Play is the order of the day, as most hardware vendors have *finally* figured out that people like simple solutions.

For most of you here on Missing Manual Airlines, you'll be traveling on to farther destinations, like the Internet, and this is the last page in this chapter you absolutely need to read since your network is working. Those of you with Windows machines may want to proceed to Chapter 5 for more detailed information about networking between individual PCs, while Mac readers will find Chapter 6 more illuminating. If you've got a houseful of both systems, Chapter 7 is your next stop.

Now then, for those of you still on board waiting for your network to take off, your hold up might be one of the following:

• You once asked your ISP for a static IP address so you could run your own Web or email server.

• Your Internet service provider makes you use PPPoE to connect to the Internet.

This next section is for you.

Manually Configuring Your Router

Okay, so your basic network setup wasn't so basic; your computers are not quite yet ready to get online. No problem. This section will tell you everything you need to know to manually configure your router. (If the term "manually configure" makes you nervous, relax. It really just means "typing stuff into boxes onscreen and clicking OK.") If you've got a static IP address, read on; if you're a PPPoE person, skip ahead to "Information PPPoE People Need" on page 28.

Information Static IP People Need

If you've got yourself a static IP address, you need to obtain the following bits of info from your ISP before you can move ahead: the IP address, subnet mask, default gateway, and DNS servers. Here's a quick primer on what all this arcane technical jargon means.

The IP address

Every computer connected to the Internet, even temporarily, has its own exclusive *IP address* (IP stands for Internet Protocol). An IP address is always made up of four numbers, separated by periods. Think of your IP address as the number of your house on your street—350, 1060, or whatever. If you have a static IP address, make sure your Internet service provider has given you an address that will allow you to get out on the Internet. If the static address falls within any of three restricted ranges—192.168.0.0 to 192.168.255.255, 172.16.0.0 to 172.31.255.255, or 10.0.0.0 to 10.255.255.255—it won't let your PCs get online. These numbers all fall within the category of what's known as *private IP address ranges*. Internet engineers once decided that these number ranges should be reserved for secure private networks that can't connect to the big sprawling Internet, which is *very* public. So if you've been assigned one of these numbers, ring up your ISP and get a new one.

Subnet mask

The *subnet mask* (also sometimes called the *network mask*) is a number used to break up a large network into small, manageable pieces. Like the IP address, the subnet mask is composed of four numbers, separated by periods. Without the subnet mask, your Internet service provider's network would be one huge, unwieldy mess. But by using a combination of your unique IP address and this subnet mask, your ISP can quickly and efficiently route Internet traffic to your house.

The subnet mask is like the name of your street—Fifth Avenue, West Addison Street, and so on. When combined with your unique IP address, the Internet can find your computer at 350 Fifth Avenue or 1060 West Addison Street. Your subnet mask is also assigned to you by your ISP and determines on which of their many networks your router lives. Beyond just getting this information from your ISP, you should never have to mess around with the subnet mask.

UP TO SPEED

Internal and External Addresses

Your home network actually uses two different kinds of IP addresses. The one assigned to you by your Internet service provider is what's known as your *external* IP address. The only device that ever sees this address is your router, and this address is used solely for Internet communication.

On the other hand, the computers and other devices connected to your home network use a separate set of IP addresses, which are known as *internal* IP addresses. Internal IP addresses are used solely by your computers to communicate with your router.

Default gateway

The *default gateway* is a number that serves as your network's own "door" to the Internet. (It's also a member of the four-digits-separated-by-a-period club.) When your computer realizes that it's communicating with another computer that doesn't live on your local network, it uses this door to get to other networks.

By examining your IP address and subnet mask, your computer can tell whether you're trying to get to things like a Web site on a local computer (that is, one inside your home) or a computer out on the Internet. If the computer determines that you're using the Internet, it automatically sends the information to the default gateway—in this case, your router. The router understands both *your* network and the network Out There. It's sort of like a real estate agent that knows you as well as the sellers, and neither of you can to talk to the other without going through the agent.

Domain Name Services servers

Domain Name Services, or DNS, is like a telephone book for the Internet. Without DNS, you'd be forced to remember addresses like *http://216.239.37.99* instead of the more human *http://www.google.com.* DNS automatically translates the name into the number for you, just like a telephone book. Most Internet providers send you two DNS server addresses so that if one is unavailable, the other one picks up the load. Some ISPs even provide three addresses.

Okay, now that you've got your Ph.D. in Static IP–ology, skip ahead to "Configuring Your Router from the Web" for all the details on what to do with your collection of numbers and settings.

Information PPPoE People Need

Some ISPs still require their subscribers to use the ol' PPPoE connection method and special communications software that's sometimes built into the operating system (as is the case with Windows XP), and sometimes is a standalone program with a name like WinPoET or MacPoET. These programs help make the connection from a home computer to the Internet. If your ISP uses PPPoE, you're not out of luck, since most routers let you establish PPPoE connections if you plug in the information they need. Once your router is connected to your ISP, you don't have to use the PPPoE connection software to get online. Your computers will talk directly to your router about using the Internet and not deal directly with your ISP anymore.

Fortunately, as complicated as that all sounds, the information you need to gather is pretty simple: a PPPoE user name and password, and a service name, if your ISP is one of the small minority that still requires that. (Usually your ISP will have given you all this info in the packet of instructions you got when you signed up with them.)

Configuring Your Router from the Web

Unlike the basic network setup, this more advanced configuration requires you to manually adjust some settings in your router. You normally have two tools in your router-configuring toolbox:

• The setup CD that came in the box with the router

• Any computer in your home with a working Web browser

The method you use is up to you, but using the Web to configure your router usually gives you access to certain advanced configuration settings like some security features and PPPoE settings. You also never have to worry about losing your router's CD. When you configure using the Web, all the setting screens are always waiting patiently there for you.

Note: If you've got a Mac, sometimes you have no choice but to configure your router via a Web browser, because some router software is Windows-only.

If you want to use the CD, go ahead, and its software wizards will lead the way. If you'd like to get the router routing with your Web browser, read on.

Step 1: Perform the basic network setup on page 22

Like a tap-dance routine, every advanced network installation can be broken down into smaller, simpler steps. In your case, to get started, follow steps 1 through 6 from "A Basic Network Setup," which starts on page 22. All you need is one machine turned on and connected to the router for the configuration dance to begin.

Step 2: Open a Web browser

Every modern operating system comes with a Web browser. Windows XP has Internet Explorer, Mac OS X has Safari, and both systems can use open source browsers like Firefox. Just start up your favorite electronic window to the world.

Step 3: Connect to the Netgear RP614 (or whatever router you bought)

Like every router, the Netgear RP614 comes with a default IP address, user name, and password that you'll need for configuration. In this case, go to your browser's address bar and type in *http://192.168.0.1*. Enter the default administrative user name (*admin*) and password (*password*).

You may wonder why you're able to connect to this Web site when you can't yet get on the Internet. That's because you're not actually traveling out on the World Wide Web; instead, you're making a connection to your router, which lives at the Web address you just typed in.

If you are using a brand of router other than Netgear, the default IP address, user name, and password may be different. The table below provides you with the default IP addresses, user names, and passwords for routers from several popular manufacturers.

Vendor	Configuration address	Default user name	Default password
Belkin	192.168.2.1	<blank>	<blank>
D-Link	192.168.0.1	admin	<blank>
Linksys	192.168.1.1 or 192.168.15.1	<blank>	admin
Microsoft	192.168.2.1	<blank>	admin
Netgear	192.168.0.1	admin	password

Step 4: Go to the configuration window

When you first connect to the Netgear router, you're greeted with a welcome window letting you know that your polite router is willing to walk you through your setup. Skip this wizard, since you're heading for the *settings* configuration here, as shown in Figure 2-5. Netgear is somewhat unusual in that it's included a wizard in its router's Web-based configuration; most manufacturers include this wizard on the CD instead.

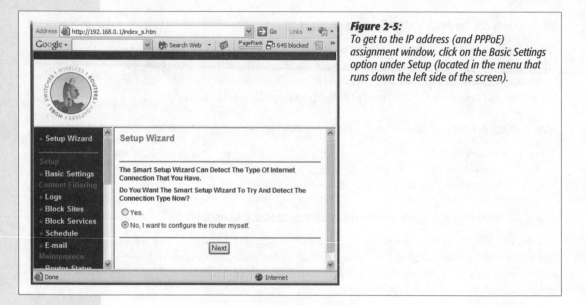

Figure 2-5:
To get to the IP address (and PPPoE) assignment window, click on the Basic Settings option under Setup (located in the menu that runs down the left side of the screen).

Step 5a: Enter all your IP address information.

Note: PPPoE people can skip to Step 5b. This one's for static IP folks only.

You have to provide more than just your static IP address here. Be ready to provide the subnet mask, the default gateway, and DNS server names, which you learned about back on page 27. Figure 2-6 shows the screen from the Netgear RP614 and gives you instructions for setting the IP address.

When you're done entering the IP address information, click the Apply button at the very bottom of the window.

Step 5b: Type in PPPoE information

Note: This step is for PPPoE people only.

Okay, now you're in the place where you can give the router your PPPoE user name and password and finally get this show on the road! Figure 2-7 shows a view of the Netgear RP614 and explains where to enter the PPPoE user name and password.

When you're done entering your PPPoE information, click the Apply button at the very bottom of the window.

At last! Your computer should be surfing the Web, and you're finally ready to look for the latest deals on ceramic dachshund figurines or the choicest vintage Wonder Woman memorabilia on eBay.

Note: Remember, if you've got a PPPoE connection, when you go online, you no longer have to use the PPPoE software that your ISP gave you.

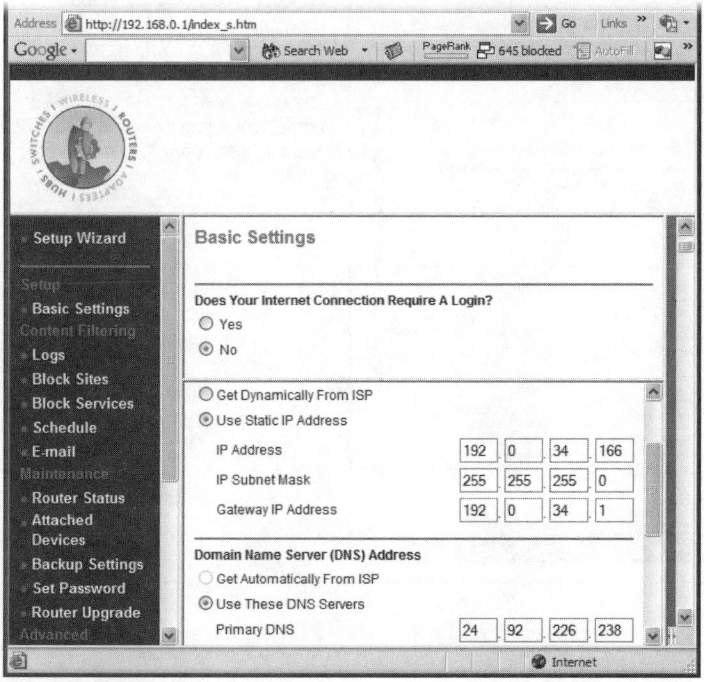

Figure 2-6:
Under the Internet IP Address section of the Basic Settings window, select the option Use Static IP Address to tell your router that you want to manually assign it an IP address. Next, type the IP address that your ISP gave you into the IP Address field, followed by the Subnet Mask and the Default Gateway. Finally, in the Domain Name Server (DNS) Address section, select Use These DNS Servers and type in the IP addresses of the DNS servers that you got from your ISP.

Going Hybrid?

Using Ethernet doesn't mean you can't also use the other types of networks like WiFi (Chapter 3) or Powerline (Chapter 4). In fact, there might come a point when you need to mix it up a bit, for instance by adding WiFi to the other end of your house so you don't have to staple a 100-foot Ethernet cable to the molding all the way down your hallway.

When you're picking out Ethernet networking equipment, make sure to think long term whenever possible. Maybe you're thinking about getting a WiFi-enabled laptop with your tax refund. Wouldn't it be much more relaxing to update your blog in front of the fireplace instead of being tethered to the drafty computer room upstairs this winter?

If you think you'll *ever* want to add wireless, consider buying a router that comes with WiFi built-in. If wireless sounds good to you right about now, let's cut the wires and move on to the next chapter.

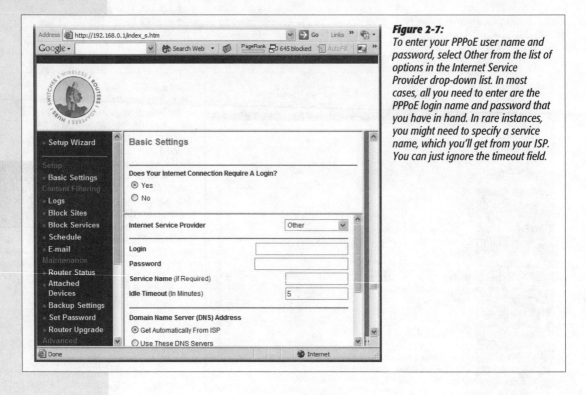

Figure 2-7:
To enter your PPPoE user name and password, select Other from the list of options in the Internet Service Provider drop-down list. In most cases, all you need to enter are the PPPoE login name and password that you have in hand. In rare instances, you might need to specify a service name, which you'll get from your ISP. You can just ignore the timeout field.

Setting Up a Wireless Network

Imagine working away on your computer anywhere in the house—with no strings attached, footloose, and fancy cable-free. You can move from room to room with your laptop and still stay connected to the Internet. Stationary desktops can join in on the fun, too, since wireless networking works on all computers, big and small. No wonder *WiFi* (short for Wireless Fidelity) is the fastest growing type of network being used by people at home today.

WiFi networks come in three distinct varieties, formally known as *802.11a*, *802.11b*, and *802.11g*, but sometimes referred to casually as *A*, *B*, and *G*. Although they have important differences, which you'll learn about in a moment, they all accomplish the same task: beaming data over radio waves. Each format also uses a central antenna to wirelessly communicate with computers, and in turn, each computer connected to the network needs to have a wireless networking card installed so it can communicate with the central station. By the end of this chapter, you'll know a lot more about how all this works.

Along the way, you'll get step-by-step instructions for setting up a basic wireless network and will learn how to secure your network to keep folks outside your home from piggybacking your network.

A WiFi Network's Main Ingredients

As you learned in Chapter 1, WiFi, just like every other type of network, needs three things to fly:

- A **router.** In WiFi's case, this router not only works to connect your home to the Internet, it also contains a WiFi antenna that beams an Internet connection to the computers in your home. WiFi routers transmit their signals according to one (or more) of the three WiFi standards in use today.

- A **wireless networking card,** which is plugged into, or internally installed on the computers you want on your WiFi network. These cards also come equipped to work with one or more of the WiFi flavors.

- And **air,** which thanks to the magic of WiFi, serves as the connective link between your PCs and your WiFi router.

As with any networking setup, you can find a zillion WiFi variations when it comes to the equipment sold in stores and the rigs your neighbors have in their homes. But most WiFi networks are something like the one represented in Figure 3-1.

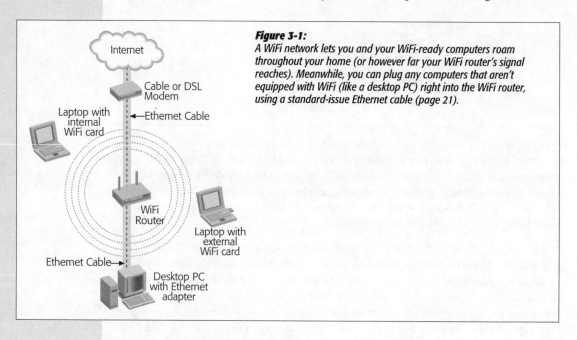

Figure 3-1:
A WiFi network lets you and your WiFi-ready computers roam throughout your home (or however far your WiFi router's signal reaches). Meanwhile, you can plug any computers that aren't equipped with WiFi (like a desktop PC) right into the WiFi router, using a standard-issue Ethernet cable (page 21).

Time to Learn Your A-B-Gs

To most people, A, B, and G are just letters of the alphabet, but these particular letters have special meaning when it comes to WiFi. Each wireless standard has three characteristics that distinguish it:

- The *radio frequency* that it uses

- The *speed* at which the network can transfer data

- The physical *range* of the wireless signal

You should consider all these factors when you're trying to figure out which kind of wireless gear to buy and install in your house.

Radio frequency

The next time you hop in the car for a drive, consider that humble radio in the dashboard. It has the power to pull music, news, sports, and mattress commercials down from the airwaves and play them out of your car's speakers. You find your favorite stations by their call letters and the number of the radio frequency they occupy on the dial, like 1010 WINS or KSSS 101.5 FM. Unless you're almost out of range, you hear just the one station you're tuned to.

This is because each radio station transmits on its very own frequency in order to prevent *signal overlap*—the chaos up and down the dial if all of a sudden a hockey game from one station and a live classical music concert from another were both pouring out of your speakers at the same time. Your home networking radio equipment works on the same concept, but it's limited to just two major radio frequencies: 2.4 gigahertz and 5 gigahertz (GHz).

UP TO SPEED

What's in a Name?

Beyond the single letter designation on the caboose of the 802.11, wireless-networking equipment has quite a few names that different manufacturers use to describe their products. Of course, you sometimes see wireless equipment referred to by its official designation of 802.11a, 802.11b, or 802.11g, but other makers ditch the digits and refer to equipment as being "wireless-A," "wireless-B," or "wireless-G."

In case you were wondering, the 802.11 prefix at the beginning of each wireless network refers to the number that the Institute of Electrical and Electronics Engineers (IEEE) assigned to the wireless-networking working group of people who labored to develop the technology several years ago. This working group was—and still is—responsible for setting the industry standards that manufacturers are supposed to follow to make sure an 802.11g wireless router by one company works the same way as an 802.11g wireless router made by another company. (Of course, manufacturers are free to add bells and whistles, like enhanced security, and even speed boosts. But the point is that the underlying 802.11g technology works the same regardless of which company's products you use.)

And then there's Apple Computer, which just loves to be different. Apple called its first wireless router the "AirPort" and followed it up with the "AirPort Extreme" and then the tiny portable "AirPort Express" mobile Base Station. ("Base Station" is how Apple usually refers to its wireless routers.) Underneath the gleaming white plastic, however, are regular wireless standards. The original AirPort is an 802.11b device, while the AirPort Extreme and AirPort Express run on the 802.11g standard.

The key difference between these two radio bands is that the Federal Communications Commission has largely deregulated the 2.4 GHz frequency, and the devices that operate on it have prospered and multiplied. The 5 GHz band is not quite as busy because it remains under some regulation, especially in other countries where governments reserve certain frequencies for official use or reluctantly regulate them for use by the public.

The 2.4 GHz standard is widely used in a variety of devices in the United States. Your cordless phone at home probably operates in the 2.4 GHz range, as do many wireless baby monitors. Your microwave's radiation might even affect your electronic gadgets that use the 2.4 GHz frequency.

Of the three WiFi standards in use today (brace yourself, there are more coming), 802.11a is the only one that operates on the 5 GHz frequency. It's also the least popular, mainly due to its lack of compatibility with its B and G brethren.

802.11b and 802.11g are the reining king and queen of the WiFi ball. They both operate on the 2.4 GHz radio frequency and, because of this, play nicely together. That means you can have a B card in your laptop and be able to connect to a G router with no problem at all. Neither B nor G will talk to A, though, and they don't even let A sit with them at the cool networks' table in the wireless cafeteria.

That said, some hardware manufacturers do sell equipment that can handle A, B, and G all at once, but this can be a pretty expensive investment. Besides, B and G are doing a fine job supporting home networking needs on their own. B, which was first out of the gate, is currently the most popular and best-supported standard, but G is quickly gaining ground thanks to falling prices and zippier speeds. In fact, if you're starting your network from scratch, you'll want to stick with G.

POWER USERS' CLINIC

Wireless Networking Scorecard

802.11a was originally developed for business use and is less prone to interference from devices such as microwave ovens. It can also support a larger number of users logged onto the network than B or G can.

For a variety of reasons, including serious regulatory problems in Europe, A is falling out of favor as B and G soak up the limelight. G is just as fast as A is, and the equipment you'll need to run it is cheaper, too. And unless you live in a frat house, most home networks don't need to support hundreds of computers, so G will work just fine. G does suffer from the occasional frequency interference from other devices in the 2.4 GHz band, but as long as you remember to fire up that bag of microwave popcorn *after* you finish your big album download from the Napster store, you'll never notice.

Speed

The speed of a network determines how quickly you can transfer and share data between computers.

If you're sharing just an Internet connection, even the slowest wireless network is more than sufficient for your browsing needs. However, if you're installing a home network with an eye toward doing more—like sharing files, playing games head to head, or watching movies—the speed of your network becomes much more important.

Both A and G run at 54 Mbps (which translates into the mind-boggling power to send 3,240 pages of plain text per second). But G has a tendency to suffer more from interference generated by other electronic devices camped on the same radio frequency (such as baby monitors). From a pure performance standpoint, A is faster than G, but not by much, and that alone isn't enough to make up for A's other deficiencies, like a short range and lack of compatibility. At the rear of the pack, B slugs along at a maximum speed of 11 Mbps, (about 660 pages of text per second), but it does have a greater physical range than the other two.

Range

Every radio station has a limited transmission area; otherwise, you'd be hearing all kinds of cacophony coming out of your speakers as all the radio stations on the same frequency blast through at once. But as you drive farther from the station's transmission tower, its signal starts to fade before disappearing completely. Since a WiFi network uses radio waves, it has similar range limitations.

This physical range is the third key difference between the three wireless standards. Say your wireless network consists of a single WiFi router in the center of a circle. The boundaries of that circle represent the *range* of your router and, by extension, your wireless network.

Physical range is one area in which A literally comes up short compared to B and G. A has a range of only about 75 feet from the central antenna. Compare that to B's range of about 150 feet. Meanwhile, B's cousin, G, only reaches about 50 to 100 feet from the antenna. But since G shares the same radio frequency as B, G can automatically fall back to a B signal when it reaches the limit of its range, thereby extending G's range to a total of about 150 feet. So you can enjoy G's speedier connection when you're within its optimum range, but not lose your connection completely if you happen to wander beyond G's border into B territory.

A few physical and environmental factors affect all of these ranges. For example, the number of walls that stand between the network's antenna and the connected computers can diminish the signal, as can certain construction materials used in the walls themselves (metal isn't so good for wireless signals). Interference from other types of wireless devices like baby monitors and cordless phones can narrow your range, too.

So with all these elements to consider, which type of wireless network should you choose for your home?

POWER USERS' CLINIC

Alphabet Soup

Funny thing, that alphabet. You learn it one way in preschool and then decades later, some wacky engineers start tossing letters out left and right. A, B, and G are accounted for, but what did those propeller-heads do with C, D, E, and F? Actually, C through F are all in use, but they all work behind the scenes to help A, B, and G get their job done.

And just when you thought it was safe to ignore the rest of the alphabet, hardware makers are rumbling about yet another new standard: 802.11*n*. It's still a ways off, but 802.11n is supposed to be compatible with 802.11b and 802.11g, but with vastly increased range and speed. Some manufacturers even selll "pre-N" equipment that will be able to take advantage of the new technology once it is officially approved. Stay tuned!

Making the Choice

Computer stores can be intensely aggravating if you find yourself faced with a wall of obscurely named products and haven't been able to grab a salesperson to help you. The multitude of hardware choices and high-tech jargon doesn't help, so before you take that trip to your local Comp-u-Mart, here's a crib sheet to help you remember which wireless technology is which:

	802.11a	802.11b	802.11g
Speed	Up to 54 Mbps	Up to 11 Mbps	Up to 54 Mbps
Frequency range	5 GHz band	2.4 GHz band	2.4 GHz band
Range from router to WiFi-equipped PCs	About 75 feet	About 150 feet	About 50 to 100 feet (for best speed) Up to about 150 feet for reduced speeds
Cost	High	Low	Medium
Interference risk from other devices (e.g., cordless phones)	Low	High	High
Suitable for beefy multimedia files?	Yes	Probably not	Usually, unless there's significant interference

Some people like to analyze all the pros and cons of a particular question, and hopefully this chart will help you weigh all the factors, both pro and con. If you're *not* one of these people and want to know what's the best thing out there right now, the next section is for you.

G stands for great!

Fortunately, you've picked up this Missing Manual to help you in your home-networking quest, so you hit the jackpot in Easy Answer Bingo: if this is your very first network, run out now and buy 802.11g equipment. It's fast, compatible, and capable of covering most homes without a problem. G has handily beaten A in the home networking arms race and is moving up fast on the heels of B for new network installations.

Even though it's more prone to signal interference than an 802.11a network, a G system still provides excellent performance at greater distances. It's less expensive than A gear and it works with the huge amount of B equipment already hanging out in Network Land. Even if you have an older wireless card for your computer, say maybe something you got in school to use the institution's wireless network, the old B card will still work on your G network (even though you won't get the faster speeds that you'd enjoy with a G card).

So now that you know what makes all of this hardware different, it's time to go buy some gear.

Picking Out Your Wireless Hardware

Wireless networks use the same basic type of equipment as a wired network, but while the wireless hardware serves a similar function, it looks and acts a bit differently.

Wireless Routers

The central point of any WiFi network is the *wireless router* or *wireless access point.* Both these devices contain the antenna that broadcasts your network's signal. But a wireless router goes beyond simple beaming duty: as the name suggests, it also acts as a router. If you're just looking to set up a basic WiFi network and want to cut down on the number of boxes you've got cluttering your house, you want a wireless router (also sometimes known as a *WiFi router*).

Tip: Why would you buy a wireless access point? If you've already got a plain vanilla Ethernet router (page 3) handling your router duties, then you could just go for the wireless access point. But, honestly, WiFi gear is getting so inexpensive these days that it's almost always worth it to get the whole enchilada—router and WiFi antenna—packed into one box: the WiFi router.

You probably want your wireless router to have a built-in Ethernet switch (page 6), because this gives you several Ethernet ports on your router (Figure 3-2). That's useful if you want to give access to your network to someone such as a visiting cousin with no wireless card for her laptop.

Figure 3-2:
Top: A WiFi router beams your network's connection throughout your home.

Bottom: The backsides of most WiFi routhers have built-in switches, which are handy if you've got a desktop PC that you want to plug directly into the router.

Built-in 4-point switch

A Quick Bite of the Apple

Macintosh owners looking for an easy solution have probably heard all about Apple Computer's hangar full of wireless products: the AirPort, AirPort Extreme, and portable, pocket-sized Airport Express.

If you're a Mac devotee, you're probably used to buying gleaming white equipment right from the Mother Ship—all of which has been optimized to work specifically with your Macintosh computer. Apple's own home networking equipment is no exception. If you're a total Machead and your house is full of nothing but Macintosh machines, setting up a wireless network with one of Apple's Base Stations can be a breeze, especially because Apple's operating system, Mac OS X, is on excellent speaking terms with its hardware and compatibility is a cinch.

GEM IN THE ROUGH

Proprietary Speed Boosting

If you want to spend up to $150 or so, you can get a router that uses its maker's own super-secret proprietary technology to boost the network's speed. Linksys calls its technology "SpeedBoost," while D-Link calls its "Super-G."

One thing to remember with these performance-enhancing technologies: they're manufacturer-specific enhancements, so unless you use equipment from the same company for every wireless device on your network, you won't see the speed increase. Also, bear in mind that these tweaks won't make your Internet surfing any faster, but they may increase the speed of your network *inside* your home, an advantage if you're exchanging files or gaming.

If you're a PC person, you've likely been ignoring Apple's product announcements for years (until the iPod came out anyway). But the company's current wares—the AirPort Extreme and the AirPort Express, shown in Figure 3-3—do work with Windows. The AirPort Express even says "Mac + PC" right on the box, which is a big cardboard Welcome mat for the Windows soul who's spent 20 years feeling incompatible with those in the Apple corps.

Figure 3-3:
Like many of the company's products, from iPods to iBooks, Apple's wireless Base Stations come decked out in gleaming white with chrome accents.

Left: The Airport Express for Windows and Macintosh systems plugs right into the wall, can quickly connect up to 10 computers, and even lets you wirelessly stream iTunes music to a connected stereo. (See page 172 for more about how that works.)

Right: The spaceship-shaped AirPort Extreme is built to handle up to 50 computers on its network and even has a 56K modem port on the back in case you need to dial into your own home network when you're on the road. Also, if your broadband connection ever conks out and you're desperate, you can use the modem port to dial-in to the Internet.

The original AirPort, which used the B standard, was Apple's first entry into the wireless world, but the company has retired the AirPort, in favor of its spiffy new G hardware, the AirPort Extreme and its little Mini-me, the AirPort Express (Figure 3-3). Both use the G standard and work with computers that have G or B cards. Apple sells its own AirPort and AirPort Extreme wireless cards for its Macintosh desktop and laptop machines, but PCs equipped with B or G cards from other companies can also connect to AirPort Extreme networks.

Apple's hardware is known for its stylish sophistication and savvy design, and its wireless router is no exception. The AirPort Extreme Base Station looks like a tiny peaked-dome spaceship or a piece of futuristic modern art. If you'd prefer to keep your router out of sight, the small, boxy AirPort Express plugs right into the wall outlet and can be tucked discreetly away behind the couch.

Although they have similar names, the two Base Stations were designed for different uses. The larger AirPort Extreme can connect up to 50 computers and comes with a jack for an external antenna in case you need to increase the network's range with a little extra signal boost. It's also got a 56K modem tucked inside so you can easily dial right into your home network if you're traveling and realized you left the files you need on your home machine.

The AirPort Extreme Base Station may look good, but some people may not care for its lack of clearly explained ports on the back. Apple does provide some symbols next to each jack (a telephone handset next to the modem port, for example), but you may have to refer to its manual to see exactly what all the symbology means back there. The flashing lights on the front can also be hard to interpret without a guidebook. ("What's that you say, AirPort? Our ISP's down right now and we don't have Internet access? Should I go for help?")

The mobile AirPort Express can connect only 10 computers to its wireless network at once. But it also features an audio line-out port so you can connect it to your stereo and wirelessly blast music from your iTunes library through the speakers from wherever the computer happens to be in the house (page 172).

Tip: Both the AirPort Express and AirPort Extreme include a USB port that lets you connect a USB-enabled printer. Once the printer is hooked up, everybody on the network can convert their documents from bytes to bond paper over the airwaves with nary a cable in sight.

The Wireless Router Shopping List

Prices for some common models follow:

- **802.11g wireless router with four-port Ethernet switch:** from $75 up to $150 for proprietary speed-booster models from companies like Linksys and D-Link.

- The **Linksys WRT54G** (featured later in this chapter in the role of "wireless router") costs about $75 and includes a four-port Ethernet switch and a firewall (a device that adds a layer of protection from intruders; page 8).

• **Apple's Airport Extreme Base Station,** which works with all B and G systems, sells for $200; the smaller AirPort Express mobile Base Station works with B and G systems as well, and goes for around $120.

Regardless of which wireless router you buy, you'll also need a wireless network adapter for each computer you'd like to connect to your wireless wonderland.

The Wireless Network Adapter Card

The *wireless network adapter* gives your computer the voice it needs to talk to the wireless router. Wireless network adapters come in different forms, depending on your computer.

Newer PC laptops, like those that use Intel's Centrino or Sonoma mobile technology, have the wireless adapter built right in, because that's part of the Centrino deal. Designed for road warriors, the Centrino systems all include a wireless card, energy-efficient processors, and long-life batteries right out of the box. And on the other side of the fence, all Apple laptops now ship with wireless Airport Extreme cards already installed.

If your laptop or desktop didn't come with wireless powers, you can buy a wireless card for it. Like wired Ethernet adapters (page 18), wireless network adapters come in a three basic varieties: PCI cards for desktop computers, USB adapters for any computer with a USB port, and PC Cards that fit in laptop card slots (Figure 3-4). If you need to install a PCI wireless network adapter, skip back to page 20 and follow the instructions for installing the wired variety—it's the exact same process.

Figure 3-4:
Like their wired cousins, WiFi network adapters come in several varieties, including (clockwise from top left) a PCI card that you install inside your desktop machine, a USB network adapter that you connect to an available USB port, and a PC card that you plug into a laptop's card slot.

Wireless network adapter shopping lists

The table below shows approximate prices for wireless network adapters as of this writing:

802.11b (works with 802.11g)	$30–$40	$30–$40	$30–$70
802.11g (works with 802.11b)	$65–$75	$50–$70	$60–$70
Apple AirPort Extreme	N/A	Laptops: $79	Desktops: $99

Setting Up a Basic Wireless Network

For many people, the main reason to install a home network is to share a cable or DSL Internet connection among a couple of computers. Maybe you've got a desktop computer that, all of a sudden, needs to share its broadband connection with a newly arrived WiFi-ready laptop. Or perhaps you've just signed up for broadband and want all your PCs to join in on the high-speed fun. Whatever the reason, you're in the right spot if you've got one or more computers and you want to get them set up on a WiFi network.

The setup instructions covered in the steps below should work for the vast majority of prospective home networkers. But since it's not practical to describe *every* possible computer and WiFi equipment combination, you're going to read about one *particular* setup: a desktop computer running Windows XP and a Windows XP laptop with a built-in 802.11g card. The router in the starring role for this network production is a Linksys WRT54G unit, which uses the 802.11g standard and includes a four-port Ethernet switch.

Of course, you might be running different operating systems at home, or have an additional computer you want to invite to the wireless party, or have some other slight variation. The cool thing about networking in the 21st century is that whichever company you buy your WiFi gear or your computers from, the setup has become a pretty uniform process. The smart engineers that created WiFi, and the related gadgets and software that make use of it, designed things so your network works no matter what you connect to it—as long as you properly connect all the parts.

So your equipment might vary from the equipment used in this example. Heck, the Linksys router might not even be available by the time you read this paragraph. It doesn't really matter all that much. Even though WiFi routers come in all shapes and sizes, at heart, they all perform the same service: beaming that juicy WiFi signal throughout your home.

By the time you complete the following steps, all your computers should be able to connect to the Internet. And when you're bored with browsing the Web and catching up on email, flip on ahead to Part 2 of this book to learn how to get your computers to share files and other documents with each other over your new home network.

Note: If you're one of those sophisticated folks who uses a static *IP address* (an Internet address for your computer that never changes) or your Internet provider requires that you use an older connection method called *Point-to-Point Protocol over Ethernet* (*PPPoE*), follow the steps listed below, and then move on to the section called "Manually Configuring Your Router" on page 47.

1. **Buy a wireless router.**

   This example uses a Linksys WRT54G, an 802.11g wireless router with a four-port Ethernet switch. But these instructions should get you connected as long as you've got some kind of WiFi router with a built-in Ethernet switch (page 35).

2. **Buy and install wireless network adapters for all the computers you want to wirelessly connect to your new network.**

   Figure 3-4 gives you the lowdown on all the different WiFi network adapters you can add to laptop or desktop computers. As is the case in this example setup, you may well have one desktop computer that's already happily online with a *wired* Ethernet connection. *That* computer doesn't need a wireless network adapter, since you can just plug it right into the wireless router (more on that in step 6).

3. **Turn off all your computers.**

4. **Unpack and plug in the wireless router.**

   Free the router from its cardboard box and connect its power cord to an electrical outlet. (Most models don't have separate power switches and will power up as soon as you plug the unit into the wall.) You should place this router fairly close to your cable or DSL modem, since you're going to have an Ethernet cable running between the two devices.

5. **Connect your broadband modem to the router.**

   In this exercise, the assumption is that before you got started, your desktop computer was happily tooting along with its personal private connection to your broadband modem. In order to let other computers wirelessly partake of the broadband connection, you're going to add a wireless router into the mix, as shown in Figure 3-5.

   Connect your DSL or cable modem's Ethernet cable to the port marked *WAN* or *Modem* on the router. The port might also be called *Internet* or *Cable/DSL*. (*WAN* [or Wide Area Network] is the term for networks that connect to one another across vast geographic boundaries. Your personal network here is called a *LAN*, or Local Area Network.)

   If you're building this whole wireless rig from scratch (that is, if you've never had a computer connected to a broadband modem), you should go from here directly to step 8.

6. **Connect the desktop computer to the router. (Though this step refers to PCs, it works the same for Macs.)**

   Plug an Ethernet cable (page 17) between one of the Ethernet ports on the router and the Ethernet port on the PC. If you want to connect the desktop PC wirelessly, you'll need to get it a wireless card so it can communicate with the wireless router.

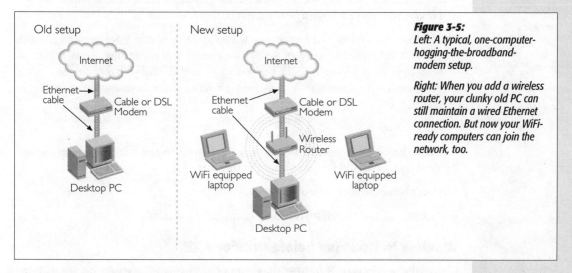

Figure 3-5:
Left: A typical, one-computer-hogging-the-broadband-modem setup.

Right: When you add a wireless router, your clunky old PC can still maintain a wired Ethernet connection. But now your WiFi-ready computers can join the network, too.

   All versions of Windows, as well as Mac OS 9 and Mac OS X, have the ability to automatically get the Internet access settings they need from the router. The router turns around and automatically gets *its* information from your Internet service provider. (How does the router do this? A little trick called *Dynamic Host Configuration Protocol,* or DHCP. See the box "DHCP: The Host with the Most" back on page 25 if you want to know more.)

7. **Turn on the desktop PC.**

   Once you restart the desktop computer, you should be able to open up a Web browser and start surfing from this computer.

8. **Turn on your laptop.**

   The Windows XP laptop will need some extra steps to get an Internet connection up and running. After you log onto Windows, a balloon box pops up in the Notification Tray (at the bottom-right corner of your screen) to tell you "one or more wireless networks are available."

Note: This example uses a laptop running Windows XP, but you might be running a different version of Windows or might be using Mac OS 9 or Mac OS X on your laptop. If that's the case, skip steps 9 to 12 and move on to the appropriate section for your operating system. One quick word of advice before you go: be sure not to leave this chapter without reading "Securing Your Wireless Network" on page 52; it tells you everything you need to know to make sure your network is secure.

---

9. **Click the message balloon telling you about the available wireless networks.**

The Wireless Network Connection dialog box opens.

10. **Find your wireless network in the "Choose a wireless network" list and select it.**

A list of available wireless networks appears. If the laptop detects more than one wireless network, they'll all be listed here, so if your neighbors have WiFi networks set up, you may see network names you don't recognize. If you're using a Linksys router, you'll see a wireless network named *linksys*.

The name of a wireless network is called its *SSID,* or Security Set Identifier, which is used to identify the name of the network the router is running. Every manufacturer uses its own default SSID, but you can—and should—change this to a name of your own choosing. You'll find directions for changing the SSID in Figure 3-10.

11. **Click Connect.**

Click the connect button to attach your laptop to the wireless router. Voilà! Your laptop should be able to use the Internet.

12. **Don't forget to secure your network.**

"Securing Your Wireless Network" on page 52 has details.

Wireless Networking before Windows XP

Unlike the versions of Windows that lumbered through the world before it, Windows XP has a lot of features that make tasks like connecting to a wireless network nice and simple. Antique versions of Windows, including Windows 95, 98, Millennium Edition, and 2000 don't have these advanced wireless features, mostly because nobody was really thinking about wireless networks back when they dominated the earth. But while these older versions of Windows don't make the networking stuff as easy as Windows XP does, you can still get wirelessly connected. But it does take a little more work, and the steps may vary depending on which wireless network adapter you have.

If you are running an older version of Windows, be sure to check the system requirements for any piece of wireless-networking hardware you're thinking of buying. When it comes to Windows 95 or Windows 98, some wireless network adapters won't work at all. Many wireless adapters require support for USB, and since USB ports didn't even start showing up regularly in PC hardware until the late 1990s, these older systems totally missed the boat—because the boat hadn't been built yet. Windows 98 Second Edition, released in 1999, did catch the USB boat, as did all future versions of Windows from that point on.

Unfortunately, until Windows XP came along and standardized things, it was completely left up to the WiFi hardware people to figure out how to get their adapters to work with Windows, and everybody had a different way of making the connection. If you're adding a wireless network adapter to your older Windows system, use the manufacturer's installation and configuration instructions.

Going Wireless on a Macintosh

Macintosh computers have a well-earned reputation for elegance, simplicity, and ease of use, and using a wireless network with a Mac or a group of Macs is no exception.

If you've got an AirPort card installed and you want to connect to a wireless router (regardless of whether it's made by Apple or some other company) just click the Airport menu bar icon (Figure 3-6) and choose the name of the network you want to connect to. Wireless life isn't much tougher if you're running Mac OS 9; you'll find the list of available networks on the control strip's Airport module. Or you can select → AirPort to launch the AirPort utility and pick your network's name from the "Choose network" drop-down list.

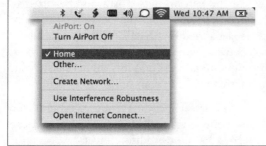

Figure 3-6:
Once you've got an Airport card installed, you can use the menu bar icon to turn off your AirPort card (for battery savings in a laptop), to switch from one AirPort network to another (in schools or companies that have more than one), and to check your wireless signal strength (by counting the "waves" coming out of the icon on your menu bar).

Manually Configuring Your Router

Okay, so what happens if your basic network setup turns out to be not-so-basic? No problem. The two most likely culprits are that you've got a static IP address or your Internet service provider makes you use a PPPoE connection. In either case, you've probably got to take matters into your own hands and manually configure your WiFi router. (If the term "manually configure" makes you nervous, relax. It really just means "typing stuff into boxes on screen and clicking OK.") If you've got a static IP address, read on; if you're a PPPoE person, skip ahead to "Information PPPoE People Need" on page 49.

Information Static IP People Need

If you have a static IP address, you need to obtain the following bits of info from your ISP before you can move ahead: the IP address, subnet mask, default gateway, and DNS servers. You'll need all this arcane technical jargon to configure your router correctly. All these terms are described in the following sections.

The IP address

Every computer connected to the Internet, even temporarily, has its own exclusive *IP address* (IP stands for Internet Protocol). An IP address is always made up of four numbers separated by periods. Think of your IP address as the number of your house on your street—350, 1060, whatever. If you have a static IP address, make sure your Internet service provider has given you an address that works. If the static address falls within any of three restricted ranges—192.168.0.0 to 192.168.255.255, 172.16.0.0 to 172.31.255.255, or 10.0.0.0 to 10.255.255.255—it won't work for getting on the Internet. These numbers all fall within the category of what's known as *private IP address ranges.* Internet engineers once decided that these number ranges should be reserved for secure private networks that can't connect to the big sprawling Internet, which is *very* public. So if you've been assigned one of these numbers, ring up your ISP and get a new one.

Subnet mask

The *subnet mask* (also sometimes called the *network mask*) is a number used to break a large network into small, manageable pieces. Like the IP address, the subnet mask is composed of four numbers, separated by periods. Without the subnet mask, your Internet service provider's network would be one huge, unwieldy mess. But by using a combination of your unique IP address and this subnet mask, your ISP can quickly and efficiently route Internet traffic to your house.

The subnet mask is like the name of your street—Fifth Avenue, West Addison Street, and so on. When combined with your unique IP address, the Internet can find your computer at 350 Fifth Avenue or 1060 West Addison Street.

Your subnet mask is also assigned to you by your ISP and determines on which of their many networks your router lives. Beyond just getting this information from your ISP, you should never have to mess around with the subnet mask.

UP TO SPEED

Internal and External Addresses

Your home network actually uses two different kinds of IP addresses. The one assigned to you by your Internet service provider is what's known as your *external* IP address. The only device that ever sees this address is your router, and this address is used solely for Internet communication.

On the other hand, the computers and other devices connected to your home network use a separate set of IP addresses, which are known as your *internal* IP addresses. Internal IP addresses are used solely by your computers to communicate with your router.

Default gateway

The *default gateway* is a number that serves as your network's own "door" to the Internet. (It's also a member of the four-numbers-separated-by-a-period club.) When your computer realizes that it's communicating with another computer that doesn't live on your local network, it uses this door to get to other networks.

By examining your IP address and subnet mask, your computer can tell whether you're trying to get to things like a Web site on a local computer (that is, one inside your home) or a computer out on the Internet. If the computer determines that you're using the Internet, it automatically sends the information to the default gateway—in this case, your router. The router understands both *your* network and the network Out There. It's sort of like a real estate agent that knows you as well as the sellers, and neither of you can to talk to the other without going through the agent.

Domain Name Services servers

Domain Name Services, or DNS, is like a telephone book for the Internet. Without DNS, you'd be forced to remember *http://216.239.37.99* instead of the more human *http://www.google.com.* Instead, DNS automatically translates the name into the number for you, just like a telephone book. Most Internet providers send you two DNS server addresses so that if one is unavailable, the other one picks up the load. Some ISPs even provide three addresses.

Okay, now that you've got your Ph.D, in Static IP–ology, skip ahead to "Configuring Your Router with a Browser" for all the details on what to do with your collection of numbers and settings.

Information PPPoE People Need

Some ISPs still require their subscribers to use the ol' PPPoE connection method and special communications software that's sometimes built into the operating system (as is the case with Windows XP), and sometimes is a standalone program with a name like WinPoET or MacPoET. These programs help make the connection from a home computer to the Internet. If your ISP uses PPPoE, you're not out of luck since most routers let you establish PPPoE connections if you plug in the information they need. Once your router is connected, you won't have to use the PPPoE connection software anymore.

Fortunately, as complicated as that all sounds, the information you need to gather is pretty simple: a PPPoE user name and password, and a service name, if your ISP is one of the small minority that still requires that. (Usually your ISP has given you all this info in the packet of instructions you got when you signed up with them.)

Configuring Your Router with a Browser

Unlike the simple network setup, this more advanced configuration requires you to manually adjust some settings in your router. You normally have two tools in your router-configuring toolbox:

• The setup CD that came with your router

• Any computer in your home with a Web browser

The method you use is up to you, but using the Web browser to configure your router usually gives you access to certain advanced configuration settings like some security features and PPPoE settings. You also won't have to worry about losing your router's CD. When you configure using the Web browser, all the setting screens are always waiting patiently there for you.

If you want to use the CD, go ahead, and its software wizards will lead the way. If you'd like to get the router routing with your Web browser, read on.

Step 1: Perform the basic wireless network setup

Like a tap-dance routine, every advanced network installation can be broken into smaller, simpler steps. In your case, to get started, follow steps 1 through 7 from the "Setting Up a Basic Wireless Network" section of this chapter, which starts on page 43. As you've discovered, you're not browsing the Internet yet. All you need is one machine turned on and plugged into the router for the configuration dance to begin.

Step 2: Open a Web browser

Every modern operating system has a Web browser included these days. Windows XP has Internet Explorer, Mac OS X has Safari, and both systems can use open source browsers like Firefox. Just start up your favorite electronic window to the world.

Step 3: Connect to the Linksys WRT54G (or whatever router you've got)

Like every router, the Linksys WRT54G comes with a default IP address, user name, and password that you'll need for configuration. In this case, go to your browser's address bar and type in *http://192.168.0.1*. Enter the default administrative user name (if you've got a Linksys router, leave this box blank) and password (for Linksys use *Admin*).

You may wonder why you're able to connect to this Web site, when you can't yet get on the Internet. That's because you're not actually traveling out on the World Wide Web; instead, you're making a connection to your router, which lives at the Web address you just typed in.

If you're using a different brand of router, the default IP address, user name, and password might be different. The table below provides you with the default management IP addresses, user names, and passwords for routers from several popular manufacturers.

Vendor	Configuration address	Default user name	Default password
Belkin	192.168.2.1	<blank>	<blank>
D-Link	192.168.0.1	admin	<blank>
Linksys	192.168.1.1 or 192.168.15.1	<blank>	admin
Microsoft	192.168.2.1	<blank>	admin
Netgear	192.168.0.1	admin	Password

Step 4: Get to the configuration window

When you first connect to the Linksys router, you're greeted with a window that provides you with details on the device's basic configuration. The Internet Connection Type drop-down list says "Automatic Configuration—DHCP," which Figure 3-7 shows.

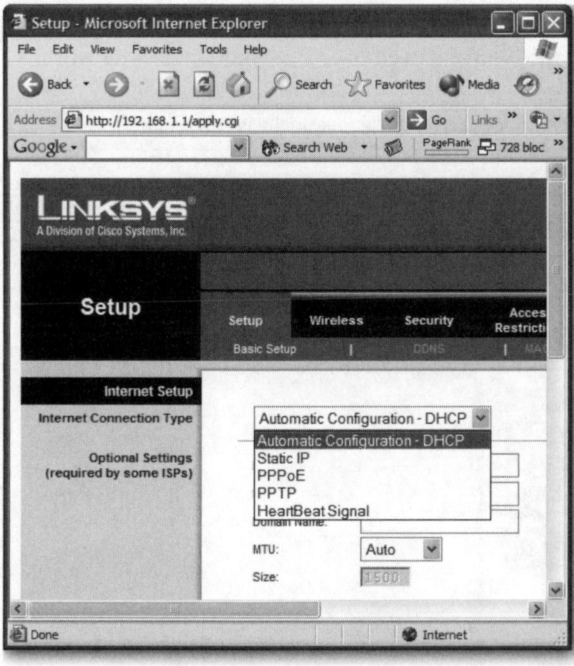

Figure 3-7:
Pick the appropriate entry from the Internet Connection Type list. If you have a static IP address, select this option. If you're setting up a PPPoE connection, select the PPPoE option instead.

If you're using a different brand of router, you screen will look different, but you should be able to find the static IP or PPPoE configuration screen.

Step 5a: Provide IP addressing information

To manually configure your router with a static IP address, you also need to enter the subnet mask, the default gateway, and the domain name servers (discussed starting back on page 47. Figure 3-8 shows the screen from the Linksys WRT54G.

Note: PPPoE people can skip this step, as it's for static IP people only.

When you're done entering addressing information, click the Save Settings button at the very bottom of the window.

Step 5b: Provide PPPoE login information

Figure 3-9 shows a screenshot from the Linksys WRT54G after the Internet connection type box is changed to PPPoE. The two fields that need your attention are User Name and Password.

When you're done entering the PPPoE information, click the Save Settings button at the very bottom of the window.

At last, you're ready to browse the Web. But don't whip out that credit card and start ordering goodies just yet, because you still need to secure your wireless network.

Note: Static IP people can ignore this step because it applies only to the PPPoE people.

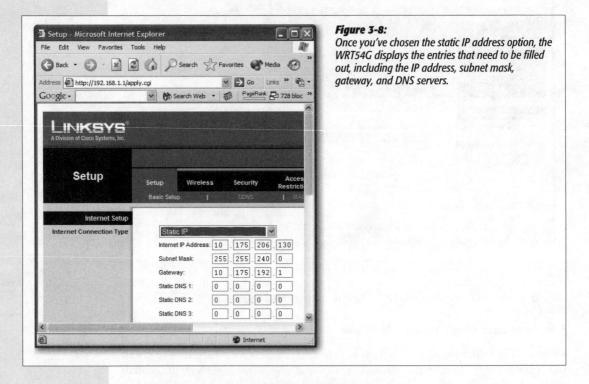

Figure 3-8:
Once you've chosen the static IP address option, the WRT54G displays the entries that need to be filled out, including the IP address, subnet mask, gateway, and DNS servers.

Securing Your Wireless Network

From the beginning, wireless networks have suffered from poor security. All that data flying over the airwaves is tempting prey for determined snoops on the hunt for personal information like passwords, credit card numbers, and your mother's maiden name.

If you live out in the country and your closest neighbor is miles away, you might not worry so much about eavesdroppers, unless the cows in the field next door have wireless laptops and a bone to pick with your backyard grilling habits. But if you live in a high-rise or other densely packed living quarters, things are different, since it's much easier for criminals, neighbors, or any combination of the two to try to pick up stray signals from vulnerable wireless networks.

Fortunately, there are some simple steps you can—and most definitely *should*—take to protect your personal information. While no level of security will completely protect you, you can put up enough of a defense to deter casual and intermediate intruders.

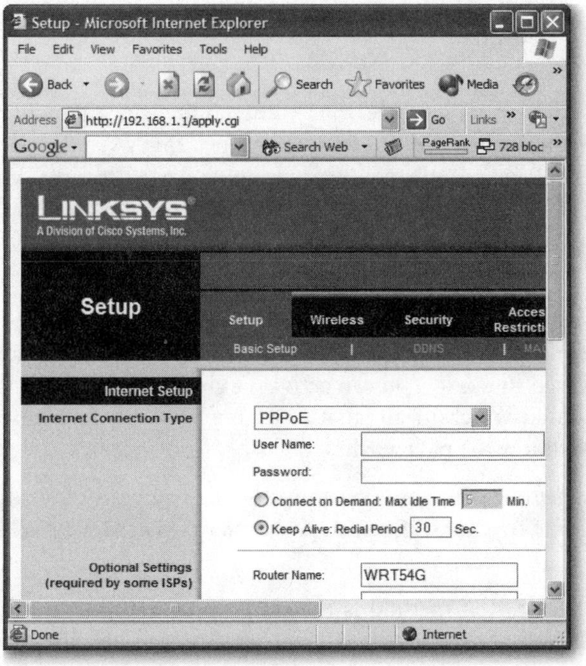

Figure 3-9:
Enter the PPPoE user name and password that your ISP gave you.

The Language of Security

One reason many people hesitate to batten down their home network is the intimidating thicket of terminology and choices awaiting them when they enter the world of wireless security. And unfortunately, as of now, there's no such thing as a simple solution (the equivalent, say, of a home alarm system where you just punch in a code). But if you're willing to learn just a few words and phrases—things like *SSID, authentication*, and *WEP*—you'll at least be able to decide what kind of security setup makes sense for you, and find out how to go about setting it up.

Service Set Identifier (SSID)

Everything has a name, even your wireless network. Your router beams out a *Service Set Identifier*, or *SSID*, which announces your wireless network's name to any nearby WiFi-enabled computers. Every manufacturer starts you off with a suggested SSID—for example, D-Link's is *default*, while Linksys proudly uses *linksys* and Belkin opts for *WLAN*. The table below shows the SSIDs used by some leading router manufacturers.

Vendor	Default SSID(s)
Linksys	linksys
Belkin	WLAN or belkin54g
D-Link	default
Netgear	NETGEAR
Microsoft	MSHOME

Unfortunately, these WiFi shout-outs increase your vulnerability, since they literally broadcast your network's existence to any computer that's WiFi-ready, whether or not you want to. Page 56 tells you everything you need to do if you want to silence the SSID (and how to let PCs you know and trust go ahead and make a manual connection).

Authentication

When you turn on your computer, you might have to type in a user name and password before you're allowed to use it. You can activate a similar feature—called *authentication*—on your router, which means that anyone who wants to connect to your network will need to know the password.

Here's where you'll need to get out your acronym soup spoon. You've got four different authentication methods to choose from: Open System, Shared Key/WEP, WPA, and WPA-PSK.

- **Open System.** This authentication method is the simplest of the four, but it's also the most insecure. Under an Open System, any computer can join the wireless network and receive any nonencrypted traffic. This is the type of authentication you have if you set up your router and don't take any steps to secure it.

- **Shared Key/WEP.** The next level up is Shared Key authentication, which is slightly more secure than Open System. Shared Key means that all wireless devices on your network share the same password (which geeks sometimes call a *key*). The key is any combination of letters and numbers, and it acts as the password you (and anyone you allow) use to log onto your network. Shared Key works in conjunction with Wired Equivalent Privacy (WEP), which you'll learn about in the next section.

- **WPA-PSK.** This mouthful of letters stands for WiFi Protected Access Pre-Shared Key. It's similar to WPA (the next item in this list), but it's suitable for home networks because it doesn't require special hardware to run it. It works like the Shared Key method but has more advanced security features and offers more protected communication for the network's traffic. To use WPA-PSK, you need to create a secret key on your router and use wireless network adapters that support the WPA-PSK standard.

- **WPA.** WiFi Protected Access is one of the newer authentication methods, and it's slowly creeping into home networking hardware (among others, Apple's AirPort Extreme Base Station uses it). But not all hardware manufacturers have adopted this standard, which means you might prevent certain people from joining your network if you use this method (since their WiFi cards might not be WPA-ready).

With all of these choices, which method should you use for your home network? For reasonable security and compatibility with the widest variety of wireless network cards, Shared Key/WEP is your best option (read on to find out how to set this up on your network). Open System is way too open and the WPA systems haven't become widely adopted for home-networking systems yet, even though they probably represent the future of wireless security.

Wired Equivalent Privacy (WEP)

Before you get started securing your network, it helps to know a little more about WEP. *Wired Equivalent Privacy* is an encryption method that locks up and protects data traveling back and forth across your network.

Note: WEP can't be used with WPA and WPA-PSK, since these newer systems use their own encryption recipe (which happens to whip WEP hands down, which is why they're likely to be the future of wireless security once they become a little more widespread).

The level or intensity of the encryption is controlled by the length of a cryptic code—called a *key*—which is used in conjunction with a mathematical algorithm to scramble and unscramble your network's data. Most routers give you three increasingly strong key lengths (40, 64, and 128) to choose from; which one you select depends on the level your router and your network adapters support. You install the key in both your router and the computers on your network (you'll learn how to do both those things in the sections that follow).

Note: Higher encryption levels can result in slower data transmission speeds because the computer has to use some of its power to deal with encrypting and decrypting data.

Once you pick a particular encryption level, you need to make sure all your wireless network adapters can handle that level. For example, if you have a card or device on the network that can't handle 128-bit encryption, you'll have to drop the level down to the highest level all the devices on your network can handle.

Note: Newer wireless routers and access points support 256 bits of encryption for even stronger security. Older routers can sometimes be upgraded to support this level, so check your router manufacturer's Web site to see if this is possible.

There is a downside to WEP: it's been cracked. That means someone has figured out a way to unscramble its code and decrypt the data by using sneaky software.

WEP doesn't secure your network as well as it should and probably never will, which is another reason WPA is moving up fast as the better way to protect networks. But even though it's not perfect, WEP sticks a barrier in front of potential trespassers and will deter most amateur bandwidth bootleggers.

Securing Your Router

To go ahead and actually secure your network, you need to change the settings on your router, as well as on any computers that you want to connect to the network. Think of it this way: it's like you're installing a new lock on your door and once you do, you need to give keys to anyone who you want to allow into your house. You should make the changes in this order: first, to the router and then to each desktop computer. (That order is important: if you change things in the opposite order, you won't be able to log onto your WiFi network.)

Suppose you want to secure the wireless network described earlier in this chapter. In particular, say you want to turn off the SSID broadcast and turn on WEP encryption—both of which would make your network more secure than most people's and yet still make it reasonably easy to use. Here's what you need to do.

Note: As with the instructions for the initial network setup, the numbered steps that follow are meant specifically for the Linksys WRT54G router. But the choices you'll face if you've got a different model should be fairly similar.

First, flip back to page 49 and follow steps 1 to 3 (which will get you to the manual configuration window for your router), and then continue by doing the following:

1. **Go to the Wireless Settings page and click the Wireless option on the main heading in the window.**

    The first thing you're going to do is turn off the SSID broadcast, which you'll do in the next step.

Note: If you've got an Apple Base Station, use the Airport Admin Utility (found in Applications → Utilities) instead of a Web browser. Once you've launched it and opened the configuration panel for your Base Station, look on the AirPort tab for the AirPort Network section. There you'll see a checkbox, which you can turn on to create a closed network. You can also click the Change Wireless Security button in that section to turn on WEP or WPA.

---

2. **Change the SSID broadcast option to Disable on the Basic Settings page (Figure 3-10).**

    Figure 3-10 also shows you how to change the name of your SSID.

3. **Click the Save Settings button.**

    You won't lose your connection to the wireless network, because you're already connected to your network's current SSID. From this point on, though, new wireless computers within range won't be notified that your wireless network exists.

---

4. **Go to the Wireless Security configuration page.**

Now you're going to turn on the WEP encryption. Look again at the page shown in Figure 3-10. Click the Wireless Security link, which is immediately to the right of Basic Settings.

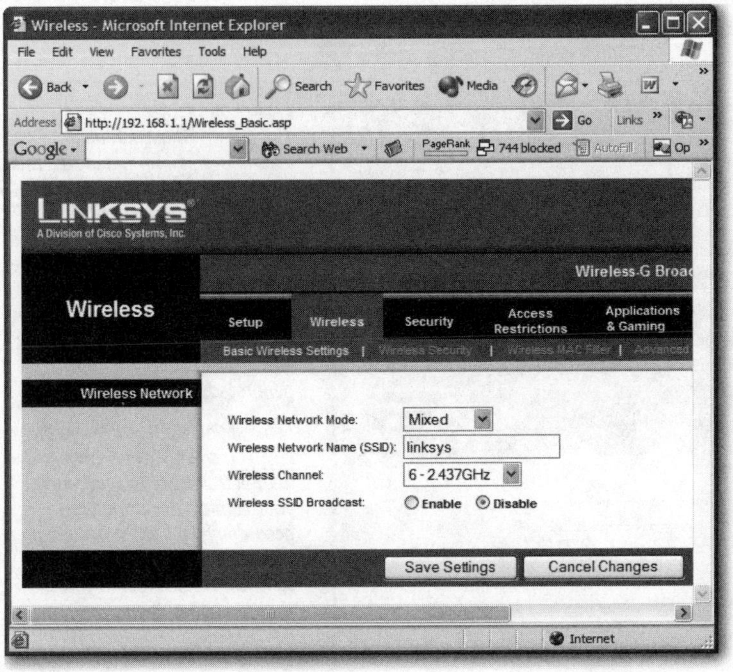

Figure 3-10:
Once you disable the SSID broadcasting function, your router will no longer shout out its name to anybody within distance of your network. Most routers let you easily disable this feature.

If you want to change your SSID (that is, your network's name), just enter a new name in the Wireless Network Name (SSID) box.

5. **Change the Security Mode to WEP.**

To activate WEP encryption, change the entry in the Security Mode box by clicking the pull-down menu and selecting WEP.

6. **Type a password into the passphrase box.**

Your router will use this password to generate a series of four keys, only one of which you'll actually use when securing your network (the leftover keys, as you'll learn in a moment, are the virtual equivalent of backup, or alternate keys). In this example, you'll create a 40-bit key. For 40-bit security you only need to use a five-character long password to generate the 10-character key that 40-bit encryption needs. You can type more characters, but they'll be ignored. If you select a higher bit encryption level, you'll need to use a longer passphrase. For 128-bit security, for example, the passphrase must be at least 13 characters long, which generates a 26-character key.

7. **Click the Generate button.**

This step actually uses the password you typed to generate the keys. The keys probably look like a bunch of gobbledygook, which may give you an idea of why security developers came up with the idea of using a password to generate the key. It's a heck of a lot easier to come up with the word *skippy* than to think up four different variations of the key *6CA8CB0BC6*. Figure 3-11 shows you an example of a key.

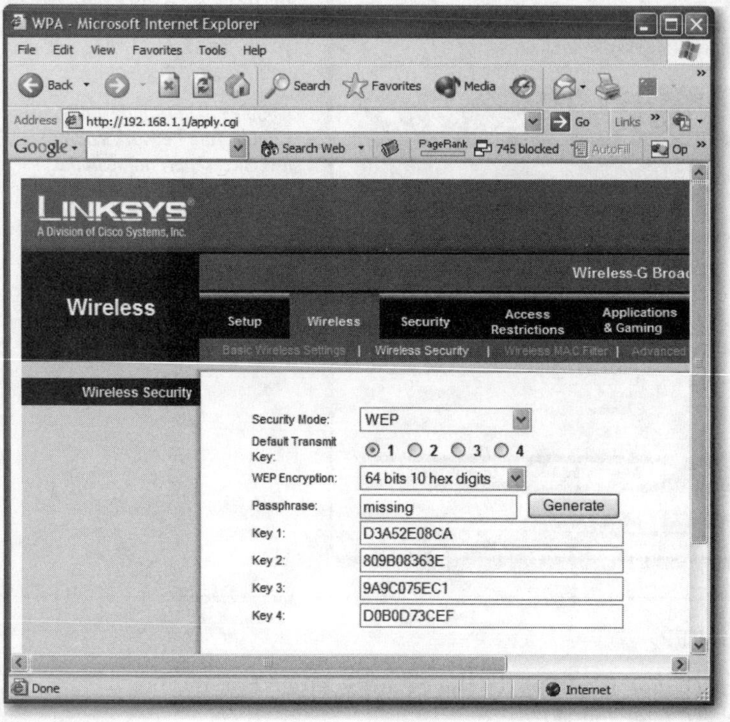

Figure 3-11:
The password used in this example—missing—generated four keys. Since this example uses 40-bit security, only the first five letters—missi—are actually needed to create the key. At the top of the screen, there's an option for Default Transmit Key, which is set to 1. This means that the first key will be used out of the four generated.

Later, if you want to change the key, you can always change the default transmit key and modify your connected computers accordingly. It's like having four different super-secret passwords, so if you think somebody has guessed one of them, you can easily change to one of your other keys to lock out the intruder again in a flash.

8. **Write down the key *and* the passphrase you selected.**

As shown in this example, the router is using the first key generated, so write down this series of letters and numbers. Make sure that everything is capitalized, just like the router has it.

At this point, if you're connected from a wireless computer, you won't be able to use the Internet anymore. Even worse, you won't even be able to connect to your router, because you just pulled the carpet out from under your wireless connection by turning on the router's WEP encryption. Read on to find out how to fix this.

Tip: Keep both the key and the password some place you'll remember, because you'll need the key if a friend comes over, and you'll need the password if you want to recreate a new set of identical keys.

Adjusting Your PC's Security Settings

Now you need to give your computer and any laptop-toting friends the key to get back on the network. That's what the next four sections cover. Pick the section that covers your computer's operating system.

Windows XP

For Windows XP owners, modifying your WiFi connection is pretty easy.

1. **Open up Network and Internet Connection properties.**

   Go to Start → Control Panel → Network and Internet Connections and click Network Connections. In the Network Connections window that appears, double-click Wireless Network Connection. The Wireless Network Connection Status dialog box appears.

2. **Click the Properties button.**

   The Wireless Network Connection Properties dialog box appears.

3. **Click the Wireless Networks tab (Figure 3-12, top).**

   With no wireless networks visible, your Windows XP computer won't be able to automatically connect anymore, so you need to manually add your wireless network, which you'll do in the next step.

4. **Click the Add button.**

   The "Wireless network properties" dialog box appears.

5. **Enter your network's SSID info and your WEP key as explained in Figure 3-12, bottom.**

6. **Save the settings.**

   Click OK until all the dialog boxes go away. When you're done, Windows XP automatically reconnects to your router. Even better, all the traffic between your computer and your router is now safe from spies.

Windows 95, 98, 98SE, ME, 2000

To change your wireless networking configuration under these older operating systems, you need to use the software that came with your wireless network adapter and follow the instructions provided by the adapter's manufacturer. Microsoft improved wireless network adapter support in Windows XP, but older versions can be inconsistent because Microsoft left it up to the hardware makers to decide how their products behave.

Some hardware vendors don't make you use the weird-looking key that was generated by the router and let you just use the password directly. With that information, the computer can figure out what the keys are supposed to be. However, be prepared to type in the funky string of letters and numbers for the manufacturers who don't do this favor for you.

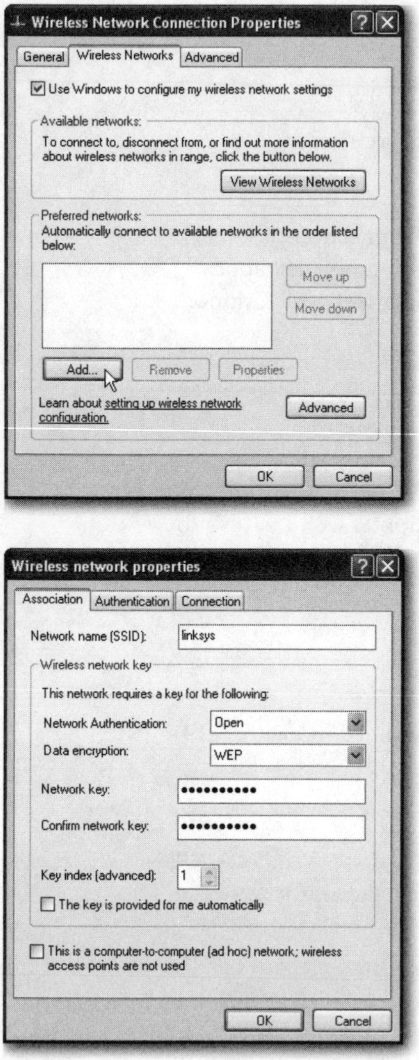

Figure 3-12:
Top: On the Wireless Networks tab of the Wireless Network Connection Properties dialog box, the "Preferred networks" box is probably blank. Click the Add button to open up a screen similar to the figure below.

Bottom: Here's where you type in the SSID for your network. In this example, it's linksys. Next, change the data encryption option to WEP and turn off the checkbox next to "The key is provided for me automatically" since you need to manually enter the key. In the "Network key" and "Confirm network key" boxes, type in the first key that was generated by your router. This string of letters and numbers will be either 10 or 26 characters long, depending on which level of WEP encryption you chose.

Mac OS X

Mac OS X also provides an easy way to change your wireless configuration.

1. **Open up your AirPort card's preferences.**

   Click the AirPort wireless adapter icon in the Mac's menu bar. (The icon looks like a fan-shaped triangle of little sound waves.) Click the icon to get the pull-down menu and select *Other...* from the list.

2. **Select WEP as your AirPort card's encryption method.**

   From the Wireless Security drop-down menu, choose WEP Password (see Figure 3-13).

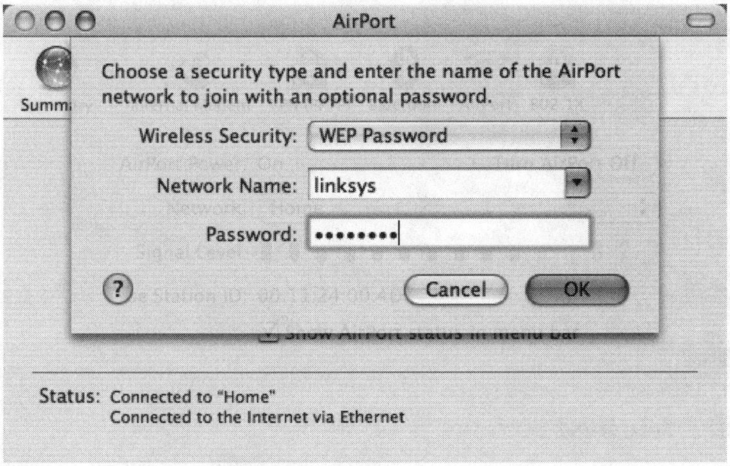

Figure 3-13:
Type the WEP key that was generated by your router and click OK. Your Mac OS X computer will connect to the wireless network and you'll be back on the Internet, but now your data transmissions will be encrypted to keep out those network nosy Parkers.

3. **Enter a network name.**

   Enter your wireless network's SSID. For example, if you were using the Linksys router, you'd enter *linksys*.

4. **Enter the 10- or 26-character WEP key.**

Mac OS 9

Here's how to change your wireless settings if your computer's running Mac OS 9.

1. **Open up the AirPort configuration utility.**

   Go to Macintosh HD → Apple Extras → AirPort and double-click the AirPort icon.

2. **Type the name of your wireless network's SSID.**

   Since SSID broadcasting is disabled, you won't be able to just select a network. In the SSID/network box, type the name of your network. In this example, it's *linksys*.

3. Type the WEP password when prompted (Figure 3-14).

Tip: The AirPort Setup Assistant that comes with Apple's AirPort Extreme and AirPort Express Base Stations will walk you through the WEP steps when you set it up.

Figure 3-14:
Type the WEP key that was generated by your router and click OK. Your Mac OS 9 computer will get right back on the Internet with its data safely scrambled between computer and router.

Security on Apple Base Stations

Apple's AirPort Extreme and AirPort Express stations come with the AirPort Setup Assistant software to walk you through setting up your AirPort network (page 40), but the security portion of the setup program may be confusing for people new to the whole wireless ballgame.

Here are the bits of information you should fill in during the AirPort setup to keep your network as secure as possible.

- **Network Name.** What other routers call an SSID, Apple's hardware describes in good old English. Give your network a name right here.

- **Network Password.** You can keep intruders from lounging on your AirPort network by requiring a password. The password should be 5 (40-bit) or 13 (128-bit) characters long for maximum compatibility with most wireless adapter cards.

- **Verify Password.** Your AirPort Base Station wants to make darn sure that you typed your password correctly. Type it again.

- **WEP Key Length.** The AirPort Base Station provides two levels of WEP encryption. The weakest is 40-bit encryption; 128-bit encryption provides better security.

Note: If you're running Mac OS X 10.3, or later, or Windows XP on all of your wireless computers, you can use a much stronger form of encryption than WEP. WiFi Protected Access (page 55) is a much tougher encryption nut to crack, but you need to make sure your wireless network adapters can support it.

The Base Station password

Apple gives you the ability to assign a different password to the Base Station itself, separate from the password required to join the network. By default, the Base Station just uses the network password you chose earlier in the setup process. This gives anybody connected to the network the power to change the Base Station settings, including the level of encryption. If you don't want to allow others to mess around with the Air-Port, assign a separate password for the Base Station during the setup process.

Going Hybrid?

Almost all wireless networks use other types of network technology at some point. At the very least, your broadband modem uses an Ethernet cable to connect to your wireless router. But what if you want to extend these wired/wireless partnerships even further? The simplest step is to make sure the wireless router you buy comes with plenty of Ethernet ports. That way, if you've got devices you want everyone on the network to use—for example, a printer, or a network attached hard drive (page 185)—you can just plug the gadget directly into your wireless router. But in the next chapter, you'll also read about another type of networking technology, called Powerline, that gets along very nicely, both with Ethernet and WiFi. Powerline uses the existing electrical wiring in your home to extend the reach of your network. Flip the page to find out more.

Setting Up a Powerline Network

Ethernet and WiFi tend to hog all the networking glory, but there's a third way of linking your computers, and it's gaining some attention in the home-networking industry. *Powerline* networks use the electrical wiring already in your home to link your computers together.

In this chapter, you'll learn about Powerline's nuts and bolts and how to install a Powerline network in your home. If you've already done some networking but were stymied on how to extend your network into some hard-to-reach spot—the basement or an attic office, for example—you'll learn how to add Powerline onto your existing Ethernet or WiFi network.

Note: You might sometimes see Powerline referred to as *HomePlug*—that's the name of the official networking standard all Powerline devices use. To make matters worse, some hardware makers pile on even more monikers by slapping their own names, such as HomeLink or PlugLink, on their Powerline products.

Deciding If Powerline Is Right for You

Powerline is an impressive and easy-to-use network technology, but it's a little different from Ethernet and WiFi, the current networking champs. While Powerline devices can theoretically work all by themselves, most companies have focused their energy on developing products that work *with* your existing network's Ethernet or wireless router. In practice, most people use Powerline as a supplement to the main network, sort of like adding a room over the garage to get more living space in your house. Figure 4-1 shows a typical Powerline network setup.

Now that you know what a typical Powerline setup looks like, here are a few points to consider before deciding whether Powerline's for you:

- **Powerline's good for extending your network to hard-to-reach spots.** If your PCs are spread far and wide across your house (say, greater than 150 feet apart, which is too far for WiFi to reach, or would require an unsightly mass of Ethernet cables), Powerline's a great alternative.

- **Powerline's not the fastest network on the block.** With a maximum speed of 14 megabits per second (Mbps)—compared to Ethernet's current standard of 100 Mbps—Powerline networks aren't exactly going to win the Indianapolis 500 of networking technologies. And that's the *theoretical* maximum speed—in reality, a Powerline network will probably coast along at 5 to 8 Mbps. These speeds are fine for low-bandwidth tasks like surfing the Web and email, but you'll likely get frustrated by speed lags and slow performance if you try to use your Powerline network for muscular chores like copying large files between computers or streaming digital movies.

Note: When your power system is hindered, Powerline automatically falls back to speeds as slow as 1 Mbps, which is probably slower than your broadband Internet connection. Surge protectors, uninterruptible power supplies, electrical interference filters for stereo equipment, drills, hairdryers, and microwave ovens can also create harsh conditions on your electrical system that results in poor Powerline network performance.

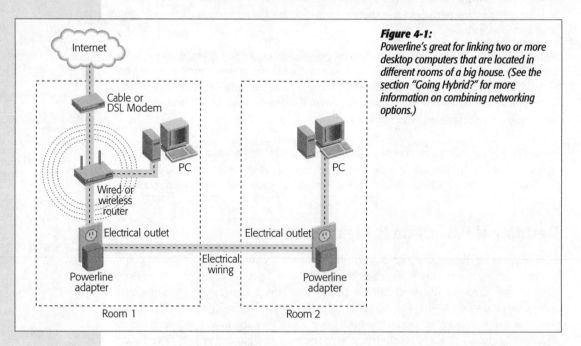

Figure 4-1:
Powerline's great for linking two or more desktop computers that are located in different rooms of a big house. (See the section "Going Hybrid?" for more information on combining networking options.)

- **You can't use more than 16 Powerline devices on your network.** Powerline's technical standard limits the number of devices you can pile on your power lines to 16. This 16-and-under restriction probably won't affect a family home network, but could put a crimp in the plans of someone trying to set up a small office network with Powerline equipment. (In contrast, the wired Ethernet networks described in Chapter 2 have no limit on the number of computers that can connect.)

Picking Out Powerline Hardware

If you're still game, you're going to need to bring three things to the Powerline setup party: a Powerline network adapter, a router, and some cables.

Powerline Network Adapters

Like every type of network, Powerline requires the use of network adapters (page 5)—sometimes also called *bridge adapters*—that let your computer to talk to the Internet and to other computers hanging out on the network. If you've been reading this book from the beginning, you know that Powerline adapters (Figure 4-2) look a bit different than those used by Ethernet and WiFi networks.

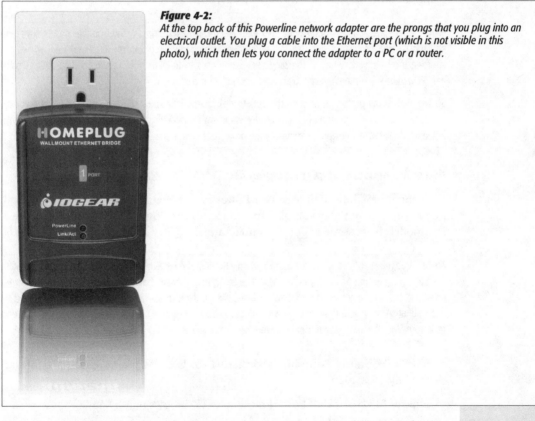

Figure 4-2:
At the top back of this Powerline network adapter are the prongs that you plug into an electrical outlet. You plug a cable into the Ethernet port (which is not visible in this photo), which then lets you connect the adapter to a PC or a router.

Powerline network adapters come in two varieties: Ethernet and USB. Both versions use their respective cable types to plug into the appropriate port on your computer. (If your computer doesn't have an Ethernet port, check out page 20, which tells you how to open up your system and install one.) Unfortunately, there's no such thing as a Powerline adapter that you can install *inside* your computer. You always have to use a Powerline-to-Ethernet or Powerline-to-USB adapter. If you do have an Ethernet port on your PC, you'll want to use the Ethernet Powerline adapter, because it's speedier than its USB counterpart.

Note: Most Powerline equipment is Windows-only. While this factoid is not much of a problem for 95 percent of the world, it tends to depress Mac people. Luckily for them, though, a company called SMC Networks (*www.smc.com*) is now making Powerline networking equipment that works with all-Macintosh networks. Macwireless.com also has some Mac-friendly Powerline devices (search under "Powerline").

You always need to have at least *two* Powerline network adapters on your network. You need one for each computer you want to connect to the network, and you also need a Powerline adapter to connect to the Ethernet port on your router. The Powerline adapter you connect to your router has to be of the Ethernet persuasion, but it doesn't matter whether the router you're plugging into is wireless (Chapter 3) or plain-old Ethernet (Chapter 2)—either way, both work with Powerline.

Note: Powerline adapters don't work well with electrical power strips, uninterruptible power supplies, and most surge protectors, because this equipment sometimes filters out the high-end frequencies on your electrical network—which is the range Powerline uses to transmit your network's data. Always connect Powerline equipment *directly* to an electrical outlet for best results.

Sockets with surge protection right on the outlet (look for the little colored button marked Reset if you're not sure if you have a protected outlet) render your Powerline device useless. Belkin (*www.belkin.com*), however, does make a Powerline-friendly surge protector that you may want to check out.

Powerline network adapter shopping list

Remember, you'll need at least two Powerline adapters—one for your router and one for every computer you plan to connect to the Powerline network. Here are a few models from some popular manufacturers.

Note: Mac mavens, listen up: in the list below, only the SMC EZ Powerline adapter includes encryption software that you can turn on directly from a Mac. The encryption software that comes with other adapters *works* on a Mac, but you've got to *activate it* from a Windows machine (page 70 tells you everything you need to know about securing your Powerline network). Bottom line: if you're living in a Mac-only household, buy your gear from SMC. If you've got a mix of Macs and PCs, then you can buy from any Powerline manufacturer.

- SMC EZ Connect Powerline-to-Ethernet (or USB) adapter (Windows and Mac friendly): $50 each

- Linksys PLUSB10 USB Powerline adapter (Windows only): $65

- Linksys PLEBR10 Ethernet Powerline adapter (Windows only): $65

- Netgear XE102 Ethernet Powerline adapter (Windows only): $50

- D-Link DHP100 Ethernet Powerline adapter (Windows only): $50

A Router with a Built-in Ethernet Switch

Routers (page 3) are the traffic cops of every home network. They help distribute your Internet connection among all the computers on your network. As you learned earlier in this chapter, Powerline device manufacturers have pretty much decided that it doesn't make sense to make a Powerline-only router. Instead, if you've decided to use Powerline, you need to first get yourself an Ethernet or a WiFi router (make sure whichever you get comes with a built-in switch, which most do nowadays). Ethernet router details await you on page 16; check out page page 33 for a quick primer on WiFi routers.

Cables

You need two different kinds of cables when using Powerline:

- The **electrical power lines** behind your walls, which you can't really change without potentially electrocuting yourself. Powerline network adapters use the electrical wires in your walls to communicate with the router and the computers on your network.

- A **USB or USB cable** that connects the Powerline network adapter to your computer or router. If you buy an Ethernet Powerline adapter, make sure you have a standard Ethernet cable (page 21) to connect the network adapter to the computer's Ethernet port. If you've got a USB Powerline adapter—you guessed it—you need a USB cable.

Cable shopping list

You can find USB cables in just about any computer shop or office-supply store, in varying lengths (prices vary by how long the cable is, but expect to pay between $10 and $20). You can even find them at Wal-Mart, which is one of the few places in America where you can buy frozen waffles, a bathrobe, Turtle Wax, and computer-networking supplies all under one roof.

Ethernet cable pricing also depends on the length of the cable. Big-chain computer stores may charge you $25 to $35 for a measly 10 feet of cable, but you can find the same length of cord for anywhere from $3 to $7 if you carefully scout the Web, Wal-Mart, or smaller, independent computer shops. Ethernet cable comes in several grades or *categories* (page 22). Buy the cables marked Category 6 if you can; if you can't Category 5 or 5e work, too.

Setting Up a Basic Powerline Network

Now that you know what goes into a Powerline network, you're ready to learn how to set one up. By the end of this section, you'll be able to jump on the Internet from any of the Powerline-connected computers in the house.

To get a simple Powerline network up and running so all your computers can browse the Internet at once, follow these steps:

1. **Make sure you've got an Ethernet or WiFi router up and running.**

   Pop back to page 26 for information on how to set up an Ethernet router. Page 47 tells you everything you need to know to set up a WiFi router.

2. **Buy your Powerline equipment.**

   Remember that you need at least two Powerline adapters and that at least one of them has to be an *Ethernet* Powerline adapter for the connection to your router.

3. **In the room with the router, plug the Ethernet Powerline adapter into the electrical outlet on wall.**

   Try to use an outlet close to the router to keep the amount of cables snaking through the room to a minimum.

4. **Connect the Powerline adapter to the router.**

   Plug one end of an Ethernet cable into the Ethernet port on the Powerline adapter and the other end into a free Ethernet port on the router. Make sure both ends of the cable click into place to ensure a good connection.

5. **Plug a Powerline adapter into the wall next to each computer and then connect the adapter to the computer.**

   In each room where there's a computer, plug a Powerline adapter into an available electrical outlet. Connect the appropriate cable (USB or Ethernet) between the Powerline adapter and either the computer's USB or Ethernet port.

6. **Go!**

   At this point, all of your computers should be able to get to the Internet. Not too hard, eh?

Although your computers are on the Internet at this point, the data moving around your network isn't safe from nosy neighbors. That's because the Powerline signal could possibly "leak" out of your house via the electrical lines you share with the rest of the neighborhood (page 71). This can be a big problem, especially if you live in close quarters with your neighbors, as in an apartment building. The next section shows you what you need to do to make sure you're secure.

Securing Your Powerline Network

If you don't want your neighbors to potentially pop onto your network, you'll want to install the encryption software that comes with every Powerline adapter. Encryption protects your network by wrapping up all your traveling data into a package, and only you and the Powerline hardware have the key to unlock it.

Note: Without encryption, a neighbor or another tenant in your apartment building could plug a Powerline adapter into one of their own electrical outlets and be able to see everything on your network. A Powerline signal can travel more than 1,500 feet over electrical lines before becoming unusable, so people living in apartment complexes, townhouse condo communities, and neighborhoods where single family homes are shoved up against each other are particularly at risk for signal leakage.

FREQUENTLY ASKED QUESTION

Identical Looking Devices

Why do many Powerline adapters from different hardware companies look exactly the same?

When you're doing your shopping research for Powerline hardware, you may notice that many of the standard Ethernet-to-Powerline network adapters look very similar to each other. If you browse through online manuals and setup screens on each company's Web site, you might even notice that many of them use identical software and the same factory-set password.

So what gives? Are hardware makers that unoriginal that they all copied the first person who made Powerline adapters?

Actually, this serious case of device déjà vu stems from the fact that there are only a couple of different electronics companies that make the communications hardware found inside *all* of the different Powerline bridge adapters. Home-networking manufacturers like D-Link, Netgear, IOGEAR, and Belkin buy these standard components and then slap their own labels on them. One good thing about this uniformity: the different brands work really well together if you've got hardware from a couple companies mixed in together on your Powerline network.

Turning on your adapters' encryption involves a few steps. You activate the first adapter's encryption from any *one* of the PCs that you've just hooked up. Then, from that PC, you can activate the encryption on all the *other* Powerline adapters. All the Powerline adapters will use the same password, and you'll just have to set this encryption up one time; from then on, you'll be Powerlining with full encryption protection. Here's how it works.

Note: The following instructions explain how to install the encryption software included with the D-Link DHP100 Ethernet-to-Powerline bridge. But if you've got a Powerline adapter from Netgear, IOGear, or Belkin, you'll be going through almost exactly the same setup, because each device uses the same program to activate encryption. If you're using a different brand, these instructions will probably work, but if not, check out the manual that came with your device.

---

1. **Insert the CD that came with your Powerline adapter and start the installation wizard.**

   You can perform this installation from any computer on your network that's plugged into a Powerline adapter.

2. **From the CD's main menu, choose Install Encryption Software.**

3. **Click the Next button on the next three screens.**

The first screen welcomes you to the installation process; the second screen asks you to accept the license agreement; and the third screen asks you to enter an optional user name and organization name (and lets you pick whether the software can be used just by you or by all users on your PC).

4. **Click Install to install the software.**

5. **Click Finish on the next screen.**

6. **Restart your PC.**

Your PC and the attached adapter are now using encryption, albeit using a standard password that anyone can get by going to D-Link's Web site. Therefore, you'll learn how to change the password in the next few steps. And that's also where you'll activate the encryption on any other PCs you've got that are using Powerline adapters (as well as the adapter attached to your router).

7. **Start the D-Link Configuration Utility.**

Double-click the D-Link Configuration Utility (Figure 4-3) on your desktop, or go to Start → Program → D-Link PLC → D-Link Configuration Utility.

Figure 4-3:
Double-click the D-Link Configuration icon to start the D-Link Powerline utilities. Obviously, if you're not using a D-Link device, you're going to see a different icon, but you get the idea.

8. **Click the Security tab (Figure 4-4).**

Here's where you're going to set the password for the Powerline adapter that's connected to your PC (as opposed to any of the other Powerline adapters out there on your network). This password is the same one that you're going to eventually use on any other Powerline adapters that you've got, so make sure you write it down. Enter your new password in the box below where it says Network Password. Then click Apply, and then click OK.

9. **Click the Advanced tab.**

This is where you're going to set the passwords for any other Powerline adapters you've got on your network.

Tip: The Advanced tab is also useful if you have a Macintosh on your network and are not using the Mac-friendly SMC EZ Powerline adapter. By changing the password from a Windows computer and doing so for all your adapters at once, the adapter connected to your Mac is also updated with the new password.

---

10. Write down the factory-assigned password that came with each additional Powerline adapter on your network (that is, each adapter that's *not* connected to the computer you're using right now).

You'll find the password on the Powerline adapter itself, and it should look something like this: *MX96-DHEE-U9Y3-BXJB*.

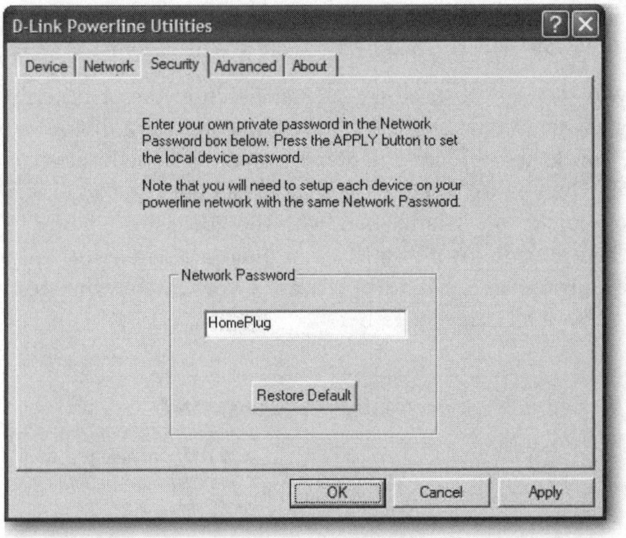

Figure 4-4:
The factory setting for the D-Link's password is HomePlug. It's case-sensitive, meaning that Homeplug and HomePlug are different passwords as far as the computer is concerned.

11. **Enter the device password in the Device Password text box.**

Click Add. The password appears in the Remote Password list box. Continue entering the device password for all the Powerline adapters on your network.

12. **In the Remote Password list box, select all the device passwords.**

13. **In the Network Password text box, enter the password you created back in step 8. Click Set All. Then click OK, and you're done.**

Now that you've got your Powerline network set up and secure, surely you're ready to do more than simply surf the Internet? Those of you with Windows machines may want to continue on to Chapter 5 for more detailed information about networking *between* individual PCs, while Mac readers will find Chapter 6 more illuminating. If you've got a houseful of both systems, Chapter 7 is your next stop. But before you move on, you may be interested in learning about other ways that Powerline can work with Ethernet and WiFi networks.

Going Hybrid?

The basic Powerline setup you learned about in this chapter is not the only way you can use Powerline in conjunction with other types of networks. You might, for example, want to set up a WiFi zone (page 10) in a far, far corner of your house.

This challenge is especially common for people who've got basement or attic offices or playrooms that they want to blanket with WiFi coverage. The problem these people face is that their WiFi router's stuck back in some *other* part of the house and the far corner is, well, too far away to be reached by a standard WiFi antenna.

Powerline can help you out. The procedure can take a little bit of time, but it involves performing steps you've already learned, or will soon learn, if you're willing to read Chapter 2 (on Ethernet) and Chapter 3 (on WiFi). The basic steps are pretty straightforward: you set up a network that uses Powerline to link your broadband modem to your far-off room. Then, with the Powerline adapter in the far-off room, rather than plugging it into a PC, you plug in a *wireless access point* (page 39), whose sole purpose in life is to broadcast a wireless Internet connection. Figure 4-5 shows how it all comes together.

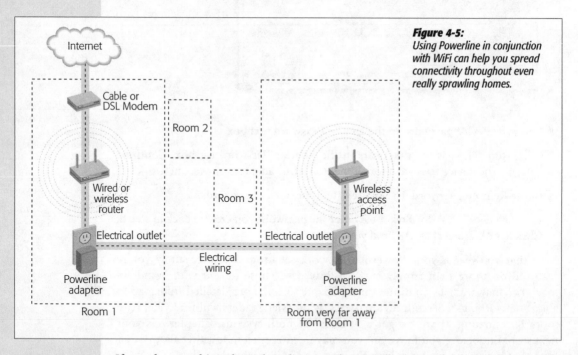

Figure 4-5:
Using Powerline in conjunction with WiFi can help you spread connectivity throughout even really sprawling homes.

If you do something along these lines, you're actually using all three of the network types discussed so far and have officially won the Triple Crown of home-networking. Congratulations!

Part Two: Using Your Network

2

Using the Network with Windows Computers

Surfing the Web from your newly networked computers is fun, no doubt. But some of the best parts of having a home network revolve around what's going on *inside* your house. You, proud network owner, have got your own wide world of resources waiting for you on the PCs sitting right within your home. The files, folders, disk drives, and printers—in fact, almost anything you can attach or store inside any computer on your network—can be shared among all your PCs. Sharing requires taking three basic steps:

- **Naming the PCs and people on your network.** Every computer needs a name. And, in many cases, you'll want to create *user accounts* for everyone on all the PCs you want them to have access to. You'll learn much more about both procedures in the first part of this chapter, but the user accounts in particular are a great way to keep everyone's stuff private and looking exactly the way everyone wants it to look.

- **Designating *what* you want to share with others.** You can share—or not— pretty much any file, folder, or hard drive that's attached to your computer. The second part of this chapter shows you how to designate what you want to share, as well as what you want to keep private.

- **Learning how to access the items others have shared on their PCs.** Once everyone's set up their computers to share, the next step is learning how to get to other people's stuff. This step is a piece of cake.

Note: This chapter covers how to share resources among Windows computers. If you've got some Macs in your mix, you'll want to read this chapter and then skip ahead to Chapter 7, where you'll learn about sharing with the Apple lovers in your life.

Naming PCs on the Network

Even though, under the hood, computers use cryptic numbers called IP addresses (page 26) to keep track of each other, you, lucky modern-operating-system-owner, get to use real names to identify the PCs on your network. These names will be of great help later on, when it comes time to actually find other computers on your network.

Windows computers are also kind enough to let you put them into groups—called *workgroups*—that are especially useful if you have *lots* of computers to handle. While not particularly helpful for a home network with only a few computers, someone at Microsoft long ago made the decision that *every* Windows computer will belong to some kind of workgroup.

In the next two sections, you'll learn how to assign or change the name and workgroup of all your Windows computers.

Setting Up the PC's Name

All computers come shipped from the factory with computer names that don't always make sense. If you just bought a new Dell, for example, its name might be something like EJKL776JJRTYUI456. Fortunately, you can change the factory-assigned name to something easier to remember like "PC1," "DiningRoom," or "Fluffy."

The name you pick for your computer can be just about anything you want—as long as it contains only the letters A–Z (lowercase too), the numbers 0–9, dashes, spaces, and some other special characters, such as apostrophes. When naming your computer, the only real rule of thumb is this: keep it simple.

Computer naming procedures work very differently depending on the version of Windows you're running. If you've got Windows XP or 2000, use the steps in the following section. (Windows 95/98/98SE/ME readers: use the instructions starting on page 81.)

Note: Windows computer archaeologists have come up with a valuable shorthand method for referring collectively to Windows 95, 98, 98 Second Edition, and Millennium Edition: Windows 9x. To save a few trees, you'll see that moniker used throughout this chapter.

Windows XP and Windows 2000

To change the name of the computer:

1. **Go to the Control Panel.**

   In Windows XP, go to Start → Control Panel. In Windows 2000, go to Start → Settings → Control Panel.

2. **In the Control Panel, double-click the System icon.**

   If you don't see the System icon, in the left part of the window, in the Control Panel option box, click the Switch to Classic View option. Doing so changes the Control Panel view to something a little easier to manage and also puts the System icon on the screen for you.

3. **In the System Properties dialog box, click the Computer Name tab.**

   You manage your computer's name from this tab.

4. **Click the Change button.**

   The Computer Name tab shows you your computer's current name, plus some other information—such as the workgroup. To change the name, in the lower part of the Computer Name screen, click the Change button. The Computer Name Changes dialog box pops up.

5. **Give the computer a new name (Figure 5-1).**

   At the top of the Computer Name Changes dialog box, in the "Computer name" box, type the new name of your computer.

6. **Click OK to save your changes.**

   A message box pops up, letting you know you need to restart your computer.

Older versions of Windows

For those of you running older versions of Windows, including Windows 95, 98, and ME, your computer probably has a factory-specified name, too. Windows makes it easy to change this. To do so:

1. **Go to the Control Panel.**

   Go to Start → Settings → Control Panel.

2. **In the Control Panel, double-click the Network icon.**

   Windows 9x considers the computer name part of your computer's networking configuration. Go configure.

3. **From the Network control panel window, click the Identification tab.**

4. **Give the computer a new name (Figure 5-1).**

   At the top of the dialog box, in the "Computer name" field, type the new name of your computer.

---

5. **Click OK to save your changes.**

A message box pops up, letting you know you need to restart your computer.

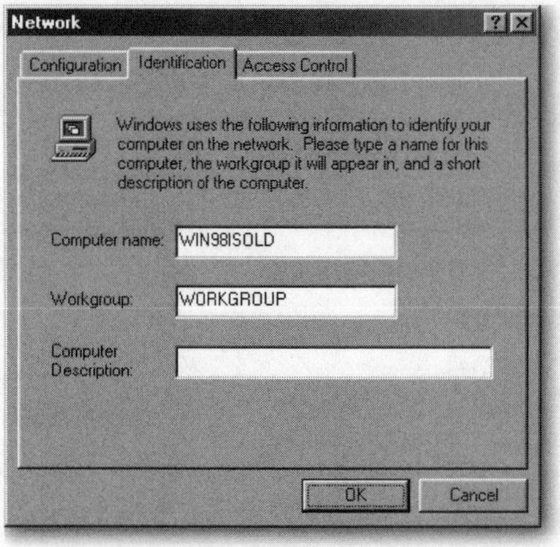

Figure 5-1:
Top: In Windows XP and Windows 2000, use this window to make changes to your computer's name and workgroup. Don't worry about the "More" option. It's only there for Windows gurus with much larger networks.

Bottom: The computer name and workgroup change process is pretty straightforward. For all versions of Windows, remember that the maximum length of the workgroup name is 15 characters, and it can't be the same as any computer name.

Setting Up the Workgroup Name

Truth be told, if you're anything like the average small home network operator, you won't spend much time dealing with your PCs' workgroup names. The most important thing is to make sure every PC belongs to the *same* workgroup. The workgroup name is for big company network setups, in which, say, all the PCs in the marketing department share one workgroup name, while the sales team's PCs use another name. Breaking down the computers into these smaller groupings makes it easier for people in each division to find stuff on their colleagues' computers.

But because of the way Windows handles networking, your PC has to have a work-group name. In most cases, you won't have to worry about this, since every new computer today comes from the factory with the MSHOME workgroup name already assigned. (Older PCs may use the name WORKGROUP.) But if for any reason you do want to change the workgroup name, the next few sections show you how.

Windows XP and Windows 2000

Changing the workgroup name in Windows XP and Windows 2000 works the same way. Just follow these instructions:

1. **Go to the Control Panel.**

   In Windows XP, go to Start → Control Panel. In Windows 2000, go to Start → Settings → Control Panel.

2. **In the Control Panel, double-click the System icon.**

   If you don't see the System icon, in the left part of the window, in the Control Panel option box, click the "Switch to Classic View" option. Doing so display's the System icon.

3. **In the System Properties dialog box, click the Computer Name tab.**

4. **Click the Change button.**

   The Computer Name Changes dialog box pops up.

5. **Give the computer a new workgroup name (Figure 5-1).**

   At the bottom of the dialog box, in the Workgroup field, enter the new work-group name. Use something like "OurHouse" or "Cow Barn 1." The work-group name can't be the same as any computer name in the workgroup.

6. **Click OK to save your changes.**

   A message box pops up, indicating that you need to restart your computer.

Older versions of Windows

To change the workgroup name in an older version of Windows, do the following:

1. **Go to the Control Panel.**

   Go to Start → Settings → Control Panel.

2. **In the Control Panel, double-click the Network icon.**

3. **In the Network control panel window, click the Identification tab.**

4. **Give the computer a new workgroup name (Figure 5-1).**

   In the middle of the dialog box, in the Workgroup field, enter the new work-group name. Use something like "OurHouse" or "Cow Barn 1." The work-group name can't be the same as any computer name in the workgroup.

Creating and Managing User Accounts

For years, teachers, parents, and computer lab instructors struggled to answer a difficult question: How do you rig one PC so that several different people can use it throughout the day without interfering with each others' files and settings? And how do you protect a PC from damage by mischievous (or bumbling) students and employees? And now you, home network administrator, are hereby welcome to join this chorus of despair. How *are* you supposed to keep all the people on your network from driving each other batty?

The answer lies in *user accounts.* Microsoft designed both Windows XP and Windows 2000 to be multiple-user operating systems. On these machines, anyone who uses the computer must *log on*—click (or type) their name and type in a password—when the computer turns on. You may remember that when you first installed Windows XP or Windows 2000 or fired up a new Windows XP/2000 machine, the computer asked you for a name and password. You may not have realized it at the time, but you were creating your PC's first *user account.*

> **Note:** PCs running Windows 9x sometimes require you to log on as well, depending on how things are set up. While not as powerful (or as secure) as Windows 2000 and XP, logging into a Windows 9x computer with a separate account provides some of the same organizational benefits, but without the super-security of Windows 2000 and XP.

POWER USERS' CLINIC

The Domain Game

You've just learned a little bit about workgroups and Windows computers, but there's another way that Windows machines can participate on a network: by being part of a *domain.* A *domain network* is a group of computers and other network gear that's centrally maintained by an administrator, thanks to a special master computer called a *domain controller,* which allows domain administrators to set up and troubleshoot all files and security settings on all domain PCs without having to visit each one in person.

All versions of Windows can operate in either workgroup *or* domain mode with one exception: Windows XP Home Edition cannot be a member of a Windows domain.

Domains offer some powerful advantages over the workgroup model of networking…for the workplace. Home network operators don't need this power or complexity. In particular, domains make it easier for the tech folks at your office to control who can access certain areas on a Windows

server, and they also make it easier for the tech team to manage the vast number of people on the network.

In a domain, a user's account (page 82) is created only once, and *any* computer that is a member of the domain can then use it. In contrast, under the workgroup model, user accounts need to be created on each individual computer. Since employees are constantly coming, going, and transferring, this time-consuming manual administration can add up to a whole lot of work. A domain also requires a server running a beefier (and much more expensive) version of Windows.

Since you have only a few computers in your home, the workgroup model is the best choice, and this book covers only the workgroup model. If you're interested in learning more about how Windows fits into the domain model, take a gander at *Windows XP Pro: The Missing Manual.*

Upon logging in, you discover your Windows universe just as you left it, including these elements:

- **Desktop.** Each person with a separate account sees a different set of shortcut icons, folder icons, and other stuff left out on the desktop.

- **Start menu.** If you reorganize the Start menu, you won't confuse anybody else who uses the machine. No one else can even *see* the changes you make.

- **My Documents folder.** Each person sees only his own stuff in the My Documents folder.

- **Email.** Windows XP and 2000 maintain a separate stash of email messages for each account holder—along with separate Web bookmarks, MSN Messenger contact list, and other online details.

- **Favorites folder.** Any Web sites, folders, or other icons you've designated as Favorites appear in *your* Favorites menu, and nobody else's.

- **Internet cache.** This folder stores a copy of the Web pages you've visited recently for faster retrieval.

- **History and cookies.** Windows maintains a list of recently visited Web sites independently for each person; likewise, it also maintains a personal collection of *cookies* (Web site preference files).

- **Control Panel settings.** Windows memorizes the Control Panel preferences each person establishes, including keyboard, sound, screen saver, and mouse settings.

- **Privileges (Windows 2000 and XP only).** Your user account determines what you're allowed to do on *other* computers on the network, especially which files and folders you can open and modify.

In other words, the multiple-accounts feature provides two distinct advantages. First, if you physically share the same computer with one or more people, accounts let you hide everyone else's junk (this benefit really doesn't have anything to do with home networking, but hey, who's keeping score?). Second, accounts can be a great security tool since, by setting them up for other people on your computer, they can help you control access by visitors to your PC from across the network.

But this second point about security comes with a big caveat. When it comes to people who arrive at your PC from *across the network* (as opposed to those who sidle up and physically log on), the security advantages of setting up multiple accounts are mainly limited to folks with Windows XP Pro or Windows 2000 on their systems.

For all you Windows XP Home–owners out there (not to mention you people in the back with your Windows 9x jalopies), you can set up accounts until Bill Gates is a senior citizen, and they won't help you protect the files on your PC. To be sure, *all* Windows users get to decide *which* files to share; but if you've got Windows XP Home Edition, then you're either sharing these designated files with everybody or with nobody. (There are a few exceptions to this rule that you'll learn about, but they don't have anything to do with the existence of user accounts.)

So, if you're still interested in learning more about user accounts, read on. The next few sections tell you how to set them up in each Windows varietal. If you're not interested, skip ahead to page 96, where you'll learn how to select the things on your computer that you want to make available to others on the network.

Tip: If you have Windows XP, and you're hungry for the kind of user account control you remember from Windows 2000, you're in luck: you can use the same account management tool Windows 2000 provides. Page 90 tells you everything you need to know.

Deciding How Many Accounts to Create

In the next few sections, you'll learn about all the different methods Windows offers for creating accounts. But before you proceed, it helps to have a rough idea of how many accounts you want to create. Here are some good rules of thumb:

- **Add one account for each person on your network who you want to access your PC.** For example, if your name is Moe, and you're living in a three-computer house with your pals Larry and Curly, you'd want to add accounts for Larry and Curly on your machine (which presumably already has an account named Moe).

- **For each account you create for a given person, use the same name and password.** Moe, for example, might want his account on his own machine to have the user name set to BIGMOE and the password set to NYUCKNYUCK. To make things run smoothly, Larry and Curly should use that same name and password combination when setting up Moe's accounts on *their* machines.

Managing Accounts in Windows XP

Windows XP user accounts come in two flavors: Administrator and Limited. Administrator accounts are specialized, all-powerful, all-knowing accounts. In contrast, Limited accounts are…limited in what they let their owners do.

You'll probably want the account on your own PC to be an Administrator account. With this kind of account you can:

- Create or delete accounts and passwords on the PC.

- Install new programs (and certain hardware components).

- Make changes to certain Control Panel programs that are off-limits to non-administrators.

- See and manipulate any file on the computer.

Anyone who isn't an administrator is an ordinary, everyday Limited account holder. "Limited" people have everyday access to certain Control Panel settings—the ones that pertain to their own computing environments. However, most other areas of the PC are off-limits, including everybody else's My Documents folders, Windows system files, and so on. A Limited account holder's entire world consists of the Start menu, her My Documents folder, the Shared Documents folder, and any folders she creates. She also can't install software.

Note: If there was a file that a Limited account holder wanted to access that was left on another account holder's Desktop, the file wouldn't be reachable since it's outside the Limited user's accessible work space.

As you go about creating accounts for other people who'll use your PC, Windows offers you the opportunity to make each one an administrator just like you. Not everyone needs this level of access, though. Bestow these powers upon only those who need the abilities described in the list above. Remember, because Administrator accounts aren't restricted at all, someone who logs into your computer as an Administrator can access *any* file.

Tip: If a Limited account holder manages to download a computer virus, its infection is confined to his account. If an *administrator* catches a virus, on the other hand, every file on the machine is at risk.

That's a good argument for creating as few Administrator accounts as possible. In fact, some Windows pros don't even use Administrator accounts *themselves.* Even they use Limited accounts, keeping one Administrator account on hand only for new software or hardware installations, account or password changing, and similar special cases.

Adding an account

Windows XP makes adding accounts easy. Go to Start → Control Panel, and then click the User Accounts icon. Then click the "Create a new account" link (which you see only if you are an administrator). A wizard guides you through the selection of a name and an account type, as shown in Figure 5-2.

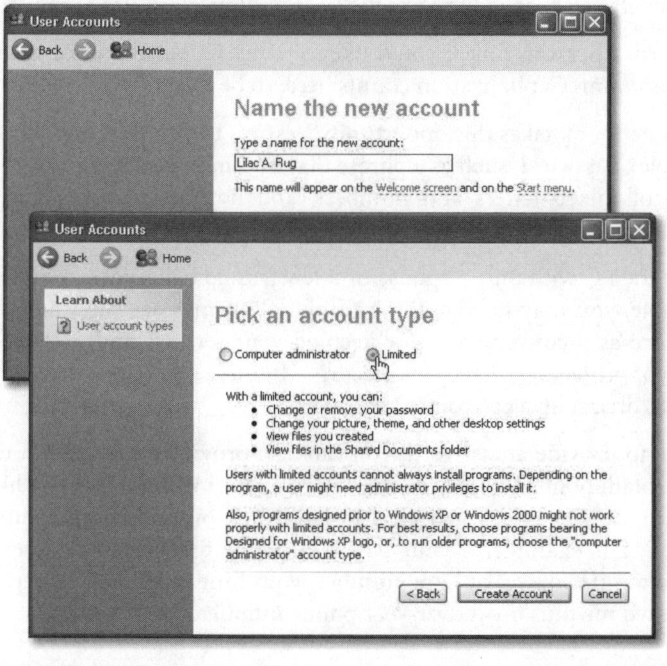

Figure 5-2:
Top: "Name the new account." Informal names like Robert or Chuck are fine. If you're in an office, maybe you'll want to use something more formal like first initial plus last name. Capitalization doesn't matter, but most punctuation is forbidden.

Bottom: "Pick an account type." This is the master control that lets you specify whether this unsuspecting computer user will be a computer administrator or a limited user.

When you're finished with the settings, click the Create Account button (or press Enter). After a moment, you return to the User Accounts screen (Figure 5-2), where the new person's name joins whatever names were already there. You can continue adding new accounts forever (or until your hard drive is full, whichever comes first).

Tip: If you never had the opportunity to set up a user account when installing Windows XP–if you bought a PC with Windows XP already on it, for example–you may see an account named Owner already in place. Nobody can use Windows XP at all unless there's at least *one* Administrator account on it, so Microsoft is doing you a favor here by creating the Owner account as an administrator.

Just use the User Accounts program in the Control Panel to change the name Owner to one that suits you better. Make that account your own using the steps in the following paragraphs.

Editing an account

Although the process of creating a new account is swift and simple, it doesn't offer you much in the way of flexibility. You don't even have a chance to specify the new account's password, let alone the all-important tiny picture that appears next to the person's name and at the top of the Start menu (rubber ducky, flower, or whatever).

That's why the next step in creating an account is usually *editing* the one you just set up. To do so, once you've returned to the main User Accounts screen, click the name or icon of the freshly created account. You arrive at the screen shown at the top in Figure 5-3, where—if you're an administrator—you can choose from these options:

- **Change the name.** Windows offers you the opportunity to type in a new name for this person and then click the Change Name button—just the ticket when one of your family members gets married or joins the Witness Protection Program.

- **Create a password.** Click this link if you'd like to require a password for access to this person's account. Capitalization counts here, so be careful.

   The usual computer book takes this opportunity to stress the importance of having a long, complex password, such as a phrase that isn't in the dictionary, something made up of mixed letters and numbers, and not "password." This is excellent advice if you create sensitive documents and work in a big corporation.

   But if you share the PC with only a spouse or a few trusted colleagues in a small office, for example, you may have nothing to hide. You may see the multiple-users feature more as a convenience (for keeping your settings and files separate) than a way of protecting secrecy and security. In these situations, there's no particular need to dream up a convoluted password.

   If you do decide to provide a password, you can also provide a hint (for yourself or whichever family member's account you're operating on). This is a hint that anybody can see (including bad guys trying to log on), so choose something meaningful. For example, if your password is the first person who ever kissed you plus your junior-year phone number, your hint might be "First person who ever kissed me plus my junior-year phone number."

Later, if you ever forget your password, you can view this hint at sign-in time to jog your memory.

By the way, it's fine for you, an administrator, to create the *original* passwords for new accounts. But don't change people's passwords later on, *after* they've been using the computer for a while. If you do, you'll wipe out various internal security features of their accounts, including access to their stored Web site passwords and stored passwords for shared folders and disks on the network.

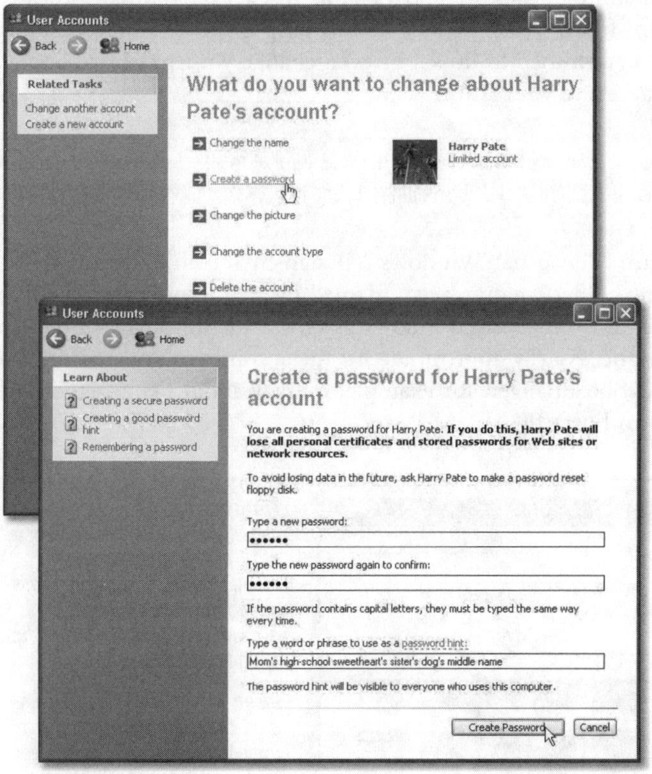

Figure 5-3:
Top: Here's the master menu of account-changing options that you, an administrator, can see. (If you're a Limited account holder, you see far fewer options.)

Bottom: You're supposed to type your password twice, to make sure you didn't introduce a typo the first time. (The PC shows only dots as you type, to guard against the possibility that some villain—such as your wily cat—is snooping over your shoulder.)

Make the new user's files private. If you click the button labeled "Yes, Make Private," Windows takes a minute to mark everything in this account's *user profile folder* off-limits to other account holders. (The user profile folder is the one bearing the account holder's name in the Documents and Settings folder on your hard drive.) Henceforth, if someone else tries to open any of this account's files or folders (when logged in under her own name), she'll get nothing but a curt "Access is denied" message. You can also click No if you don't want to make this account's files private.

Note: The private-folder feature is available only on hard drives you've formatted using the *NTFS* (New Technology File System) scheme. NTFS is a method that lets you assign extremely particular permissions to files and folders. You can, for example, allow Joe access to the games folder but only to look at what's in there, not to use it. If you're using Windows XP, it's a safe bet that your hard drive uses the NTFS format. If you're interested in learning more about NTFS, Microsoft has a nice writeup about it at *www.microsoft.com/ windowsxp/ using/setup/expert/russel_october01.mspx.*

(Technically, making a folder private even shields it from the eyes of the machine's Administrator account holders—but it's a pretty flimsy shield. A determined administrator can burrow past this wisp of protection to examine your files, if she's determined to do so, or even change your password late one night to gain full access to your stuff.)

Tip: You can make *any* of your own folders private—or unprivate, for that matter. Just right-click the folder; from the shortcut menu, choose Properties; click the Sharing tab; and turn "Make this folder private" on or off.

• **Change the picture.** The usual Windows XP sign-in screen (Figure 5-4) displays each account holder's name, accompanied by a little picture. When you first create an account, however, Windows assigns a picture at random—and not all of them are necessarily appropriate for the account you're creating. Not every extreme-sport headbanger, for example, is crazy about being represented by a dainty flower or butterfly.

Figure 5-4:
Left: If you like to change your picture with your changing moods, there's a shortcut to this dialog box. Just click your account picture at the top of the open Start menu.

Right: Here's where you change a user account's picture, which appears on the Welcome screen and atop the user's Start menu.

If you like the selections Microsoft has provided (drag the vertical scroll bar to see them all), just click one to select it as the replacement graphic. If you'd rather use another graphics file from the hard drive instead—a digital photo, for example—you can click the "Browse for more pictures" link (Figure 5-4). Windows shows you a list of the graphics files on your hard drive so that you can choose one, which Windows then automatically scales down to postage-stamp size (48 *pixels*—the little dots that make up the display on your screen—square).

- **Change the account type.** Click this link to change a Limited account to an Administrator account, or vice versa.

- **Delete the account.** See the next section.

You're free to make any of these changes to any account at any time.

Deleting an account

It happens: somebody graduates, or you dump someone. Sooner or later, you may need to delete a user account from your PC.

To delete a user account, you, an administrator, must open the User Accounts program, click the appropriate account name, and then click "Delete the account."

Windows XP now asks you if you want to preserve the contents of this person's My Documents folder. If you click the Keep Files button, you'll find a new folder, named for the dearly departed, on your desktop. (As noted in the dialog box, only the documents, contents of the desktop, and the My Documents folder are preserved, *not* programs, email, or even Web favorites.) If that person ever returns to your life, you can create a new account for him and copy these files into the appropriate folder locations.

If you click the Delete Files button, on the other hand, the documents are gone forever.

A few more important points about deleting accounts:

- You can't delete the account you're logged into.

- You can't delete the last remaining Administrator account. One Administrator account must always remain.

- You can create a new account with the same name and password as one that you deleted earlier, but in Windows XP's head, it's still not the same account. It won't have any of the original *secondary* passwords (for Web sites, encrypted files, and so on).

- You shouldn't manipulate accounts manually (by fooling around in the Documents and Settings folder, for example). Create, delete, and rename them only by using the User Accounts program in the Control Panel. Otherwise, you'll wind up with duplicate or triplicate folders in Documents and Settings, with the PC name tacked onto the end of the original account name (Bob, Bob.KITCHEN, and so on)—a sure recipe for confusion.

The Guest account

You might not like the idea of having to create an account for everyone in your family on every computer. How much worse would it be if you started having to create accounts for people that drop by to visit? Fortunately, Windows offers you a special account called *Guest.*

The Guest account is ideal for situations where somebody is just visiting you for the day. Rather than create an entire account for this person, complete with password, hint, little picture, and so on, you can just switch on the Guest account.

To do so, open the User Accounts program in the Control Panel. If you're an administrator, you'll see an icon for the Guest account at the bottom of the screen (Figure 5-5). Click it; on the next screen, click the button labeled "Turn On the Guest Account." That's all there is to it.

When the visitor to your home is finally out of your hair, healthy paranoia suggests that you turn off the Guest account once again. (To do so, follow precisely the same steps, except click "Turn Off the Guest Account" in the final step.)

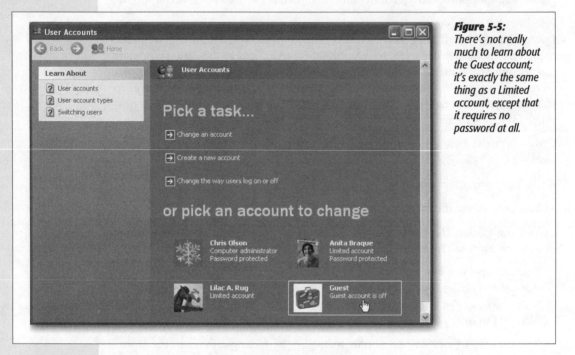

Figure 5-5:
There's not really much to learn about the Guest account; it's exactly the same thing as a Limited account, except that it requires no password at all.

Managing Accounts in Windows 2000

Windows 2000 includes a slightly more complex, but more powerful, user account management tool than the Windows XP account creation wizard. (In fact, Microsoft hasn't actually removed the Windows 2000 tool from Windows XP, so XPers can listen up, too.) The Windows 2000 account management utility lets you handily manipulate both users and *groups* (a collection of user accounts that share the same access to files and folders on your computer).

Groups are particularly useful when you have lots of accounts to which you want to assign similar kinds of *permissions*. (Permissions, which you'll learn much more about on page 102, are Windows's way of restricting or granting access to a file.)

Windows 2000 comes with a number of predefined groups. Three groups in particular are important:

- **Administrators** in Windows 2000 are the same as administrators under Windows XP (page 84). Administrators have powerful privileges to do all sorts of things to your computer that others cannot.

- **Standard users** are a little less almighty than administrators, but can do a little more than Restricted accounts (which you'll read about next). Accounts in this group can create new accounts, and modify and delete them at will—but only accounts that they themselves have created. Standard accounts can also create new *shared resources* (such as files, folders, and printers, explained more later in this chapter), assuming the account holder has access to the resource.

- **Restricted users** are identical to Windows XP's Limited accounts (page 84). Restricted account holders have access only to those Control Panel settings that pertain to their own computing environments—such as the desktop background and display settings. However, most other areas of the PC are off-limits, including everybody else's My Documents folders, Windows system files, and so on.

Tip: If a Standard or Restricted account holder manages to download a computer virus, the infection will be confined to her account. If an *administrator* catches a virus, on the other hand, every file on the machine is at risk.

That's a good argument for creating as few Administrator accounts as possible. In fact, some Windows pros don't even use Administrator accounts *themselves:* they use Standard accounts, keeping one Administrator account on hand only for new software or hardware installations, account or password changing, and similar special cases.

Windows includes a lot of other built-in user groups that are useful in larger networked environments. For your home networking purposes, you'll probably never need to use them.

The next few sections show you how to create, change, and delete users and groups.

Adding an account

To get started creating accounts in Windows 2000, go to Start → Settings → Control Panel and double-click the Users and Passwords option. If you're using Windows XP, go to Start → Run and type *control Userpasswords2.*

A User Accounts dialog box appears. To add an account, just click the Add button. A wizard consisting of three screens (the last one is shown in Figure 5-6) guides you through the selection of a user name, password, and account type. The first screen asks you to create a user name (which is what the person types to log onto the computer). You can also enter an optional full name and short description of who the user is.

The second screen requests the all-important password, and the last screen asks you to assign the account to a group. Windows graciously provides buttons for you to put the new user into either the Standard or Restricted group (see Figure 5-6).

When you're done, you return to the User Accounts screen where the new person's name joins whatever names were already there. You can continue adding new accounts forever (or until your hard drive is full, whichever comes first).

Figure 5-6:
If you want to make the new user a completely unrestricted computer administrator, select the Other option and then click the down arrow and select Administrators from the list of available groups.

Editing an account

To make changes to an account, return to the main User Accounts screen and either double-click the name of the account or select the name and click the Properties button. The new dialog box that launches lets you:

- **Change the user name.** Are you tired of logging in as *jdoe* and want to log in as John Doe's lesser-known younger brother Jim Doe? Go ahead and change your user name to *jimdoe*.

- **Change the full name.** Have you gotten married, divorced, or joined the Witness Protection Program recently? Type your new name here.

- **Change the description.** Type a new description for the user.

- **Change the account type.** Click the Advanced tab and select a new group.

One thing you can't do from the User Accounts screen is change the user's password. To change a user's password, select the user from the list and then, in the lower part of the User Accounts window, click the Reset Password button. A window pops up asking for the new password. You'll need to type the new password twice just so Windows knows that you got it right.

You're free to make any of these changes to any account at any time.

Deleting an account

Account deletion in Windows 2000 works the same as in Windows XP. Take a look at page 89 for details. Here's the short version: click on the account you want to delete and press Delete on your keyboard.

The Guest account

The Guest account is ideal if you've got someone in your home who's just visiting for the day. Rather than create an entire account for this person, complete with password, hint, little picture, and so on, you can just switch on the Guest account.

Note: For instructions about how to add a Guest account in Windows XP, see page 89.

To do so:

1. **From the Control Panel, open the Users and Passwords screen.**

   Choose Start → Settings → Control Panel. Then click Users and Passwords.

2. **Go to the Advanced tab.**

   There are only two tabs at the top of the User Accounts window: Users and Advanced.

3. **Click the button marked Advanced.**

   Don't confuse this with the tab of the same name. The Advanced button is in the middle of the window, near the right side.

4. **Click the Users folder.**

   The Users folder is in the left pane of the resulting window, above Groups.

5. **Double-click the Guest account.**

   More than likely, you see the Guest account icon with a red X in the lower-right corner indicating that the Guest account is disabled.

6. **Turn off the checkbox marked "Account is disabled."**

   Click OK. When the visitor to your home is finally out of your hair, you can safely turn off the Guest account once again. (To do so, follow precisely the same steps, except turn on the "Account is disabled" checkbox in the final step.)

Managing Accounts in Windows 95, 98, and ME

Even ancient versions of Windows let you create user accounts. But accounts in Windows 95, 98, and ME do a lot less compared to the accounts you get in modern versions of Windows, especially when it comes to security. In fact, the Windows 9x account feature is useful only if multiple people share a single computer and want to keep their files separate from one another *on the same computer*.

Out of the box, Windows 9x does not support multiple users. To enable this feature, you need to first run the Enable Multi-user Settings wizard.

1. **Open the Users window.**

   Go to Start → Settings → Control Panel and double-click the Users option. A box pops up, asking if you wish to enable multi-user settings. Click Next to begin the process.

2. **Choose Add user.**

   Each account needs to have a user name, which identifies who is currently logged into the computer. Enter a name in this window for the account you want to create for yourself.

3. **Choose the settings you want to personalize (Figure 5-7).**

   Windows 9x lets you, as the initial account holder, decide what items you want all accounts to be able to personalize—for example, the desktop or the Start menu. When an item is designated as personalized, each user gets his own version of it. If it's not personalized, each user shares a common version. For example, if you opt to personalize the desktop, each user can adjust common desktop settings (like the background). If you don't personalize a particular area, everyone uses the same copy, which means that everyone sees whatever changes have most recently been made.

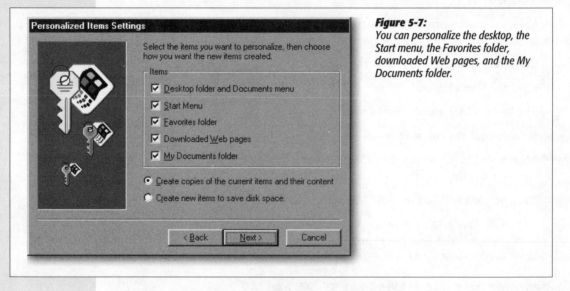

Figure 5-7:
You can personalize the desktop, the Start menu, the Favorites folder, downloaded Web pages, and the My Documents folder.

4. **Restart your computer and log in.**

   Once you finish with the personalization wizard, you need to restart your computer and log in as the user you just created.

Adding an account

Windows 9x gives you a number of different ways to create a new account:

- **Log in as the new user.** You might be asking yourself how you can log in as a user that doesn't yet exist. But it really does work in Windows 9x. If you enter a user name that doesn't exist at the Windows 9x login screen, Windows pops up a message indicating that you haven't logged in at this PC before and is even so kind as to let you retain your settings for future visits.

- **Copy an existing user.** Do you have an account already set up and just want to copy the account's preferences? Figure 5-8 shows you how.

- **Create a user from scratch.** Sometimes it's best to just start anew. To create a new user, click the button marked New User (see Figure 5-8). Windows asks you for the new name and password, as well as for which items to personalize.

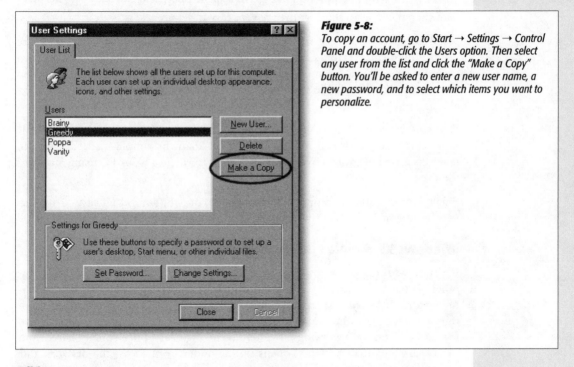

Figure 5-8:
To copy an account, go to Start → Settings → Control Panel and double-click the Users option. Then select any user from the list and click the "Make a Copy" button. You'll be asked to enter a new user name, a new password, and to select which items you want to personalize.

Editing an account

In Windows 9x, you can make only a few changes to a user account once you create it. You can change a user's password and change the personalization settings for that user. That's it. If you need to change a user's name, you're out of luck. You need to create a new account with the new name and delete the old one. To edit an account, go to Start → Settings → Control Panel and double-click the Users option. Select the account you want to change and click the Change Settings button. To change a user's password, click the Set Password button. Be aware that you need to know the user's old password in order to change it.

Delete an account

When you delete an account, you also delete that user's preferences and personal files, so be careful! To delete an account in Windows 9x, from the User Control Panel, select the user and click the button marked Delete. Windows asks if you *really* want to do this deed. If you do, click Yes. Otherwise, click No.

Sharing Your PC's Files and Folders

Okay, so you've named your computers, you've set up any user accounts you wanted to create, and now it's time for the last big step: deciding what network resources—files, folders, printers, and so on—you want to make available.

All versions of Windows can share resources with other computers on the network. As you might expect, the newer Windows descendents—Windows XP and 2000—come with lots of configurable options. Windows 95, 98, and ME aren't all bad when it comes to sharing: they're very easy to set up.

Windows gives you three methods for sharing files and folders. First, if you're using Windows XP (Home Edition or Pro), you can use *Simple file sharing,* which basically gives you a big on/off switch that you can flick on almost anything on your computer. Simple file sharing's really easy to use, but it's about as customizable as a pitchfork.

Standard file sharing, available in Windows XP Pro or Windows 2000, is a little more complex (but much more full-featured) than the simple method. You can really exercise full control over who gets access to what on your PC using Standard file sharing.

Finally, for you folks running Windows 95, 98, or ME, you get an easy-to-use but very basic system that's fairly comparable to Simple file sharing.

Windows XP Simple File Sharing

If you're working on a home network, and you have nothing to hide from the other people in the house, you may appreciate Windows XP's new *Simple file sharing* feature. It lets you share any folder (or your *whole* hard drive) with a minimum of red tape and complexity. If your housemate Harold needs a peek at that spreadsheet you were working on yesterday, no big deal—once you've shared your My Documents folder, he just opens up the folder from across the network and, presto, he's spreadsheeting.

If it's just you and your spouse, or you and a trusted co-worker, this simple file-sharing scenario is almost ideal: maximum convenience and minimum barriers. On the other hand, when you share a folder this way, anybody on the network can not only read your files, but also change or delete them. In other words, Simple file sharing isn't especially secure. Kids horsing around on the computer, young geniuses experimenting with your data, or a disgruntled co-worker could, in theory, send important data to Never-Never Land.

To get started, you first need to activate Simple file sharing on your PC. To do so, choose Tools → Folder Options from the menu bar of any desktop window (or open the Folder Options icon in the Control Panel). Click the View tab, scroll all the way down to the bottom of the Advanced Settings list, and click "Use Simple File Sharing (Recommended)." This is also how you turn Simple file sharing off. Enabling Simple file sharing just tells Windows that you're ready to start sharing your folders with the world—nothing is actually shared just yet. You still have to decide *which* folders to make available for others to see.

Sharing your own folders

It's easy enough to "publish" any of your folders or disks for inspection by other people on your network. (Actually, sharing a folder, as you're about to do, also makes it available to other people who log into this PC under their own accounts, sitting at it in person.)

The trick is to use the Properties dialog box, like this:

1. **Right-click the disk or folder icon of the folder or disk that you want to share.**

   As you probably already know, your disk icons appear when you choose Start → My Computer.

Note: If you log in using a Limited account (page 84), you may share only the disks and folders to which you've been given access. If you've logged in using the Administrator account, on the other hand, you can share *any* disk or folder, but you should still avoid sharing critical system folders like the Windows folder and the Program Files folder. There's no reason other people on the network would need to get to these folders anyway—and if they did, they could do serious damage to your PC.

---

2. **From the shortcut menu, choose "Sharing and Security."**

   The Sharing tab of the Properties dialog box opens (Figure 5-9). (If you don't see a "Sharing and Security" command, just choose Properties from the short-cut menu—and then, in the resulting dialog box, click the Sharing tab.)

   If you're trying to share an entire disk, you now see a warning to the effect that, "sharing the root of a drive is not recommended." Click the link beneath it that says, "If you understand the risk but still want to share the root of the drive, click here" and then proceed with the next step.

3. **Turn on "Share this folder on the network" (Figure 5-9).**

   The other options—the Share name, Comment, User limit, and permissions button—in the dialog box spring to life.

4. **Type a name for the shared disk or folder.**

   This field is the name other people see when they open their My Network Places windows. Make this name as helpful as possible. For example, you may want to name the kitchen computer's hard drive *Kitchen Documents Drive*.

Tip: If any of the other PCs on your network aren't running Windows XP or Windows 2000, the shared folder's name can't be longer than 12 characters, and most punctuation is forbidden. You can type it here all right, but—as a warning message will tell you—the other machines won't be able to see the shared disk or folder over the network.

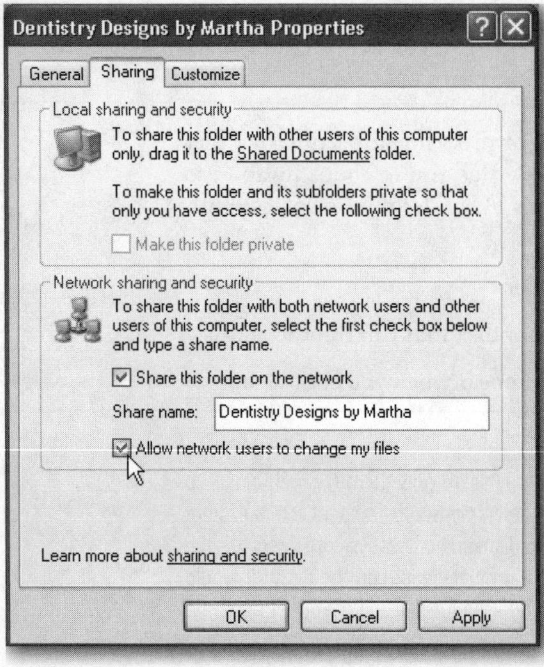

Figure 5-9:
Here's the Sharing tab for a disk or folder on a Windows XP workgroup computer. (The dialog box refers to a "folder" even if it's actually a disk.) You can turn on "Share this folder on the network" only if "Make this folder private" is turned off. (If a folder is private, you certainly don't want other network citizens stomping around in it.)

5. **Decide whether you want to let others change your files.**

   If the "Allow network users to change my files" checkbox is turned on, you provide carte blanche, unrestricted access to the files inside the folder or disk that you're sharing. In this case, someone on your network can connect to your computer, change your files, and then save over the original copy. (In technical lingo, you've established a "read-write" shared folder.) Be careful! For example, if you share the whole C: drive and allow others to change your files, a less technical person might try to clean up your disk by deleting the Windows folder. This would, in essence, turn your computer into a really expensive paperweight.

   If the "Allow network users to change my files" checkbox is turned *off*, you create a "look, don't touch" policy. Other people on the network can open and read what's inside this disk or folder but won't be able to save changes, rename anything, delete anything, or deposit any new files. (In technical lingo, you've established a "read-only" shared folder.)

Remember, however, that making the shared folder read-only means that *you* won't be able to modify its files from another computer on the network, either. You've just run up against one of the fundamental shortcomings of Simple file sharing: you must give full access to your files to either *everybody* on the network or *nobody*.

Note: Turning off the "Allow network users to change my files" checkbox isn't much of a security safeguard. True, other people on the network won't be able to change what's *in* your folder—but there's nothing to stop them from copying stuff *out* of it. Once they've saved copies of your files on their own hard drives, they can do with them whatever they like. They just can't copy the changed files back *into* your shared folder or disk. In other words, if you don't want other people to see or distribute what's in your folders (using Simple file sharing), don't share them.

---

6. **Click OK.**

   As shown in Figure 5-10, the icon changes for the disk or folder you just shared. It's also gained a new nickname: you may hear shared folders geekily referred to as *shares*.

Shared Documents   Local Disk (C:)   CD Drive (D:)

Figure 5-10:
When you share a folder or a disk, a tiny hand cradles its icon from beneath—a dead giveaway that you've made it available to other people on the network.

Notes on Simple file sharing

The preceding steps show you how to make a certain folder or disk available to other people on the network. The following footnotes, however, are worth skimming, especially for Windows 2000 veterans who may be used to a totally different file-sharing system:

- You can't share individual files—only entire folders or disks. If you need to share an individual file, put it inside its own folder.

- The "Share this folder on the network" checkbox is dimmed for *all* folders unless you've enabled Simple file sharing (page 96).

- Unless you specify otherwise, sharing a folder also shares all of the folders inside it, including new ones you create later. If your "Allow network users to change my files" checkbox is on, you are giving permission to change or delete files in all of those folders, too.

   If you right-click a folder inside a shared folder and inspect the Sharing tab of its Properties dialog box, you'll find the Sharing checkbox turned off, which can be a bit confusing. But you'd better believe it: those inner folders are actually shared, no matter what the checkbox says.

- On the other hand, it's OK to right-click one of these inner folders and *change* its sharing settings. For example, if you've shared a folder called America, you can make the Minnesota folder inside it off-limits by making it private (page 87). Similarly, if you've turned *off* "Allow network users to change my files" for the America folder, you can turn it back *on* for the Minnesota folder inside it.

- Be careful with nested folders. Suppose, for example, you share your My Documents folder, and you permit other people to change the files inside it. Now suppose you share a folder that's *inside* My Documents—called Spreadsheets, for example—but you turn *off* the ability for other people to change its files.

  You wind up with a strange situation: both folders, My Documents and Spreadsheets, show up in other people's Network Places windows, as described earlier in this chapter. If they double-click the Spreadsheets folder, they won't be able to change anything inside it. But if they double-click the My Documents folder and open the Spreadsheets folder inside it, they can modify the files.

- You're not allowed to share important system folders like Windows, Program Files, and Documents and Settings. If you've set up your PC with multiple user accounts (page 82), you can't share folders that belong to other people, either—only your own stuff. The exception: you can share them when you've logged in using the Administrator account (page 84).

Standard File Sharing—Windows XP Pro and Windows 2000

If you need more security and flexibility than Simple file sharing affords—or if your computer is part of a corporate domain (page 82)—the time has come to tackle Standard file sharing.

Note: If you're using Windows XP Home, Standard file sharing isn't an option. Windows XP Home supports only Simple file sharing.

The process of sharing a folder is much the same as it is in Simple file sharing, except that there's an additional step: specifying who else on the network can access the shared folder or disk and what they're allowed to do with it.

First, you need to pick which files you want to share and then share them. Next, you have to decide who can access your files and what they can do—that is, if they can just see them or also change them. The next two sections show you what you need to do.

Note: Before you can create Standard file shares, you must disable Windows XP's Simple file sharing feature; page 96 shows you how.

Step 1: Turn on sharing

After you've located the drive or folder you want to share, turn on sharing by following these steps:

1. **Right-click the disk or folder icon.**

2. **From the shortcut menu, choose Sharing and Security (in Windows 2000, it's just called Sharing).**

   The Sharing tab of the Properties dialog box opens (see Figure 5-11). If you've ever seen this dialog box when using Simple file sharing in Windows XP, you'll notice that it looks quite a bit different now.

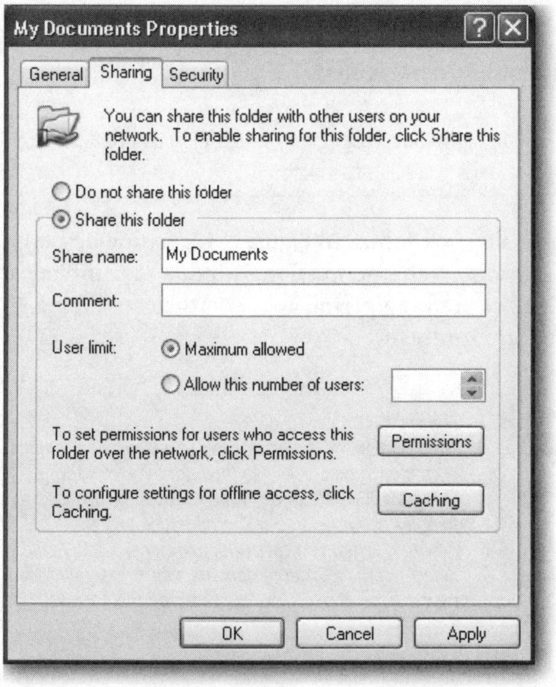

Figure 5-11:
Take a look at the Sharing tab for a disk or folder on a Windows XP standard share system or a Windows 2000 system. From here, you can share this folder, specify the maximum number of people who can access it at once, and specify who can access the share and to what degree.

3. **Turn on "Share this folder."**

   The other options in the dialog box become active.

4. **Type a name for the shared disk or folder.**

   This field is the name other people see when they open their My Network Places windows. Windows proposes the name of the folder as the share name, which is fine, but you can change it to anything you like.

   If you want to limit the number of network users that can access the shared file or folder simultaneously—to avoid slowing down your PC, for example—click the "Allow this number of users" radio button, and specify the maximum number of people who can access the share at one time (3 or 5, for example).

If you were to click OK at this point, you would make this item available to everyone on the network. But before leaving the dialog box, take a moment to survey the security options. This, after all, is one of the advantages of Standard file sharing.

Step 2: Select who can access your files and decide what they can do

When you make a folder or drive available to the network, you don't necessarily want to give your co-workers permission to run roughshod over the files inside it. In many cases, you may prefer to share a folder or drive *selectively*. You might want to make the family-budget spreadsheet accessible to only the responsible adults but off-limits to everyone else in the house.

Fortunately, you can limit access on an individual (or group-by-group) basis, thanks to the Permissions button shown in Figure 5-12.

Note: If you're using Standard file sharing, then your visitors from across the network must have an account on your PC (unless they're logging in using the Guest account).

When you click it, you get the dialog box shown in Figure 5-12. Setting up permissions involves three steps: opening up the permissions window, identifying the person (or group) to whom you're granting permission, and then specifying how much access you want to grant him (or them).

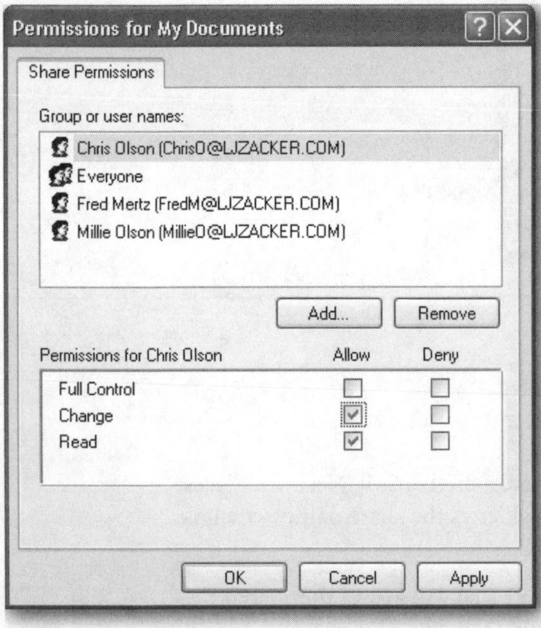

Figure 5-12:
The Permissions dialog box lets you control how much access each person has to the folder you're sharing. Using the top list, specify which people (or groups of people) can access your shared folder over the network. When you click Add, another window (called Select Users or Groups) appears, which lets you add new groups or users to your share permissions list.

1. **Launch the Permissions dialog box.**

   Click the Permissions button. A Permissions dialog box appears (Figure 5-12). The top half of the box lists the account holders or groups that have currently been granted permission to the share; the bottom half tells you how much access Windows has granted each person or group.

   When you first share a folder or disk, you'll see only the Everyone group in this list. (As you might expect, the Everyone group, is composed of anyone who has access to your computer.) If you're on a workgroup (page 78) network, you'll see that the Everyone group starts out with Full Control permission. If you're on a *domain* computer in a corporation, the Everyone group starts out with only Read permission, which offers more security. More about these permissions settings in a moment.

Tip: When a permission checkbox is selected but also shaded gray, it means that its permissions settings have been inherited from the folder that it's in.

---

2. **Select who can access your files.**

   Now you can start assigning permissions on a person-by-person (or group-by-group) basis. Until you add a user to the list, they can't access the shared resource. Figure 5-12 shows you how to add new users to the "Group or user names" list.

Note: See page 78 for details on groups—and remember that an individual account's permissions take precedence over group permissions.

---

3. **Now decide what those who can access your files can do with them.**

   Click the name of a person or group in the list. Set the appropriate permissions by turning on the relevant checkboxes. You've got three options:

   Read: This person (or group of people) encounters a "Look, But Don't Touch" policy when he tries to open this folder from across the network. He'll be allowed to open and read what's inside (and run any programs he finds there), but he won't be able to save changes, rename anything, delete anything, or deposit any new files.

Note: Other people on the network can *copy* folders and files from a Read folder or disk onto their own computers. From there, they can do whatever they like. But they can't copy the changed files back to your shared folder or disk.

   Change: The person or group you've selected can not only open the shared files, but they can also edit and even delete them. They can also put new files and folders into the shared folder or disk.

Full Control: The selected person or group can run wild, fooling around not only with the contents of the disk or folder, but also with its permissions. They can change whatever permissions settings you make here, and even claim *ownership* of the folder or disk, potentially locking you out of your own files.

Note: When you first turn on sharing for a folder, it inherits the permission settings from the disk or folder it's in (that is, its *parent* folder). But if you *change* the settings for one of these inner folders, your new settings override any permissions that are inherited from parent folders.

---

4. **Click OK to close the Properties dialog box.**

You'll see that the icon for the resource you just shared has changed. A hand now cradles the icon to help you remember what you've made available to your network colleagues.

Clever Standard File Sharing Tricks

Sharing files and folders using Standard file sharing may be a lot more trouble than Simple file sharing, but it has its rewards. Only in Standard file sharing, for example, can you have interesting scenarios like these:

- You can access your files from different computers on the network, but still protect them from tampering by other people. To do so, share the file or folder, give yourself the Full Control permission, and deny all permissions to the Everyone group.

  Yes, you are also part of the Everyone group—but an individual's permissions always override any group permissions that may affect that person. As a result, you end up with Full Control over your files, and no one else can even read them. On a home network, you can start working on a document in the bedroom upstairs—and then, when you go downstairs to cook dinner, you can continue working on the kitchen computer while the pasta is boiling. Meanwhile, the kids can be using their own computer, but won't be able to see what's in your file or folder.

- You can also create a *drop box:* a folder into which people can deposit documents for you, but that is otherwise off-limits to them.

  For example, you might create a drop box so that employees can leave insurance claim forms they've filled out with a word processor. After sharing the folder, you could grant yourself (and other people in your department) Full Control—but you would give everyone else in the company only the Change permission. Now people in other departments can copy their claim forms into the drop-box folder, because they have permission to create new files in it. But because they lack the Read permission, they can't open the folder to see what's inside.

- If a certain folder on your hard drive is really private but you still want to be able to get to it over the network, you can hide the folder so that other people on the network can't even *see* it.

The secret is to type a $ symbol at the end of the share name. For example, if you name a certain folder My Novel, anyone else on the network will be able to see it. But if you name the share My Novel$, it won't show up in anybody's My Network Places window. They won't even know that it exists. (It still shows up on your machine, of course. It will also be visible to other network computers if you shared the disk on which the folder sits.)

Windows 95, 98, and ME users: you're out of luck on this one. This trick works only on Windows 2000 and Windows XP computers.

POWER USERS' CLINIC

NTFS Permissions vs. Share Permissions

Windows XP Pro offers two separate and overlapping systems for protecting folders. First, there are the *NTFS permissions* (complex permissions useful mostly for very large networks); second, there are the *share permissions* described in "Step 2: Select who can access your files and decide what they can do." Each system lets you choose which network citizens (or groups of them) may view, make changes to, or have full control over certain folders.

Understanding the ramifications of the two separate and overlapping permissions systems involves some serious technical slogging. Here are the most important differences:

- NTFS permissions guard a folder, no matter how someone tries to get at it—from across the network or plunked down in person at the PC. Share permissions, on the other hand, govern access *only* from over the network. Suppose you've got a folder full of confidential files. Hoping to protect them from inspection by your co-workers, you might turn off all forms of access using share permissions—but all you've done is keep people hanging out elsewhere on the network out of your folder. Co-workers who sit down at your machine can still rifle through your private files.

- Nobody can access shared files from across the network unless they have both share permissions and NTFS permissions to those files. Even if somebody has given you Full Access using one permissions system, if the other is set to No Access, you're out of luck. Simply put, you have access based on the most restrictive set of permissions.

- NTFS permissions are far more flexible than share permissions. For example, there are five or six degrees of NTFS standard permissions, compared with only three levels of share permissions. NTFS permissions can also protect individual files, whereas share permissions affect only entire folders.

If you think maintaining a duplicate set of overlapping permissions is complex and confusing for your small home network, imagine being a corporate network administrator whose job it is to keep them all straight—not only for each folder on each computer, but for each person on the network. It's a mind-boggling amount of variables to juggle.

As a result, most network administrators simply grant everyone Full Access to network shares, effectively eliminating share permissions as the complicating factor. The administrators then use NTFS permissions to control access to specific files and folders, confident that these settings correctly protect shared folders and disks *both* from across the network and from each individual PC.

Using NTFS permissions is most decidedly a power-user technique because of the added complexity it introduces. Entire books have been written on the topic of NTFS permissions alone. For an overview of how to get started setting NTFS permissions, check out *Windows XP Pro: The Missing Manual.*

File Sharing in Windows 95, 98, and ME

Windows 9x computers lack many of the advanced file-sharing security features of their newer counterparts. For example, you can't protect the files on Windows 9x computers from someone else sitting at your computer like you can with Windows 2000 and XP computers.

On the plus side, sharing files on Windows 9x machines is a little easier than under Windows XP and 2000. Windows 9x doesn't believe in the fancy hoopla associated with Simple vs. Standard file sharing. You just share the folders you want and pick from some optional and rudimentary security options.

POWER USERS' CLINIC

Un-Hiding Hidden Folders

As sneaky and delightful as the hidden-folder trick is, it has a distinct drawback: *you* can't see your hidden folder from across the network, either. Suppose you want to use another computer on the network—the one in the upstairs office, for example—to open something in your hidden My Novel folder (which is downstairs in the kitchen). Fortunately, you can do so—if you know the secret.

On the office computer, choose Start → Run. In the Run dialog box, type the path of the hidden folder, using the typed command *Computer Name**Folder Name*.

For example, enter *kitchen**my novel$* in the Run box to get to the hidden folder called My Novel$ on the PC called Kitchen. (Capitalization doesn't matter, and don't forget the $ sign.) Then click OK to open a window showing the contents of your hidden folder. (See page 113 for more on the Universal Naming Convention system.)

---

1. **Enable file sharing.**

   A typical Windows 9x computer is not capable of sharing its files and folders until you tell it to share. To do so, go to the Network control panel and click the "File and Print Sharing" button toward the bottom of the window. To enable other users to access files on this computer, turn on the checkbox next to "I want to be able to give others access to my files."

2. **Open the folder or disk's Share properties.**

   To share a folder or disk, right-click it and select Sharing from the shortcut menu. The Sharing dialog box appears (Figure 5-13).

3. **Share the folder and give it a name.**

   To share a folder, select the "Share as" option at the top of the window. Enter a name for the folder so that people across the network will be able to identify it when they connect to your computer.

4. **Decide how much access to grant.**

   Windows 9x makes your access selections pretty easy. You can provide either read-only access, full access, or access that is password dependent.

   Read-Only. People who connect to this share can only read the contents of the files. They can't make changes to the originals. Of course, since they can read the stuff, they can also copy it to their own computer and make changes to their copy. If you want to share your files in Read-Only mode but make them available only to those to whom you've provided a password, enter your password in the box marked "Read-Only Password" (Figure 5-13). Make sure to share this password with the folks that need to get to your files.

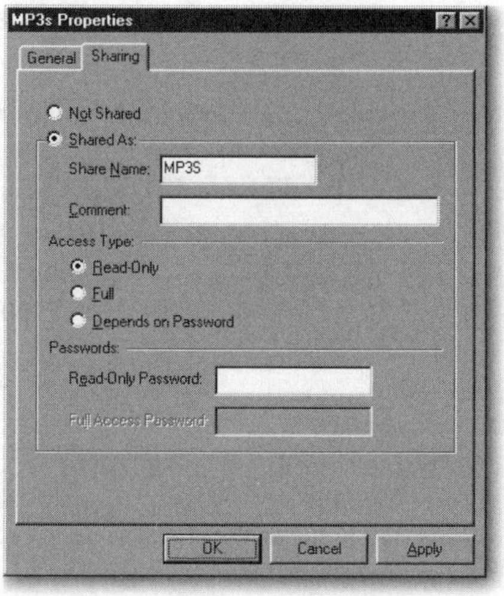

Figure 5-13:
Keep the following suggestions in mind when naming new shares:

(1) Keep the name short, but descriptive. *If possible, limit the length of the share name to eight characters to provide the highest level of compatibility with other versions of Windows. Some versions of Windows have trouble with names longer than this.*

(2) Don't use punctuation, even if Windows lets you. *Avoid using punctuation in your share names.*

Full. Remote users can both read and manipulate the files inside the shared folder. Be careful with this one! As with read-only, you can enter a password in the box labeled "Full Access Password" to restrict who has access to this share.

Depends on Password. With Windows 9x, you can allow access that is dependent upon the password the person enters when she attempts to connect to the share. When you select this option, both password boxes at the bottom of the window appear. Type the passwords into the appropriate boxes. If you leave a password blank, anyone can get into the share with that access level.

This option is particularly useful if you want to provide read-only powers to everyone except a select few people. Leave the Read-Only Password blank, provide an entry for the Full Access Password, and share it with the people who you want to grant access to.

5. Click OK.

The icon of your shared folder now features a little hand holding it.

Un-Sharing Folders

You might decide at some point that you don't want to share a particular folder anymore. No problem! Windows makes this easy. To stop sharing a particular folder, open up the Sharing properties for the folder and select the Not Shared option at the top of the window.

Sharing Your PC's Printer

Sharing files is all well and good, but what about that $1,000 color laser printer that's stuck in the basement office, chained to the computer down there? Sharing printers on your home network is a lot like sharing files. With file sharing, you made the file or folder available on the network by sharing it. Other people can then access those files by connecting to them over the network. Printer sharing works in the exact same way, but there is one additional step you have to take, which is to install the wee bit o' software that makes the printer work.

If you have printers connected to any of your computers, you probably remember having to install *drivers*—the tiny utility programs that give Windows the ability to communicate with your add-on hardware like printers, scanners, CD burners, and so on. Without the right driver, your printer won't work, because Windows won't know how to deal with it. Even when the printer is connected to someone *else's* computer, you still need to install drivers on *your* computer to use that printer over there on the other side of the network.

Note: If you share a printer that's attached to a particular PC, you have to leave that PC on for others on the network to use it. Your other options include buying a *network-ready printer,* which comes with an Ethernet jack that lets you connect the printer directly to your router (page 3). Or you can buy a router with a built-in *print server,* which is a device that lets you plug a regular printer into your router. In either case, anyone on your network can then use the printer whenever they want.

Printer sharing instructions depend on the version of Windows you're running.

Printer Sharing in Windows XP and Windows 2000

Since they're created from the same digital DNA, Windows XP and Windows 2000 both share printers the same way.

1. **Make sure you're printer is currently attached to a computer on your network.**

   If you've got a new printer, carry out whatever installation procedure came with your printer.

2. **Go to the "Printers and Faxes" control panel.**

   For Windows XP, go to Start → Printers and Faxes. For Windows 2000, go to Start → Settings → Printers.

3. **Open the Sharing dialog box for the printer you want to share.**

   To open the Sharing dialog box, right-click the printer you want to share. From the resulting shortcut menu, choose Sharing.

4. **Share the printer.**

   From the Sharing dialog box, select "Share this printer."

5. **Provide a share name.**

Just like any files and folders you may have shared, your printers need some kind of name that they'll be known by on the network. The name you select for your shared printer doesn't have to match the name that it has on the PC it's physically attached to. For example, if you have a printer named "HP LaserJet 5L" on your Windows XP computer, you can name it "The Big Red One." On your own computer, it will continue to appear as "HP LaserJet 5L," but everyone *else* will see the share name.

Note: If you try to provide a share name that is more than 12 characters in length, Windows will gently tell you that the printer may not be accessible from some MS-DOS workstations. Ten years ago, that might have been a problem. Today, about the only place a civilian home networker will see an MS-DOS–based computer is at a garage sale. In short, you can safely ignore this warning.

---

6. **Click OK.**

POWER USERS' CLINIC

Administrative Shares

When your PC is a member of a domain (page 82) and you try to share a disk, you may be surprised to see that the "Share this Folder" option is already selected, and it already has a share name (the drive letter followed by a $ symbol). As it turns out, Windows automatically shares the outer level (the *root* level) of all hard drives on a domain computer.

To be specific, it creates what's known as an *administrative share*: a shared disk that's invisible to ordinary peons on the network, but available to administrators who know its secret, hidden name. (See the bulleted list on page 104 of "Clever Standard File Sharing Tricks " for more on hidden shares, which also have the $ symbol at the end of their names.)

You're not allowed to change the permission settings for the administrative shares. You can stop sharing them, but Windows will re-share them automatically the next time you start up the computer.

But what if you want to share a drive yourself, so that other people on the network can access it?

Open its Properties dialog box, click the New Share button, and—in the New Share dialog box—specify a share name, a maximum number of users (if you like), and then click the Permissions button to set access permissions for the new share. (The administrative share permissions remain unaffected.) When you click OK, the new share name appears on the Sharing tab in the Share Name text box instead of the administrative share's name.

Notice, however, that the Share Name text box has now become a drop-down list. You can use it to choose either of the shares at the root of the drive, so that you can change the properties of each independently. You can also click the Remove Share button to delete the currently displayed share name, or click New Share to create as many shares at the root of the disk as you want. (Why you would *want* to do so is another question.)

Printer Sharing in Windows 95, 98, and ME

To share an existing printer in Windows 9x, just follow these steps:

1. **Enable file and printer sharing.**

    Windows 95, 98, and ME computers don't come from the factory ready to share their printers. First you have to activate file sharing, which you're probably already a master at. For a refresher, jump back to page 106; step 1 in the "File Sharing in Windows 95, 98, and ME" section explains everything you need to do.

2. **Open the printer's Control Panel.**

   Go to Start → Settings → Printers.

3. **Open the Sharing dialog box for the printer you want to share.**

   Right-click the printer's name and pick Sharing from the pop-up menu.

4. **Enter the details—the share name, and an optional comment and password— for this shared printer.**

   Printer share names in Windows 95, 98, and ME can't exceed 12 characters. Use the password field if you want to restrict access to this printer. Don't use this feature if you eventually intend to share this printer with Windows XP or Windows 2000 computers: the newer operating systems really hate Windows 9x passwords.

Accessing Files on Other PCs

So far in this chapter, you've been reading from the point of view of the person doing the sharing. You've read the steps for preparing a PC for sharing by other people on the network. This section details how to be one of *them*—that is, how to connect to other PCs whose disks, folders, and printers have been shared. Fortunately, doing so is extremely easy.

Method 1: My Network Places

Most people view their network contents using a special window:

- **In Windows XP or Windows ME:** choose Start → My Network Places.

- **In Windows 95, 98, and 2000:** double-click the desktop icon called Network Neighborhood.

The very first time you open the network window, you see icons that correspond to the shared folders and files on the computers of your network (including those on your own machine), as shown in Figure 5-14. Just double-click one to open it and, presto, the shared resource is yours to use.

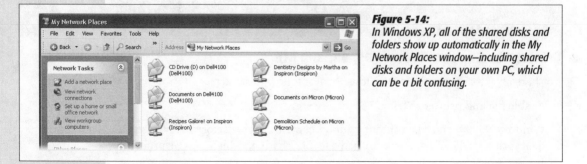

Figure 5-14:
In Windows XP, all of the shared disks and folders show up automatically in the My Network Places window—including shared disks and folders on your own PC, which can be a bit confusing.

Use "View workgroup computers" to simplify your view of network resources

If you find the My Network Places window overwhelmingly crowded as your network grows, you might find clarity in the "View workgroup computers" link at the left side of the window. It shows you the icons of the *computers* on your network—not every last shared folder on all of them. Double-click one of these computer icons to see a list of the shared folders and printers on it (Figure 5-15).

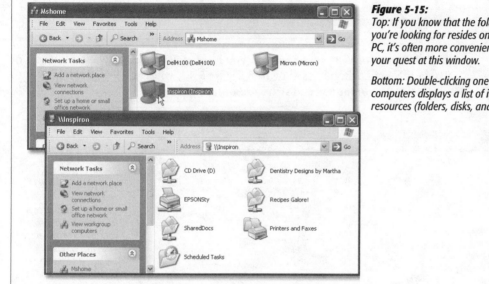

Figure 5-15:
Top: If you know that the folder or file you're looking for resides on a particular PC, it's often more convenient to start your quest at this window.

Bottom: Double-clicking one of these computers displays a list of its shared resources (folders, disks, and printers).

Older PCs: Network Neighborhood

If you're using a networked PC that's still running Windows 95, Windows 98, or Windows 2000, you won't find a My Network Places icon on the desktop. Instead, you get its ancestor: Network Neighborhood.

When you open Network Neighborhood, Windows displays an icon in the window for each computer it finds on the workgroup (see Figure 5-16), along with an Entire Network icon. (If you're on a domain network [page 82], you might see a list of domains here. Click the one you want.) Just double-click a computer's icon to see the shared disks, folders, and printers attached to it. You might have to type in the correct password to gain access.

Method 2: Windows Explorer

Instead of using the My Network Places or Network Neighborhood icon on the desktop, some people prefer to survey the network landscape using Windows Explorer. Windows Explorer is the program included in every recent version of Windows; it lets you scan the contents of your entire computer—it's kind of like a

---

Web browser for your computer. As you can probably tell, Windows Explorer can go outside your computer, too.

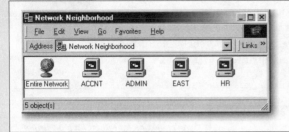

Figure 5-16:
This workgroup has four computers. The Entire Network icon lets you drill down from the workgroup to the computers—but because you see the networked workgroup PCs immediately, there's little reason to do so.

In the left pane of Windows Explorer, you'll see an icon for My Network Places or Network Neighborhood. As shown in Figure 5-17, you can click the + button to see a list of the computers and shared resources on them.

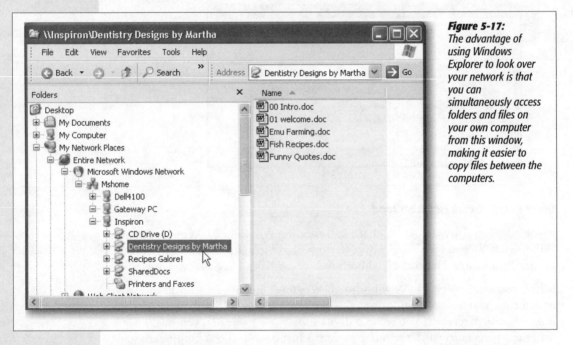

Figure 5-17:
The advantage of using Windows Explorer to look over your network is that you can simultaneously access folders and files on your own computer from this window, making it easier to copy files between the computers.

To use Windows Explorer:

- **In Windows XP or 2000:** go to Start → All Programs → Accessories → Windows Explorer.

- **In Windows 95, 98 or ME:** go to Start → Programs → Windows Explorer.

Method 3: Universal Naming Convention (UNC)

For hard-core nerds, that business of burrowing into the My Network Places folder is for sissies. When they want to call up a shared folder from the network, or even a particular document *in* a shared folder, they just type a special address into the Address bar of any folder window, or even Internet Explorer—and then press Enter. You can also type such addresses into the Run dialog box, accessible from the Start menu.

The address might look like this: *laptop**shared documents**salaries 2002.doc.*

Tip: Actually, you don't have to type nearly that much. Windows AutoComplete feature proposes that full expression as soon as you type just a few letters of it.

This path format (including the double-backslash before the PC name and a single backslash before a folder name) is called the *Universal Naming Convention* (UNC). It was devised to create a method of notating the exact location of a particular file or folder on a network. It also lets network geeks open various folders and files on networked machines without having to use the My Network Places window.

You can use this system in all kinds of interesting ways:

- Open a particular folder like this: *computer name**folder name.*

- You can also substitute the IP address (page 26) for the computer instead of using its name, like this: *192.168.1.44**my documents.*

- You can even substitute the name of a shared *printer* for the folder name.

Tips for Working with Network Files

Now that you're an expert at opening shared drives and folders from across the network, you can start using the files you find on other machines. Fortunately, there's not much to it. Here are some of the possibilities.

At the desktop

When you're working at the desktop, you can double-click icons to open them, drag them to the Recycle Bin, make copies of them, and otherwise manipulate them exactly as though they were icons on your own hard drive. (Of course, if you weren't given permission to change the contents of the shared folder, you have less freedom.)

Tip: There's one significant difference between working with "local" icons and working with those that sit elsewhere on the network: when you delete a file from another computer on the network, either by pressing the Delete key or by dragging it to the Recycle Bin, it disappears instantly and permanently, without ever appearing in the Recycle Bin of the computer you're using.

Using Start → Search

The Windows XP Search program stands ready to help you find files not just on your own machine, but also elsewhere on the network. When the Search window opens (choose Start → Search), look at the "Look in" option.

In this box, you can type the UNC path (page 113) to the computer you want to access. Or you can choose the "Look in" field's drop-down list and choose Browse (Figure 5-18). Once the browse window opens, you can browse through the network by selecting "My Network Places" (Windows ME and XP) or "Network Neighborhood" (Windows 9x, 2000).

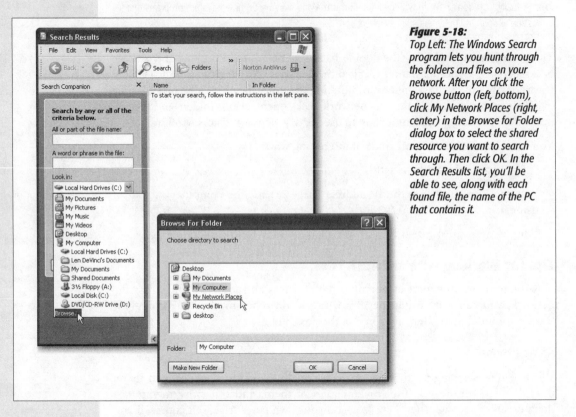

Figure 5-18:
Top Left: The Windows Search program lets you hunt through the folders and files on your network. After you click the Browse button (left, bottom), click My Network Places (right, center) in the Browse for Folder dialog box to select the shared resource you want to search through. Then click OK. In the Search Results list, you'll be able to see, along with each found file, the name of the PC that contains it.

Inside applications

When you're working in a program, opening files that sit elsewhere on the network requires only a couple of extra steps. Just summon the Open dialog box as usual (choose File → Open) and then, when it appears, click the My Network Places icon in the left-side panel (or choose My Network Places from the "Look in" drop-down menu).

Now just double-click your way to the folder containing the file you want to use. Once you've opened the file, you can work on it just as though it were sitting on your own computer.

At this point, using the File → Save command saves your changes to the original file, wherever it was on the network—unless you weren't given permission to make changes, of course. In that case, you can choose File → Save As and then save a copy of the file onto your own PC.

Creating Shortcuts to Network Places

If the networking bug has really bitten you, you may want to consider the advanced technique called *mapping shares*. Using this trick, you can assign a *letter* to a particular shared disk or folder on the network. Just as your hard drive is called C: and your floppy drive is A:, you can give your Family Stuff folder the letter F: and the hard drive in the kitchen the letter J:.

You get several benefits by mapping shares. First, these disks and folders now appear directly in the My Computer window. Getting to them can be faster this way than navigating to the My Network Places window. Second, when you choose File → Open from within one of your applications, you'll be able to jump directly to a particular shared folder instead of having to double-click, ever deeper, through the icons in the Open File dialog box. You can also use the mapped drive letter in pathnames anywhere you would use a path on a local drive, such as the Run dialog box, a File → Save As dialog box, or the command line.

To map a drive letter to a disk or folder, open any folder or disk window. Then:

1. **Choose Tools → Map Network Drive.**

   The Map Network Drive dialog box appears, as shown in Figure 5-19.

2. **Using the drop-down list, choose a drive letter.**

   You can select any unused letter you like (except B, which is still reserved for the second floppy disk drive that PCs don't have anymore).

3. **Indicate which folder or disk you want this letter to represent.**

   You can type its UNC code (page 113) into the Folder box, choose from the drop-down list of recently accessed folders, or click Browse.

Tip: Most people use the mapping function for disks and drives elsewhere on the network, but there's nothing to stop you from mapping a folder that's sitting right there on your own PC. This is useful if you frequently access a folder that's buried deep down in your hard drive and you want to get to it quickly.

---

4. **To make this letter assignment "stick," turn on "Reconnect at logon."**

   If you don't use this option, Windows forgets this assignment the next time you turn on the computer. (Use the "Connect using a different user name" option if your account name on the shared folder's machine isn't the same as it is on this one.)

5. **Click Finish.**

   A window opens to display the contents of the folder or disk. If you don't want to work with any files at the moment, just close the window.

From now on (depending on your setting in step 4), that shared disk or folder shows up in your My Computer list alongside the disks that are actually in your PC, as shown at bottom in Figure 5-19.

Tip: If you see a red X on one of these mapped icons, it means that the PC on which one of the shared folders or disks resides is either off the network or turned off completely.

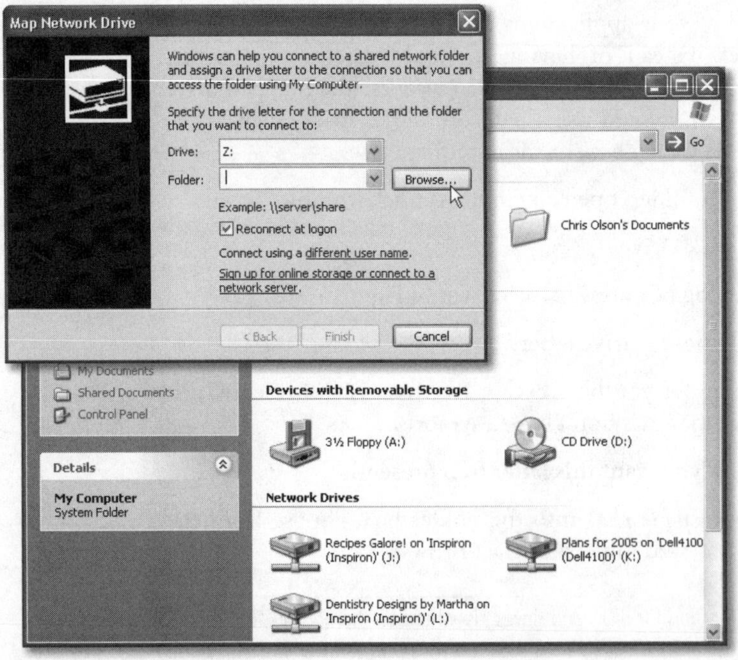

Figure 5-19:
Top: The "Reconnect at logon" option tells Windows to locate the share and map this drive letter to it every time you start your computer.

Bottom: Once you've mapped a few folders or disks to show their own letters, they show up in the Network Drives group within your My Computer Window. (Note the drive letters in parentheses—in this example, J:, K:, and L:.)

Using Printers on Other PCs

Earlier in this chapter, you learned how to share the printers connected to your Windows computer. Now, with the printer out there on the network yelling "Use me! Use me!" you need to set up each computer on your network so that it can use the printer.

Windows gives you a few ways to use a printer that's been shared by another computer:

- You can add a network printer using the Add Printer Wizard.

- You can do what the geeks do and type the *UNC path* to the printer in the Start → Run box. All these methods are described below, although method 1 is usually the easiest.

Method 1: Using the Add New Printer Wizard

To use the Add Printer wizard found in every version of Windows, follow these steps:

1. **Start the Add Printer wizard on the remote computer.**

   In Windows XP, go to Start → Printers and Faxes and double-click Add Printer. In Windows 2000, go to Start → Settings → Printers and Faxes and double-click Add Printer. In Windows 95, 98, and ME, do this by going to Start → Settings → Printers and selecting Add Printer.

2. **Add a network-based printer.**

   The first step of the wizard asks you if you're adding a *local* printer (one attached directly to your PC) or a *network* printer (one shared by another computer on the network). Since you're connecting to a printer on another computer, select the network option.

3. **Select the printer you'd like to use.**

   Specify the printer you'd like to add by browsing for it and locating it on the network.

4. **Install the software for the printer when prompted—but only if needed.**

   When you install a new printer connected directly to your computer, you sometimes have to install the driver software that makes the printer work with Windows. When you connect to a printer that's been shared, you still might have to perform this step. After you choose a printer, Windows looks at the computer sharing its printer and asks it for a copy of the printer's driver software. After receiving it, Windows decides whether it's usable.

   If Windows spurns the driver, it then asks you, the remote user, to supply it with a driver. If that happens, you'll have to have the CD that came with the printer so that you can install the driver software.

Tip: If you can't find your printer's CD, you can usually download a printer driver from the printer manufacturer's Web site.

5. **Use the printer.**

   Once the printer is successfully installed, you can print to it just as if it's connected to your computer. It will appear in the list of printers in every program and in the Printers and Faxes dialog box.

WORKAROUND WORKSHOP

Automatic Reconnections of Mapped Shares Can Be Tricky

If you select "Reconnect at logon" when mapping a shared disk or folder to a letter, the order in which you start your computers becomes important. The PC containing the shared disk or folder should start up *before* the computer that refers to it as, say, drive K:. That way, when the second computer searches for "drive K:" on the network, its quest will be successful.

On the other hand, this guideline presents a seemingly insurmountable problem if you have two computers on the network, and each of them maps drive letters to folders or disks on the other.

In that situation, you get an error message to the effect that the permanent connection is not available. It asks if you want to reconnect the next time you start the computer. Click Yes.

Then, after all the computers have started up, open My Computer or Windows Explorer. You can see the mapped drive, but there's a red X under the icon. Ignore the X. Just double-click the icon. The shared folder or disk opens normally (because the other machine is now available), and the red X goes away.

Method 2: Universal Naming Convention (UNC)

You can also demonstrate your technical prowess to your friends and family by connecting to a printer using nothing more than its universal name. For more information about this method, check out "Method 3: Universal Naming Convention (UNC)" on page 113.

However you connect to the printer, the end result is the same: your computer is able to print to the shared printer. The newly installed printer shows up in all of your programs, just like a printer directly attached to your own PC.

CHAPTER 6

Using the Network with Macintosh Computers

The first part of this book was all about setting up your home network: buying and installing routers and network adapters, getting all your Macs onto the Internet, and generally learning how to bask in the glory of being a home network maestro. Now that your Macs can communicate with the world at large, it's time to learn how to get them talking to each *other*. This chapter walks you through how to configure your Macs so that you can copy files from one machine to another (just as you'd drag files between folders on your own Mac), store your own files on any Mac in the house (while preventing others from gaining access to your stuff), and share printers among all your computers.

Tip: In Mac OS X, you can even connect to Windows machines without having to buy any additional software. To learn about that trick, see Chapter 7.

Best of all, the software you need to make this happen is built into Mac OS X (and, in some cases, Mac OS 9). Getting your Macs ready to go requires three main steps:

- **Naming the Macs and people on your network.** Every computer needs a name. And, in many cases, you'll want to create *user accounts* for everyone on each Mac you want them to access. You'll learn more about about computer names and user accounts in this chapter, but user accounts in particular are a great way to keep everyone's stuff private and looking the way they want it to look.

- **Designating *what* you want to share with others.** The second part of this chapter shows you how to flip on your Mac's *I'm-ready-to-share-my-files* switch. And you'll also learn how to navigate through the Mac's slightly intimidating world of assigning individual file and folder *permissions:* a powerful tool for controlling who has access to what on your machine.

• **Learning how to access the items others have shared on their Macs.** Once everyone's set up their computers to share, the next step is learning how to get to other people's stuff. This step is a piece of cake.

Naming Macs on the Network

Suppose you have three Macs on your home network. How do you keep them all straight? Even though, under the hood, computers use cryptic numbers called IP addresses (page 26) to keep track of each other, to avoid driving you up a tree, Apple computers also use names. When it comes to home networks, names are useful because, rather than having to figure out what's stored on the Mac at, say, IP address *123.123.4.5*, you see a name like *Mom's Mac* instead. In this section, you'll learn how to assign this important credential—a name—to your Macs.

Setting Up the Mac's Name

Make sure every Mac on your network has a name. (Your Mac may already have one, which you can check by following the steps below.) How you name your computer depends on which version of the Mac operating system you're using.

Naming your OS X Mac

In OS X, do the following to name your Mac:

1. **Open System Preferences.**

   Go to → System Preferences. (You can also double-click the System Preferences icon—the one that looks like a light switch next to an apple—in the Dock.)

2. **Go to the Sharing option.**

   From the Internet & Network section of the System Preferences window, select Sharing.

3. **Give the Mac a new name.**

   At the top of the File Sharing dialog box, in the Computer Name box, type the new name for your Mac (Figure 6-1). Go crazy with whatever name you want to use here, as long as it's 63 characters or less. Capital and lowercase letters, spaces, and numbers all work fine. The only characters you can't use are the period (.) and the at sign (@).

   There are a couple of exceptions, however. If you've got Mac OS 9 computers on your network, limit yourself to 31 characters or less. And if you've got Windows PCs on your network, check out *http://support.microsoft.com/kb/q188997/* for a bunch of Microsoft-imposed naming restrictions.

4. **Close the File Sharing dialog box.**

   That's it. You've just renamed your Mac.

Naming your OS 9 Mac

For those of you still using older versions of the Mac operating system, the steps
are a little bit different, but the idea is the same:

1. **Go to the File Sharing control panel.**

   Go to → Control Panels → File Sharing. Select the Start/Stop tab.

2. **Type in a new name for your Mac.**

   You can use capital and lowercase letters, spaces, and any characters except the
   period (.) and the at sign (@). Also, keep your name to 31 characters or less.
   There's some other stuff in this box, but for now, all you need to worry about is
   the Network Identity portion of the File Sharing control panel (Figure 6-1).

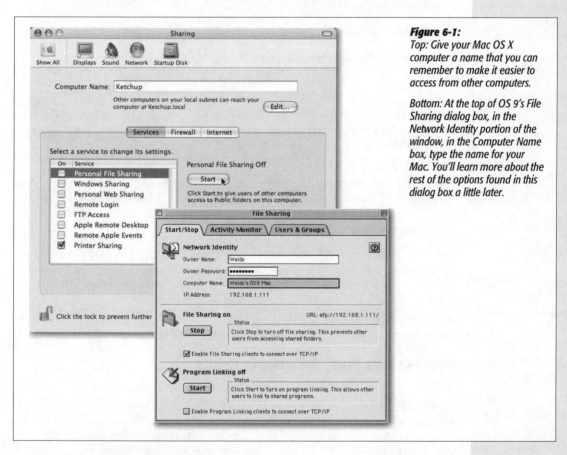

Figure 6-1:
*Top: Give your Mac OS X
computer a name that you can
remember to make it easier to
access from other computers.*

*Bottom: At the top of OS 9's File
Sharing dialog box, in the
Network Identity portion of the
window, in the Computer Name
box, type the name for your
Mac. You'll learn more about the
rest of the options found in this
dialog box a little later.*

3. **Close the File Sharing dialog box.**

   That's it. You've just renamed your Mac.

Creating User Accounts and Groups

Like its cousins, Windows 2000 and XP, Mac OS X is designed from the ground up to be a *multiple-user* operating system, thanks to powerful software underneath its flashy exterior. You can configure a Mac OS X computer so that everyone must *log in*—that is, you have to click or type your name, and enter a password—when the computer turns on. Upon doing so, you discover the Macintosh universe just as you left it, including these elements:

- Your documents, files, and folders

- Your preference settings in just about every program you use: Web browser bookmarks and preferred home page; desktop picture, screen saver, and language; icons on the desktop and in the Dock; the size and position of the Dock itself; and so on

- Your email account(s), including personal information and mailboxes

- Your personally installed programs and fonts

- Your choice of programs that launch automatically at startup

---

Note: Accounts in Mac OS 9 work somewhat similarly to Mac OS X's account system, except they're not quite as protective of the files and folders on your computer. Throughout this chapter, you'll see separate explanations of how to set up and use accounts in Mac OS 9.

This user account system means that several different people can use your Mac throughout the day, without disrupting each other's files and settings. It also protects the Mac from getting fouled up by mischievous (or bumbling) family members, employees, and hackers.

But user accounts also have *another* important purpose for home networkers: every visitor who wants to get at your computer from across the network also needs to log in. Setting up user accounts for these people lets you control where they can go on your computer. Depending on what kind of account type you give them—more on account types in a moment—they'll be able to roam about your entire computer, or end up confined to a pretty small virtual spot.

Deciding How Many Accounts to Create

Before you go crazy and set up accounts on every Mac in your home, take a minute to think about how much security you need. If it's just you and your fleet of shiny white Macs, you probably don't need to create *any* new accounts, since you can log into each Mac using the account that already exists on each computer. Similarly, if you've got house or office mates, and you're comfortable giving them complete access to all your files, then you won't need to set up any new accounts. (You *can*, of course, if you want to, but the point is you don't *have* to.) Just give your network pals your user name and password, and they can easily log in and exchange files with you. (Mac OS X is even considerate enough to let you keep working unhindered while visitors log into your Mac using your account.)

Finally, Mac OS X comes with a very handy *Guest account* feature, which you'll learn about on page 124. If the only thing you want to do is pass the occasional file back and forth on the network, you can use this Guest account to easily exchange items without having to spend time setting up a bunch of new accounts.

So now that you understand all *that,* you're free to read on and learn about the world of Mac account management, or you can skip ahead to page 134 to get started sharing the files on your Mac. If you are planning on creating new accounts for all the Macs in your house, a good rule of thumb is to create one account on each Mac for each person on your network.

GEM IN THE ROUGH

Logging In the Automatic Way

If you're the only person who will use your Mac, you can set up the system's Automatic Login feature so that the Mac always knows it's you logging in.

In Mac OS X 10.3 and later, look for this option in System Preferences → Accounts; click the Login Options button in the Accounts pane of the left side of the box.

Select the box marked "Automatically log in as" and choose the account name that you want to use every time from the drop-down list. For security, Mac OS X asks you to provide the password for this account. After providing a valid password, Mac OS X zooms right to your personal desktop without ever showing the list of available user names when you boot up the Mac in the morning.

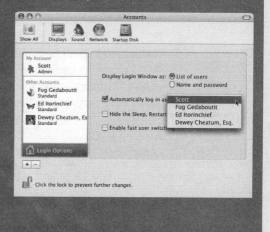

Choosing Account Types in Mac OS X

The first thing you need to decide before creating an account is what *kind* of account you want to set up. In Mac OS X, accounts come in two main flavors: Administrator and Standard.

Administrator accounts

You already have an Administrator account on your own Mac, since you need one to do things like install software or make any other big, Mac-altering changes. Among other things, Administrators are allowed to:

• Install new programs into the Applications folder.

• Add fonts (to the Library folder) that everybody can use.

- Make changes to certain System Preferences panels (including Network, Date & Time, Energy Saver, Login, and Startup Disk).

- Use the NetInfo Manager (danger, Will Robinson, danger!) and Disk Utility programs.

- Create new folders outside of their Home folder.

- Decide who gets new accounts on the Mac.

- Open, change, or delete anyone else's files.

Whether an account has administrator privileges makes a big difference as people start to connect to your Mac from across the network. As a general guideline, giving someone an Administrator account turns your Mac into an all-you-can-eat buffet. They can pretty much do whatever they want—for better and for worse.

Standard accounts

Folks with Standard accounts have everyday access to their own Home folders (they get these as soon as you set up Standard accounts for them) and to some of the System Preferences, but most other areas of the Mac are off-limits. Mac OS X doesn't even let these kinds of accounts create new folders on the main hard drive, except in their own Home folder (or in the Shared folder that's located on you Mac's hard drive, inside the Users folder).

Note: Giving Standard account holders access to an external hard drive (if they log in from across the network) requires a *ton* of extra work on your part, involving the creation of groups (page 128) and a fair amount of fiddling with the hard drive's permissions (see page 135 for details).

So when should you dole out Standard accounts? Follow these guidelines:

- If you have people on your network who you don't want meandering through your files, assign them Standard accounts.

- If you have computer novices in your house who might mess up your Mac, create Standard accounts for these people as well. That way, they can explore your computer to their heart's content and the only damage they can do is to their own stuff.

- For yourself, create Standard accounts on the other Macs in your house if you only want to access specific areas that their actual owners (for example, your college-aged offspring) want you to see.

Tip: Another option for once-a-year visitors or for anyone you don't want to assign an account to: Mac OS X comes with a built-in *Guest* account. Network visitors who sign in as guests are extremely limited in what they can do—page 151 has the details—but these accounts are useful if you just want to pass a file or two back and forth with someone on your network.

Managing Accounts in Mac OS X

Mac OS X makes it easy to create, change, and delete accounts.

Creating accounts

To create a new account, choose → System Preferences. Click the Accounts icon and then click the + button beneath the list of accounts. The controls shown in the right-side pane of Figure 6-2 appear.

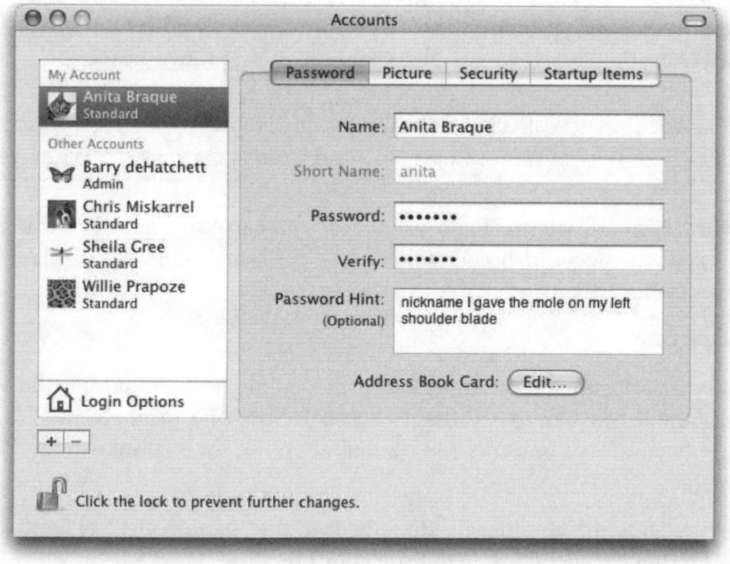

Figure 6-2:
The screen lists everyone for whom you've created an account. From here, you can create new accounts or change passwords. Notice the padlock icon at the bottom. Whenever you see it, you're looking at settings that only administrators are allowed to change—after clicking the padlock and identifying themselves by password, that is.

Mac OS X offers a long list of options for each account, as described in the following pages. None of the following steps are difficult; some of them, in fact, are kind of fun.

1. **Name the account.**

   On the first tab of the Accounts dialog box, called Password, you fill in certain information about the new account holder:

   Name. If the new account belongs to a member of the family, the name could be George or Gracie. If you're in a small business or school, you'll probably want to use both first and last names.

   Short Name. Particularly if the person's name is, say, Alexandra Stephanopoulos, she'll quickly discover the value of having a short name—an abbreviation of her actual name. When she accesses this Mac she can use the short variation. Technically, the short name is the actual account name and the name the Mac uses for the account's Home folder.

As soon as you tab into this field, the Mac proposes a short name for you. You can replace the suggestion with whatever you like. (It doesn't even have to be shorter than the "long" name.)

Password, Verify. Here's where you're supposed to type this new account holder's password (Figure 6-2). In fact, you're supposed to type it twice, to make sure you didn't introduce a typo the first time. The Mac displays only dots as you type, to guard against the possibility that somebody is watching over your shoulder.

You may want to consider setting up *no* password—leaving both password blanks empty. Later, whenever the account holder is asked for a password, he can just leave the Password box blank and log in that much faster.

Warning: If your Mac is connected directly to the Internet but you don't have a router (page 3) or a firewall (page 8), don't use a blank password. Without a router or a firewall, you want all the protection you can get.

Password Hint. If you created a password, you can leave a hint in this box. Later on, if the account holder forgets her password, the Mac displays this clue to give her a hand.

2. **Choose a picture.**

If you like the selections that Apple has provided at the right side of the window (drag the scroll bar to see them all), just click one to select it. If you'd rather supply your own graphics file—a digital photo, for example—follow one of these paths:

Drag the file. Drag the graphics file directly onto the "picture well" (Figure 6-3). Use the resulting Images window to frame your picture.

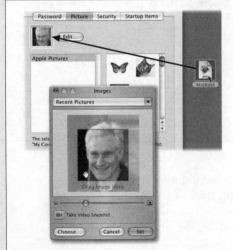

Figure 6-3:
Top: Select a photo to represent the new account.

Bottom: You can adjust its position relative to the square "frame" or adjust its size by dragging the slider. Finally, when the picture looks correctly framed, click Set. (The next time you return to the Images dialog box, you'll be able to recall the new image using the Recent Images pop-up menu.)

Use the Edit button. Click the Edit button. In the Images dialog box that appears, click Choose. You're shown a list of what's on your hard drive so that you can double-click your selection.

Use your camera. If you have an iSight camera (or a digital camcorder) hooked up to your FireWire jack, click Edit. Use the resulting Images window to frame the new user (if he happens to be sitting next to you, that is), and then click the Take Video Snapshot button.

3. **Activate any security options you want, and choose between Standard and Administrator status.**

Introduced with Mac OS X 10.3, the Security tab is the heart of Mac OS X's account security system.

The most important item here is the checkbox called "Allow user to administer this computer." This option is the big kahuna. This selection is the master switch that turns the meek Standard user into an all-powerful administrator.

Tip: If you expect Standard account holders to physically log into your Mac (rather than connecting from over the network), Mac OS X gives you a bunch of other ways to restrict what these in-person visitors can do. In the Accounts dialog box, click the Limitations tab and then restrict to your heart's content.

On this screen, you can also activate Mac OS X's (10.3 and later) much bally-hooed FileVault feature. FileVault is beyond the scope of a networking book, but in short, it's a system that lets you *encrypt* (scramble) everything in the account holder's Home folder. If you'd like to learn more about the ins and outs of FileVault, check out *Mac OS X: The Missing Manual.*

Editing accounts

Now that you've created an account, what happens if you ever need to make a change? Perhaps someone has a new name or wants a new password.

Administrators have carte blanche privileges here, but even an everyday Standard user can make *some* changes, like modifying his personal startup pictures, changing the list of things that launch automatically upon login, and, if the administrator permits, changing his own passwords. (To make changes, go to System Preferences → Accounts and select the account you want to change.)

Note: Only administrators have the right to change account names, and no one—not even mighty administrators—can change the short names.

Deleting accounts

Hey, it happens: somebody graduates, somebody gets fired, somebody dumps you. Sooner or later, you may need to delete an account from your Mac.

When that time comes, click the account name in the Accounts list and then click the little minus-sign button beneath the list. Your Mac asks what to do with all of the dearly departed's files and settings:

- **Delete Immediately.** This button offers the "Hasta la vista, baby" approach. The account and all its files and settings are vaporized forever, on the spot.

- **OK.** This button presents the "I'll be back" approach by preserving the dearly departed's folders on the Mac in a tidy digital envelope that doesn't clutter your hard drive but can be reopened in case of emergency.

In the Users → Deleted Users → [person's name] folder is a disk image file (it will have the suffix .dmg). If you double-click it, you'll find a new virtual disk icon on your desktop named for the deleted account. You can open folders and root through the stuff in this "disk" just as if it were a living, working Home folder.

If fate ever brings that person back into your life, you can use this disk image to reinstate the deleted person's account. Start by creating a brand-new account. Then copy the contents of the folders in the mounted disk image (Documents, Pictures, Desktop, and so on) into the corresponding folders of the new Home folder.

Managing Groups in Mac OS X

The inner workings of Mac OS X's file-sharing software lack one feature that was present in earlier versions of the Mac OS: the ability to easily create and manipulate *groups,* or collections of user accounts that all have similar file-access privileges. (You'll learn more about how to set these mind-bendingly complex, but powerful, privileges later on in the chapter.) Oh, creating groups can still be done, mind you; it's just not as simple as it should be.

Tip: If you're going to be spending a lot of time creating and managing groups, check out a program called SharePoints (*www.hornware.com*). It's a big timesaver.

As your networking setup becomes more complex, being able to work with subsets of the people on your network is a great timesaver. For example, you might create groups called Parents, Kids, and Animals. Later on in this chapter, you'll learn how to permit an entire group of these people to access a particular file, folder, or disk in one fell swoop.

Creating groups

To set up groups, start by opening NetInfo Manager, which is in your Applications → Utilities folder.

Defining and naming the group. Here's how you might go about creating a new group called Kids and then adding the names of three of your most dangerous offspring to it. (These steps assume that you've already created user accounts for these people, as described on page 122.)

1. **In NetInfo Manager, click the tiny padlock in the lower-left corner.**

   A dialog box appears, prompting you for an administrator's name and password. The Mac is just checking to make sure that somebody with a clue is at the helm.

2. **Type the name and password of an administrator (page 123). Click OK.**

   NetInfo presents a staggering array of network-related variables (Figure 6-4). In the second column, you'll see that one of them is called *groups*.

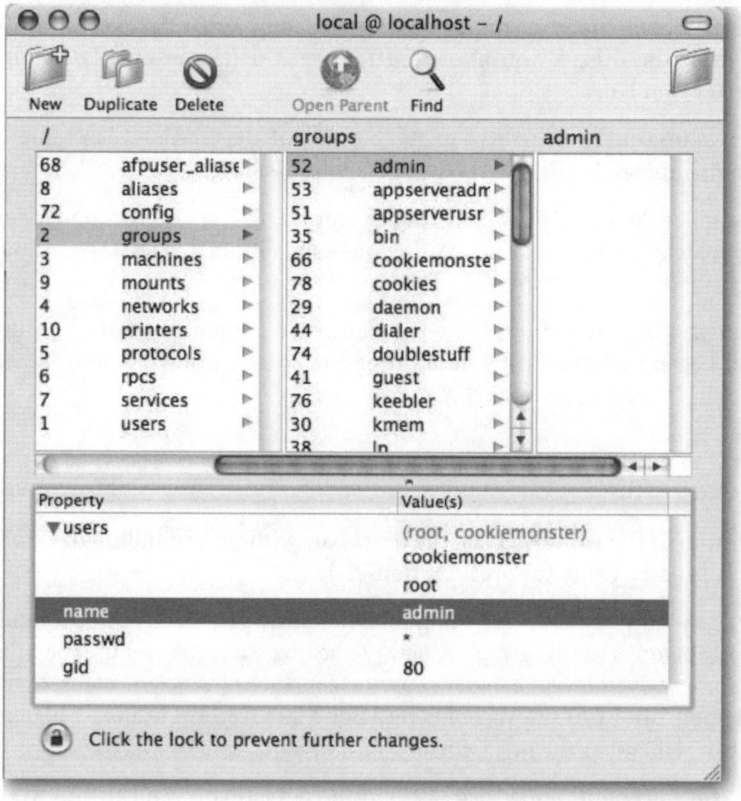

Figure 6-4:
Consider yourself warned: NetInfo Manager is an extremely technical program designed for network administrators with years of training and a vested pension plan somewhere in corporate America. Not only do you need an administrator's account to play with it, but veering off the instructional path detailed in the following pages could, in theory, get your Mac in trouble.

3. **Click "groups."**

   In the next column to the right, you'll see a list of all the canned groups that come installed with Mac OS X: admin, bin, daemon, kmem, and so on. These terms aren't especially closely related to English, but then again, Unix names were designed primarily for efficiency in typing. (Unix is the operating system that lurks in the bowels of OS X.)

You're ready to add a new group to this list. The easiest way is to duplicate one of the existing groups.

4. **Click "admin" in the list of groups, and then click the Duplicate button at the top of the window. Now click Duplicate in the confirmation message.**

You wind up with a new group in the list, called "admin copy." Note that it's highlighted, and a few morsels of information about it appear at the bottom of the window. One of them—in the Property column—says name (see Figure 6-4).

5. **Double-click "admin copy" at the bottom of the window (in the Value(s) column). Type the new name for your group, and then press Enter.**

You've just created and named a new group. To help Mac OS X keep this one separate from the others, you also need to give it a new group ID number, abbreviated *gid* in Unix-ese.

6. **If the gid value (in the third row at the bottom of the window) isn't already highlighted, double-click it. Then type *200* and press Enter.**

The ID number doesn't especially matter except that it can't be the same as any the other folders' group IDs. The existing ones are all under 100, so you should be in good shape.

At the moment, your new group lists the names of all administrator accounts (because you began this process by duplicating the admin group). Now you need to make sure that the right people belong to this group.

Adding people to the new group. The adding-people-to-a-group process takes place in the bottom half of the window.

1. **At the bottom of the window, click the users row without expanding it. Choose Directory → Insert Value (or press Option-⌘-I).**

The users row now expands, revealing individual rows for each account holder who already belongs to this group. A new_value box waits for you to type in the name of somebody you've created an account for. (Sorry, efficiency fans, there's no simple pop-up list of the accounts on your Mac; NetInfo Manager assumes that you can remember the precise name and capitalization of every account.)

2. **Type the short account name (page 125) of the person you want to add to this group, and then press Enter.**

If you want to add another person, choose Directory → Insert Value again, and then type in another name. (You can also delete someone from this group by highlighting the appropriate row and then choosing Directory → Delete Value.)

3. **When you're finished adding people, save your changes (Domain → Save Changes), and click "Update this copy" in the confirmation dialog box.**

Quit NetInfo Manager.

At the moment, you've got yourself a properly defined group, but this information is just kicking around in Mac OS X's head without any *practical* value. The next step is to tell Mac OS X which files and folders are the private stomping grounds of this group. "Advanced Permissions Control in Mac OS X" on page 135 tells you all about how to do that.

File Sharing Accounts and Groups in Mac OS 9

Just like its faster, sturdier descendents, Mac OS 9 lets you set up user accounts to help manage the various people who might want to use each Mac on your network. Unlike OS X, however, OS 9 gives you two entirely separate *kinds* of accounts:

- **Multiple Users.** These accounts are used for managing lots of people that you want to be able to log in while sitting at your Mac (as opposed to arriving from over the network). Multiple User accounts help keep everyone's files and folders separate and let you do things like restrict who can use the Mac's CD drive or install new programs. Since the Multiple Users tool doesn't really have anything to do with running a home network, you can pop over to Appendix B to read more about how to set these up, if you like.

- **File Sharing.** These accounts are what you need to create for your visitors who are logging in from across the network. And if you really want to control what your visitors see and do while accessing your Mac, once you create these accounts, you can assign various permission or restriction rights to any of your folders or hard drives—all of which are keyed to different groups of users. More on how to do that in a moment.

Note: Unfortunately, setting up Multiple User accounts doesn't do you any good when setting up File Sharing accounts, and vice versa. In other words, if you want to give someone a Multiple User account and a File Sharing account, you need to create each account separately. Chalk up another reason to consider upgrading to OS X.

But before you plow ahead and set up a zillion File Sharing accounts, consider for a moment how secure you need your Mac to be. If you don't need to restrict your network visitors, then you may very well be content to just supply them with *your* user name and password. The advantage to doing this is that, well, setting up accounts is a bit of an administrative pain, and assigning permissions to folders and disk drives is a downright chore. That said, if you *do* need this kind of control, read on. The next few sections tell you everything you need to know about File Sharing accounts.

Three types of File Sharing accounts

You can have three different kinds of File Sharing accounts on your OS 9 Mac:

- The **Owner** account is pretty similar to the Administrator account in OS X, with one important difference: you only get one of these on each OS 9 machine. Naturally, if you (or your pals on other Macs) log in from across the network as the

---

Owner, you can do pretty much whatever you want to do on the Mac you're logging into.

- **Network User** accounts are the ones you use when creating specific accounts for your people out there in Network Land. The big difference between Network Users and the Owner is that the Owner automatically has the right to open and fiddle with everything on the computer. For your Network Users, you have to specifically assign them rights to the folders and disks you want them to have access to. (Don't despair: you can take care of this in one shot by assigning them access to your hard drive, thereby entitling them to see and use everything *inside* the drive.)

- The **Guest** account is actually just a switch you flick on your Mac: once you turn it on, you've decided to let visitors log in as guests (with pretty limited rights, at least initially, to what they can do). Page 133 shows you how to activate the Guest account.

Creating new File Sharing accounts

To create a new File Sharing account, do the following:

1. **Open the File Sharing control panel.**

   Go to → Control Panels → File Sharing. The File Sharing window appears.

2. **Select the Users & Groups tab and then click New User.**

   A New User dialog box appears. For each new account you create, you need to specify three groups of settings, each of which you can see by selecting from the Show drop-down list: Identity, Sharing, and Remote Access.

   The Identity page. Enter a user name and password on this page. The user name can't exceed 31 characters and the password can't be more than 8 characters. If you want to let the new user change her password, turn on the "Allow user to change password" checkbox.

   The Sharing page. To provide some semblance of security, Mac OS 9 lets you, as the machine's master, toggle on or off a user's file sharing privileges by turning on or off the "Allow user to connect to this computer" checkbox.

   On this page, you can also provide your network visitors with the option to tap into data shared by other programs that use *Apple Events* (virtual packets of information that programs use to communicate with each other). Do so by turning on the "Allow user to link to programs on this computer" checkbox. The middle of this window also shows you a list of the groups to which this user belongs. Page 133 tells you all about File Sharing groups in Mac OS 9.

   The Remote Access page. If you want this account holder to be able to dial into your Mac from the road using the modem, turn on the "Allow user to dial in to this computer" checkbox. One drawback to this option is that it opens up your Mac to the outside world and is somewhat insecure. To practice safe computing, you can require account holders to always dial in from the same location by specifying a phone number in the "Call back at #" field. When they dial into the Mac, the Mac hangs up the phone and immediately calls back at the number you've listed.

3. **Finish creating the account by closing the new account's dialog box.**

   Click the close-window box in the upper-left corner of the dialog box. The new account now appears in the Users & Groups list in the File Sharing window.

Making changes to the Owner and Guest accounts

If you want to change the password for your Owner account, or activate the Guest account, follow these steps:

1. **Open the File Sharing control panel.**

   Go to → Control Panels → File Sharing. The File Sharing window appears.

2. **Select the Users & Groups tab.**

   To change the Owner account's password, select the account name listed to the left of the word "owner." Then click Open, and on the Identity page (see step 2 in the previous list), enter a new password.

   To activate the Guest account, select the guest name. Then click Open and on the Sharing page (see step 2 in the previous list) turn on the "Allow guests to connect to this computer" checkbox.

Tip: If you want to edit, copy, or delete any accounts, you can do so by selecting the account name from the Users & Groups tab and then clicking the Open, Duplicate, or Delete buttons, respectively. Copying accounts is useful if you've already created an account and want to use the same settings. Just duplicate the account and then change the account's name.

Creating groups

Groups are collections of File Sharing accounts. For example, at home, you might create a group called Parents into which you put your mom and dad. Later on, when you want to grant access to certain folders (you'll learn how to do that on page 140), you can give access to this group rather than to each individual member.

To create a group:

1. **Open the File Sharing control panel and select the Users & Groups tab.**

   Go to → Control Panels → File Sharing. The File Sharing window appears.

2. **Click New Group and give the group a name.**

   In the Name box at the top of the New Group window, type the group's name.

---

3. **Add users to the group.**

   (This step assumes that you've already created a few accounts.) Make sure you can see both the New Group window as well as the Users & Groups list. Now, drag the icon for the user you'd like to add to the new group to the big box on the New Group window.

Note: Groups in Mac OS 9 can't be *nested,* meaning that you can't add a group to a group, although Apple hasn't left you in a total lurch. If you try to add one group to another, Mac OS 9 automatically adds every member of the first group to the second group.

If you ever want to delete a group, highlight its name and then click the Delete button. When you delete an account, the account is automatically removed from any groups to which it belongs.

Sharing Your Mac's Files and Folders

So far, you've accomplished two tasks: naming your computer and creating user accounts. Now, it's time to tell your Mac that it should start sharing its files and folders with visitors who arrive from across the network. Once you've done that, you can decide exactly what documents everyone should be able to view and what they can do with those files. For example, should your husband have access to your work files and, if so, should he just be able to see the files or should he be able to make changes to them, too?

The steps you take depend on whether you're running Mac OS X or Mac OS 9. Each operating system is covered separately in the following sections.

File Sharing in Mac OS X

Once you establish accounts for everybody who might want to get into your Mac OS X computer—even if the only account is yours—you're ready to proceed with preparing the machine for access from elsewhere on the network.

Note: You need to be logged in as an administrator (page 123) to activate file sharing.

---

1. **Open System Preferences.**

   Click its icon on the Dock or choose → System Preferences. Either way, the System Preferences program opens.

2. **Click the Sharing icon.**

   The Sharing panel appears, as shown in Figure 6-5.

3. **In the list of checkboxes, turn on Personal File Sharing (Figure 6-5).**

   This feature takes a moment to warm up; when File Sharing is finally on, the button says Stop. Clicking the Stop button turns Personal File Sharing back off. Close the window, if you like.

Note: If you want Windows PCs on your network to be able to connect to your Mac, too, turn on Windows Sharing as well. Flip over to Chapter 7 for more information on Mac/PC cross-platform file sharing.

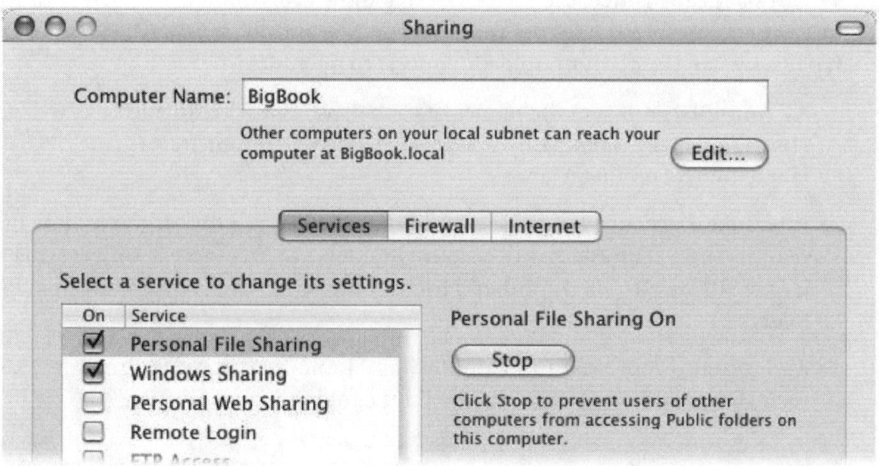

Figure 6-5:
Here's the master on/off switch for file sharing over the network in Mac OS X— the Sharing panel of System Preferences. (The toolbar has been hidden in this illustration.)

4. **Repeat this process on each Mac OS X machine in your home whose files you want to make available on the network.**

The type of account your network visitors use to sign in to your Mac (Standard, Administrator, or Guest) determines how much access they have to your computer. Page 150 lays out all the details. But if you're up for a slightly brain-bending adventure in permission setting, you can really fine-tune your system and control who gets to see what. Read on, intrepid souls.

Advanced Permissions Control in Mac OS X

Mac OS X adopts a fairly rigid scheme of permissions (*access privileges*) that lets you control what your network visitors can see and do on your Mac (view files, edit them, and so on). This section shows you a few ways to customize these permissions.

Note: To complicate matters, Mac OS X's permissions system works slightly differently depending on whether your visitors are logging in while sitting in front of your Mac or arriving from across the network. Since this is a book on home *networking,* this section covers only network access permission setting.

To modify what your network visitors can and can't do, you first need to understand a Mac OS X component called *share points*. A share point is basically a pathname (for example, */Users/chris/*) that's part of a list that the Mac's Personal File Sharing and Windows File Sharing systems consult to figure out what to make available to visitors who log in from across the network. Any item that's been designated as a share point shows up when an account holder logs in (as long as the share point is part of what the account holder is allowed to view; more on that in a moment).

Out of the box, Mac OS X provides you with only a limited number of share points: the Home directory for every account holder and the top level of each hard drive (which are available only to administrators).

What this means is that each Mac doesn't show everything on its drives to everyone who connects from across the network. Specifically, here's what each account type sees when the account holder connects to a remote Mac:

- An **Administrator** sees the names of each drive on the remote Mac as well as her Home folder. By opening up a Mac's hard drive, administrators can view all the Home folders on that Mac.

- A **Standard** account holder sees only the names of all the Home folders on the remote Mac. The Standard account holder has free access only to his own Home folder. In all the other Home folders, he can access only the Public folder.

- A **Guest** also sees only the names of all Home folders on the remote Mac. In each Home folder, all he sees is the Public folder.

Note: Just to make sure you're successfully juggling all the mental balls that are in the air right now, share points are important because they're the on/off switches that make things visible to people who log in from across the network. Once a share point exists, *then* you can make changes to a file or folder's permissions settings.

Now that you know what network visitors can see, you're ready to think about changing the permissions settings for any of these viewable items. So what kinds of changes can you make using your Mac's existing share points?

- You can modify access to each account holder's *drop box* (the folder inside each Public folder). Say you've got a full-time, high-speed connection to the Internet, and you worry about that drop box. If somebody figures out your Mac's IP address (page 26), it's conceivable that they could dump unsavory files into your drop box anonymously over the Internet.

- You can make your Public folder not quite so public.

- You can provide access to your Pictures folder (or Music, or Movies, for example) to people other than just yourself (as long as they have Administrator accounts).

But what if, say, you wanted to make the */Users/Shared* folder available to Standard account holders? That would be a problem, because that folder is not, at least to start out with, defined by Mac OS X as a share point. That means you would need to define a new share point yourself.

Alas, Mac OS X doesn't give you an easy way to create new share points. But fortunately, the good people at *www.hornware.com* offer a donation-suggested program called SharePoints. You'd use SharePoints, for example, to make your Shared folder available to other people on the network.

The best you can do then (assuming you don't want to use SharePoints and you don't want to give everyone an Administrator account) is to change permissions on the Public folder in each account's Home folder. That's because your Standard account-holding network visitors only have access to everyone's Public folders, as mentioned earlier. The next section shows you how to actually go ahead and adjust your current permission settings.

Changing access permissions for a file or folder

Changing an item's permissions affects how others can access it both when they're sitting at the computer and connected to it remotely. (Though, again, these permissions matter for remote connections only if the item is in a folder that's also a share point. Got it?)

To begin, highlight a file or folder on your hard drive. Unless you're an administrator, it must be a file or folder that you *own* (because it's in your Home folder or because you've created it yourself). Standard account holders are never allowed to mess with other people's folders.

Choose File → Get Info (or press ⌘-I). When the Info dialog box appears, expand the Ownership & Permissions panel; then expand the Details section (see Figure 6-6).

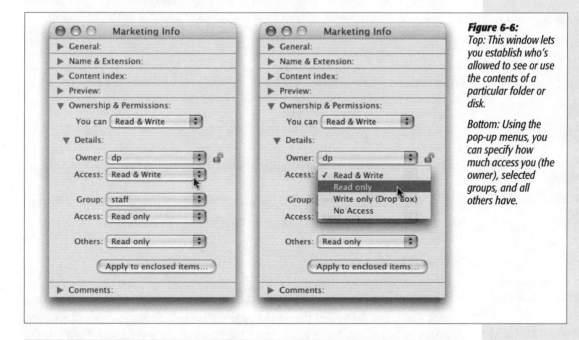

Figure 6-6:
Top: This window lets you establish who's allowed to see or use the contents of a particular folder or disk.

Bottom: Using the pop-up menus, you can specify how much access you (the owner), selected groups, and all others have.

Tip: You can also change the permissions for many folders at once. Just highlight all of them before choosing File → Get Info.

Now you see three pop-up menus: Owner, Group, and Others. (Each of the first two also offers an Access pop-up menu.) More on these designations in a moment. For now, note that the Owner Access, Group Access, and Others pop-up menus contain identical commands. They let you specify what you, the other people in your work group, and the entire network community can do with this document or folder:

- If you choose **No Access,** then you're a network tease—your family may be able to see the folder, but its name and icon will be dimmed and unavailable.

- The **Read only** option lets visitors open the folder, open the files inside, or copy the files inside; however, they can't put anything new into the folder, nor can they save changes to files they find there. Set up a *folder* like this one as a distribution point for newsletters, standard logos, or other company information. Or turn this on for a *document* that you want people to be able to read but not edit.

- The **Write only (Drop Box)** option is available only for folders. Turn it on if you want others to be able to see the folder, but not open it. All they can do is copy files into it. (Your own drop box—which Mac OS X creates automatically in your Home → Public folder—works this way, too.)

  This option is great for setting up a place where people can put documents that are intended for your eyes only. For example, students turning in homework, underlings turning in quarterly reports, and so on.

- Finally, choose **Read & Write** if you'd like your networked colleagues to have full access to the folder. They can do anything they want with the files inside, including trash them.

Note: Whenever you adjust the permissions for a folder using this method, remember to take into account the permissions of the folder it's *in* (that is, its parent folder). No matter how exquisitely you set up a drop box folder, for example, nobody will even know it's there unless it's *inside* a folder for which you've turned on at least "Read only" access.

But wait. Just when you thought this permissions business might be easy enough for you to grasp without that long-postponed Ph.D. in astrophysics, it gets more complicated.

It turns out that you can assign these different levels of freedom to different subsets of people on your network. That's why there are three different categories of pop-up menu:

- **Owner.** That's you.

  Of course, ordinarily, you have full access (Read & Write) to all your folders. You can put anything into them, take anything out of them, and do whatever you like with them. But if you feel the need to protect yourself from your own destructive instincts, you can actually limit your own access to certain folders. For example, using this pop-up menu, you can turn one into a drop box, as described below.

  If you're an administrator, in fact, you can do more than specify how much access you have. You can actually *change* the owner, so that somebody else has control over this icon. To make this change, click the padlock icon, and then choose a new owner from the Owner pop-up menu.

This is an unbelievably sweeping power. It means that you can trod roughshod over everyone else's stuff, blowing away all of the usual Mac OS X account-security mechanisms. If you feel like trashing all the files of everyone else who uses this Mac, you can do it. You, after all, are Administrator, God of the Mac. (This, by the way, is a good argument for limiting the number of people who *have* Administrator accounts. Remember: they can do the same thing to you.)

In any case, as soon as you choose a new owner from the pop-up menu, you are asked for your account password, just to prove that you're really an administrator. Type it, and then click OK.

Now you can not only change who the owner *is*, but also use the Owner Access pop-up menu to specify how much access the owner has to the file or folder.

- **Group.** In most networking systems, you can put every person in your office into certain groups, such as Marketing, Accounting, or Temps. (For details on how to set up your own groups, pop back to page 128.)

Mac OS X also comes with a whole bunch of canned, prefab groups, to which it automatically assigns everyone on the network. If you're an administrator, for example, you belong to the admin group, among others; if you're a mere peon, a Standard account holder, you're part of the staff group. (The other group names here—dialer, guest, mail, and such—exist for the benefit of network administrators and for Mac OS X itself. Mac OS X 10.3 and later even creates a group named after each account holder—very tiny groups indeed.)

If you have a Standard account, you can't change the Group pop-up menu, but using the lower pop-up menu, you can change how much access *everyone* in your group has to the file or folder.

If you're an administrator, on the other hand, you can make a selected file or folder available to any other group (and then, by using the Access pop-up menu beneath it, specify that group's degree of access). Once again, you'll be asked to prove your worthiness by clicking the padlock icon and entering your administrator password.

- **Others.** So far, you've specified how much access the *owner* of this icon has, and how much access one favored *group* gets to it. But what about everyone else?

They are the *Others,* of course. This pop-up menu specifies how much freedom *everybody else* in the network will have to the selected file or folder, including guests. Needless to say, if security is an issue where you work, you may not want to set the Others pop-up menu to permit full access.

Note: You can't give Others more access to the folder than you gave the Group people—only the same degree of freedom, or less. For example, you can't allow others Read & Write access to a folder but give your admin group just drop-box access.

If you want the change to affect all the folders *inside* the selected disk or folder in the same way, click "Apply to enclosed items." In the confirmation box, click OK.

In any case, just close the Info window when you're finished. You've just fooled around with some high-powered Unix mojo—without even knowing it.

File Sharing in Mac OS 9

Flipping on the file sharing switch in Mac OS 9 is pretty straightforward. Once you've named your Mac (page 121) and set up File Sharing accounts (page 131), here's what you need to do:

1. **Open the File Sharing control panel and select the Start/Stop tab.**

   Go to → Control Panels → File Sharing. The File Sharing window appears.

2. **Clicking Start to activate file sharing.**

3. **Turn on the checkbox called "Enable File Sharing clients to connect over TCP/IP," if the checkbox appears.**

At this point, your OS 9 Mac shares its files only withnetwork visitors who sign in using the Owner account (page 131). They can access every file, folder, and application, even if the item isn't specifically shared.

For everyone else, you need to specifically share the folder you want them to have access to:

1. **Select the folder you want to share.**

   The folder can be a high-level folder—including the entire hard drive—or a folder nestled deep inside your Mac. To select the folder, use the Finder and just click on the name of the folder.

2. **Open the folder's Sharing properties.**

   From the Finder, go to File → Get Info → Sharing. The folder's Sharing options appear.

3. **Turn on the "Share this item and its contents" checkbox.**

4. **Lock the folder (optional).**

   If you want to share a folder but don't want network visitors to make any changes to the contents, turn on the "Can't move, rename, or delete this item (locked)" checkbox.

5. **Change the folder's Privilege settings (optional).**

   Initially, the Owner account owns the folder, but you can assign a new folder owner if you like—whoever you select can do whatever she likes with it. To do so, click the name box next to Owner and select the user or group to which Mac OS 9 should assign folder ownership.

You could stop at assigning a new owner to the folder if you like. But suppose you want other people to be able to access the folder. For example, maybe you're a teacher and you want to create a virtual "drop box" into which your students can submit assignments. If that's the case, the User/Group drop-down list was made just for you. Like the Owner field, you can assign a specific Privilege level to the user or group you specify. (You'll learn about the different Privilege settings in a moment.)

Finally, take a look at the Everyone entry in the Name column (Figure 6-7). In the event you want to provide privileges to a folder to *any* user that connects to this Mac, use its Privileges drop-down menu.

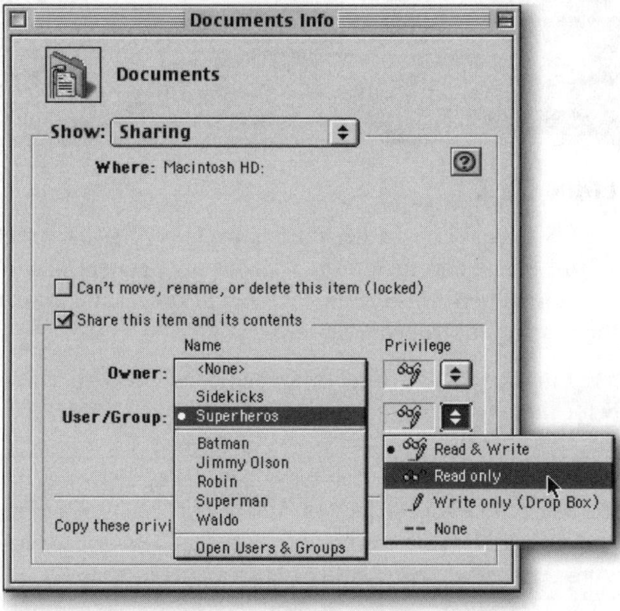

Figure 6-7:
You can't see the Everyone option in this figure since it's covered by the user list. Note that the user list contains both groups and users, as well as an option to open the Users & Groups tab on the File Sharing control panel. Also, note the different Privilege levels in the pop-up menu at the lower-right corner of the dialog box.

OS 9 gives you four different Privilege settings:

- **Read & Write** equals full access and permits the account holder to read, delete, copy, move, mangle, change, or erase the folder and its contents. Read & Write is identified by the icon with the glasses and the pencil.

- **Read only** (a glasses-only icon) offers "look but don't touch" access and lets the visitor see what's in a folder without letting him change its contents.

- **Write only (Drop Box)** (a pencil icon) provides a place for account holders to put files, but they can't see anything—including their own stuff—once it's there.

- **None** (the double-dash icon) prevents the selected user and group from accessing the folder at all.

Sharing Your Mac's Printer

File sharing is great, but Macs can help you save money, too. No longer do you have to buy a separate printer for each computer in your house. Instead, just connect your expensive laser printer to your Mac and then, Mac, Windows, and even Linux computers can easily use the printer. Pretty nifty, eh?

GEM IN THE ROUGH

Copying Privilege Settings Between Folders in OS 9

Privilege settings affect both the current folder you're assigning rights to and all its enclosed folders. In fact, if you look at the Sharing information of a subfolder inside a shared folder, a new option appears called "Use enclosing folder's privileges." When you turn this checkbox on, the subfolder inherits all the privilege settings from its parent folder. If you'd rather each individual folder have its own set of privileges, click the Copy button. This process copies the current folders privileges to *all* subfolders. If you change a permission at the top level later on, it won't be reflected in any subfolders unless you copy the privileges again.

Printer Sharing in Mac OS X

Like most things in Mac OS X, enabling printer sharing isn't very hard. Open → System Preferences → Print & Fax and turn on the "Share my printers with other computers" checkbox. Doing so performs the dual duty of putting a checkbox next to Printer Sharing in the Sharing control panel as well.

That's it. When others connect to the printer-equipped Mac OS X machine, all your printers are ready for them to use!

Note: Sharing your printers means exactly what is says. *All* the printers that *you* have access to are available to any other computers on your network. For example, if you, Mac OS X computer owner, use a printer connected to a Windows PC and you've got printer sharing turned on, then all the other Macs (including Mac OS 9 systems) can use the Windows machine's printer. There's more about how this works in Chapter 7.

Printer Sharing in Mac OS 9

Printer sharing in OS 9 is also a snap.

Note: The instructions in this section assume you have a working printer connected to your OS 9 Mac with a USB cable.

---

1. **Open the USB Printer Sharing control panel.**

   Find the control panel at → Control Panels → USB Printer Sharing.

2. **Click the Start button.**

   This doesn't actually start sharing a printer yet; it sets up your Mac to be able to do so.

---

3. **Click the My Printers tab.**

The My Printers tab opens, showing a list of your installed printers.

4. **Share your printer.**

Find your printer and share it. See Figure 6-8.

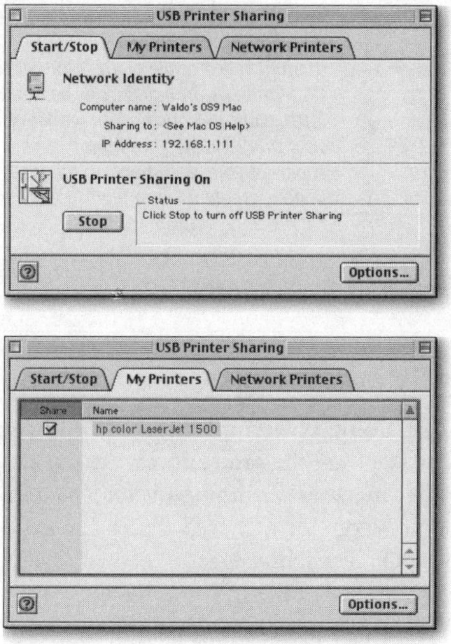

Figure 6-8:
Top: The Start/Stop tab for USB printer sharing provides you with all the pertinent details you'll need later on when you try to connect to this Mac from another Mac on the network.

Bottom: You don't have to share **all** your USB printers. If you have multiple printers, you can pick and choose which ones to share across the network. For example, you might not want to share the expensive color laser printer with others, because dang, that toner's expensive!

Now other computers can connect to this Mac and use any printers you share.

Accessing Other Macs on Your Network

At last! Now that all your Macs are configured to share their goodies, and you've set up any accounts you need, you can finally get this show on the road and actually connect with another Mac on your network (Figure 6-9).

The connection method you choose depends on which version of the Mac OS you're using. Even within the same operating system, there are different connection methods that give you and your network mates a variety of ways to access each other's machines. In this section, you'll learn about different ways to connect to other Macs and discover what you can do once you've hooked up with another Mac.

Getting Around from an OS X Mac

If you're running Mac OS X, you have it made as far as connectivity goes. Apple engineers have given you the ability to connect to pretty much any other computer—regardless of its operating system—with ease. There are a couple of methods by which you can do this. First, in Mac OS X 10.3 and later, you can use the *Sidebar*, a simple yet powerful tool for networking wizards such as yourself. Second, in all versions of Mac OS X, the *Connect to Server* option is available. You get to see both of them in action below.

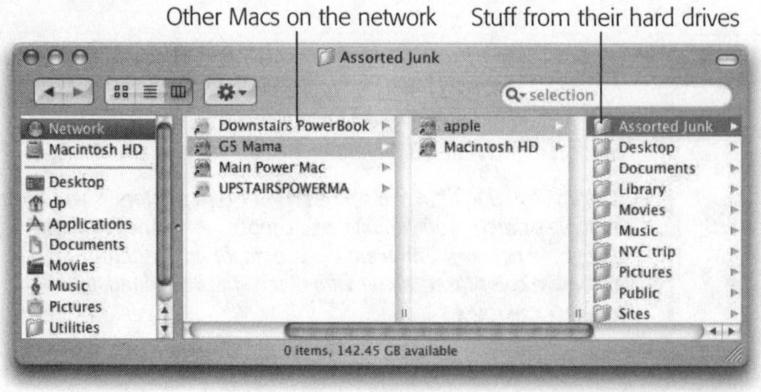

Other Macs on the network   Stuff from their hard drives

Figure 6-9:
The point of file sharing is to bring other Macs and PCs onto your own screen—in this example, the contents of the account called apple on the Mac called G5 Mama. By dragging icons back and forth, you can transfer your work from your main Mac to your laptop, give copies of your documents to other people, create a "drop box" that collects submissions, and so on.

Using the Sidebar to connect to another Mac from Mac OS X

Suppose you're seated at your Power Mac doing powerful things, but you need a file that's on the iMac down the hall. The steps are the same, no matter which version of the Mac operating system the other machine's running (as long as it's later than Mac OS 8.6). To bring its hard drive icon (or a shared folder's icon) onto your screen, follow these steps on the Mac OS X machine.

Note: Just as a friendly reminder, the Sidebar is available only in versions 10.3 and higher of Mac OS X. If you're running 10.2 or lower, you'll need to use the "Connect to Server" method discussed next.

1. **Open any Finder window.**

   Press ⌘-N, or click the Finder icon on your Dock.

2. **Click the Network icon in the Sidebar.**

   This feature is brand new starting with Mac OS X 10.3, and it's really useful. Your network is built right into your desktop.

   For several seconds, you may see nothing at all, or possibly just a Server icon, but wait it out; after 5, 10, or maybe 30 seconds, more icons appear. Depending on the complexity of your network, you may see the icons for individual Macs (Chris's iBook, PowerMac G5, and so on); skip to step 4. Or you may see an assortment of "network neighborhoods"—limbs of your network tree, as shown in Figure 6-10.

   The **Local** folder is usually the one you want. It contains the icons of all the shared Macs, Windows, and Unix machines on your network.

You may also see a **Servers** icon, which lets you know what *your* Mac icon looks like on the network. (In companies big enough to employ professional network masters, this option is where you'll find any servers they've set up for you.)

If you see an **MSHOME** icon, that means Windows PCs are being shared on the network. And the **WORKGROUP** icon displays the icons of Macs for which you've turned on Windows Sharing in System Preferences. (WORKGROUP is also the standard name for Windows machines that came before XP, so you may find some older Windows computers within that icon, too.)

Don't worry if a machine shows up in multiple places. Mac OS X is just doing its best to "listen" for the presence of every possible networking protocol.

Tip: You can also access other Macs on the network from the Open and Save dialog boxes from most applications. There, too, you'll find a Network icon in the Sidebar (expand the dialog box if necessary). Click it, and then continue with these steps.

---

3. **Click the name of the computer you want to access and then click Connect. (Figure 6-10, top.)**

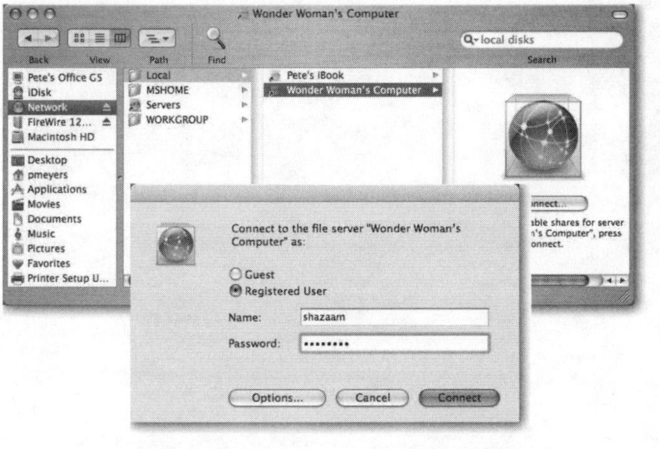

Figure 6-10:
Top: When you click Network in the Sidebar, you'll see the names of individual computers in the leftmost column. On bigger networks, you may see folder icons that represent AppleTalk zones, Windows workgroups, or other Macs. Column view, shown here, gives you the best sense of how you got where you are. Click Local, click the name of the Mac you want, click Connect. (Don't be freaked out by the appearance of your own Mac's name. That's all normal.)

Bottom: Specify your password, or if one isn't required, leave the password box blank. You can also connect using the Guest account (page 124). Click Connect.

You might see groups of machines in addition to individual computers. If you're in a big company or have older Macs on your network, some of these groups might be AppleTalk zones. If the groups aren't AppleTalk zones, they might be Windows computers shared in their workgroup. You'll learn more about connecting to Windows computers in Chapter 7.

Now the "Connect to the file server" box appears. The *file server* is actually just the Mac you're connecting to.

4. **Type your short user name (Figure 6-10, bottom).**

Type precisely what you would use to log into the networked computer if you were sitting in front of it.

If you don't have an account on the machine, on the other hand, all you can do is click the Guest button to gain some very limited access to what's on the other Mac. If the Guest button is dimmed, it means someone has turned off Guest access altogether and, unfortunately, you're out of luck.

5. **Press Tab, and then type your password.**

If you've opted for a blank password, just skip the password box. Otherwise, type your password.

6. **Click Connect, or press the Return or Enter key.**

Now a list of disks and folders on that Mac that have been *shared* for network access appears (Figure 6-11). You're free to open them and work with their contents exactly as though they were on your own Mac—with certain limitations, which are discussed below.

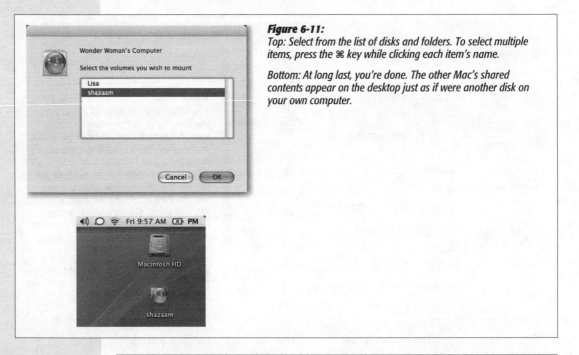

Figure 6-11:
Top: Select from the list of disks and folders. To select multiple items, press the ⌘ key while clicking each item's name.

Bottom: At long last, you're done. The other Mac's shared contents appear on the desktop just as if were another disk on your own computer.

Tip: If you drag a shared folder into the Dock, you can bring it back to your screen later just by clicking its icon. You can even drag its icon into the Startup Items window. Now the disk or folder will appear automatically each time you log in—the most effortless arrangement of all.

Using the "Connect to Server" option

The Sidebar method of connecting to networked folders and disks is practically effortless, requiring only clicking your way through folders—a skill that, in theory, you already know. But the Sidebar method lacks some advantages of the older "Connect to Server" method of Mac OS X versions gone by. Here are some of the differences:

- When you use the Sidebar to access a disk or folder, the shared icon doesn't always show up on your desktop. It's therefore hard to know when you're really connected to that disk or folder. (You can actually fix this by going to Finder → Preferences → General and turning on the "Connected servers" checkbox.

- When you use the Sidebar, if somebody shuts down the Mac you're exploring via the network, a message on *your* screen eventually appears, saying, "The alias 'chris' could not be opened, because the original item could not be found"— not exactly a crystal-clear explanation of what's gone wrong.

- The Sidebar is a mouse-only affair. You can't type in the address of the Mac to which you'd like to connect. As a result, you can access only shared disks on your network. If you want to connect to a shared disk over the Internet (using FTP, for example), you're out of luck.

- The Sidebar doesn't exist in pre-Panther (10.3) versions of Mac OS X.

UP TO SPEED

Parlez-Vous Rendezvous?

The most recent versions of Mac OS X (version 10.2 and later) include a great little networking technology called Rendezvous built right into the system. Rendezvous, which works over Ethernet and WiFi networks, checks out your Mac's network to see what's around—printers, other Macs, shared iTunes music libraries—and instantly creates sharing connections so you can print that spreadsheet, pass that file to a co-worker, or crank up the Springsteen on a friend's PowerBook without fuss.

Most Rendezvous-enabled printers will automatically show up in any print dialog box you're using. But in case your printer doesn't appear, you may need to peform a few quick steps: to find a Rendezvous-enabled printer on your network choose System Preferences → Print & Fax, and then click Printing. Click the Set Up Printers button and in the Printer List, click the Add icon. Select Rendezvous from the pop-up list, choose the Rendezvous-ready printer, and then click the Add button.

Apple has integrated Rendezvous into a number of its Mac OS X programs, offering, for example, the ability to easily share pictures from your iPhoto library with others on your local network. By showing you who's around, the technology also makes it a snap to find people to videoconference with over the iChat instant messenger program.

Rendezvous gives your Mac its own special Rendezvous name so other Macs can see you when you're on the network. This name is usually your computer's regular name with a suffix of *.local*. To find out for sure what Rendezvous is calling your Mac, choose System Preferences → Sharing. Under the box displaying your Mac's name, you'll see a line stating its Rendezvous name.

Apple is working with many hardware companies and software developers to get Rendezvous widely adopted. You can read more about the technology and its development at *www.apple.com/macosx/features/rendezvous*. Also, be on the lookout for Bonjour. That's the new name that Apple's going to start using for Rendezvous because of some, ahem, legal issues. Au revoir.

Fortunately, the pre-Panther method of summoning shared disks and folders is still alive and well. When you choose Go → Connect To Server, you get the dialog box shown in Figure 6-12. The idea is that you can type in the *address* of the shared disk you want.

Note: If you have Mac OS X 10.2 or earlier, you can't enter a URL in the Connect to Server dialog box; instead, your Connect to Server dialog box lets you browse, just like you were looking for a file or folder. Browse to the name of the computer or folder you want and double-click the item's name to connect to it.

Figure 6-12:
In Mac OS X 10.3 and later, connecting to networked disks is both easier and harder. The Sidebar method is quick and easy, but it doesn't let you connect to certain kinds of disks. The "Connect to Server" method, on the other hand, entails plodding through several dialog boxes and doesn't let you browse for shared disks, but it can find just about every kind of networked disk.

For example, from here, you can connect to:

• **Everyday Macs on your network.** If you know the IP address of the Mac you're trying to access—you geek!—you can simply type its IP address into the box and then hit Connect.

And if the other Mac runs Mac OS X 10.2 or later, you can just type its Rendezvous name; for example, *afp://upstairs-PowerMac.local/* (see the box "Parlez-Vous Rendezvous?").

Tip: To find out your Mac's IP address or Rendezvous address, open the Sharing panel of System Preferences. There, at the bottom, you'll see a message like this: "Other Macintosh users can access your computer at afp://192.168.1.24." That's your IP address. (Technically, though, you don't even need the *afp://* part—only the number.) To see your Rendezvous address, click the Edit button at the top of the System Preferences pane.

After you enter your account password and choose the shared disk or folder you want, its icon appears on your desktop *and* in the Sidebar's disk list (Figure 6-13, bottom). As a bonus, the corresponding window opens automatically. The next time you open the Connect to Server dialog box, Mac OS X will remember that address and pre-fill the Address field.

• **Macs across the Internet.** If your Mac has a permanent (static) IP address (page 223), it has the potential to work as a file server and others can connect to it from across the Internet.

• **Windows machines.** Find out the PC's IP address or computer name, and then use this format for the address: *smb://192.168.1.34* or *smb://Shirley-Dell.*

After a moment, your Mac asks you to provide your Windows user name and password. When you click OK, the shared folder appears on your desktop. You'll find more on Mac/Windows file sharing in Chapter 7.

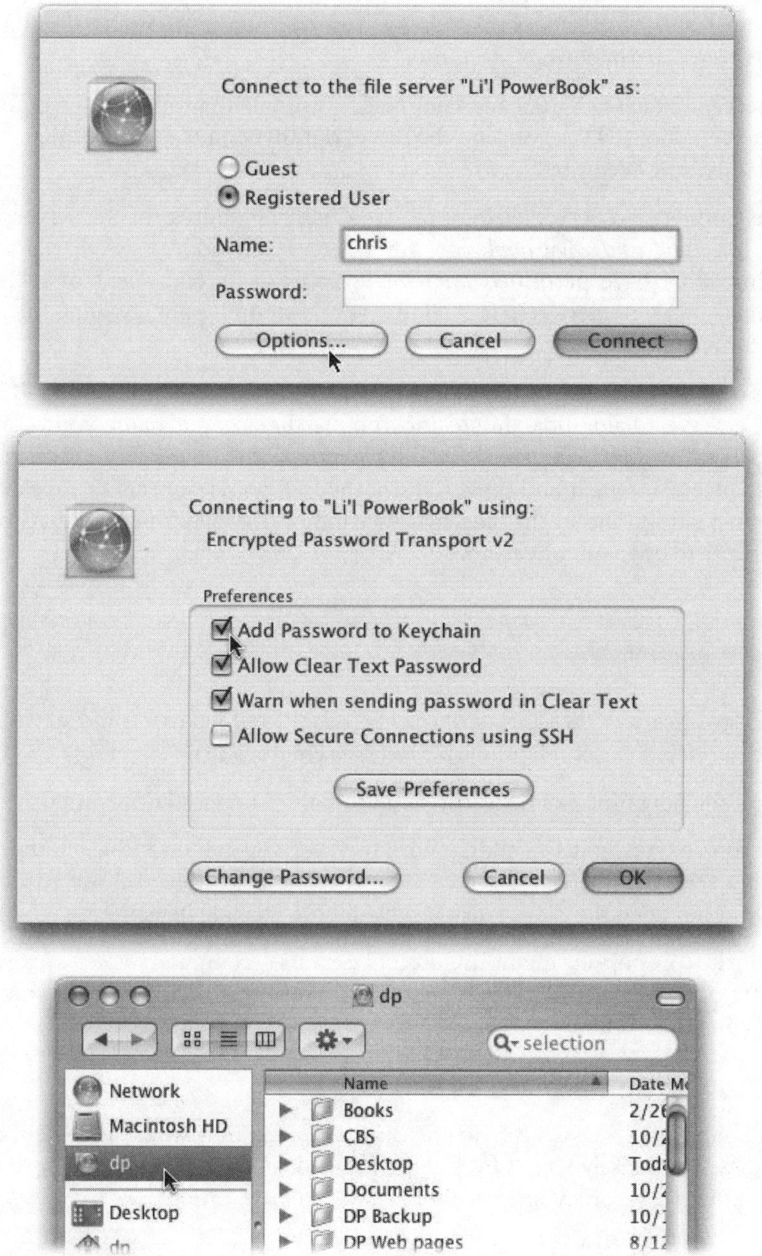

Figure 6-13:
Top: When you access another networked computer using the Connect to Server command, this dialog box asks for your name and password. Don't miss the Options button.

Middle: Clicking Options opens this useful box. The "Add Password to Keychain" button means that you won't have to type your password later (see "The Keychain" in Appendix A). If you click Change Password as you connect to another computer, you'll be given the opportunity to change your account password on that machine. A clear text password is one that isn't encrypted—a less secure, but more compatible, method of transmitting your password over the network.

Bottom: When you connect to a server using this method, its icon shows up in the sidebar, so it's easy to eject.

- **NFS servers.** If you have Unix machines on your network that use the Network File System (a program designed to let computers with different operating systems share files), you can connect to their shared resources by prefacing the machine's IP address with *nfs://* and specifying the file path to the machine. The format for connecting with NFS is *nfs://ip address* or *machine-name/pathname*. For home users, the chances that you have an NFS server are pretty slim unless you've been experimenting with Linux.

- **FTP servers.** Mac OS X 10.3 and later makes it simple to bring *FTP servers* onto your screen, too. (FTP servers are the drives out there on the Internet that store the files used by Web sites.)

  In the Connect To Server dialog box, type the FTP address of the server you want, like this: *ftp://www.apple.com* (or whatever the address is). If the site's administrators have permitted *anonymous* access—the equivalent of a Guest account—that's all there is to it. A Finder window pops open, revealing the FTP site's contents.

  If you need a password for the FTP site, however, what you type into the Connect To Server dialog box should incorporate the account name you've been given, like this: *ftp://yourname@www.apple.com*. You'll be asked for your password. Once you type it and press Return, the FTP server appears as a disk icon on your desktop (and in the Sidebar). Its window opens automatically, its contents ready to open or copy from.

Tip: If you'd like, you can even eliminate that password–dialog box step by using this address format: *ftp://yourname: yourpassword@www.apple.com.*

In each case, once you click OK, you may be asked for your name and password. You're then offered a useful Options button (see Figure 6-13).

That is not the only time-saving feature built into the Connect To Server box:

- Once you've typed a disk's address into the box, you can click the + button to add that server to the list of server favorites. The next time you want to connect, you can open the shared disk just by double-clicking its name.

- The clock-icon pop-up menu lists Recent Servers—computers you've accessed recently over the network. If you choose one from this pop-up menu, you can skip typing in an address manually.

What You Can Do Once You're In

When you tap into a Mac OS X machine, you can access only what's in certain designated folders. Precisely which folders are available depends on whether you're a *guest,* a *standard user,* or an *administrator.*

Note: Once you disconnect from a Mac (by clicking its Eject icon in the Sidebar, or dragging its Finder icon to the Trash can), you can log back in as a different user.

If you're a guest

If you're just a guest—somebody for whom an account hasn't already been set up—you won't see the usual assortment of shared disks and folders (see Figure 6-14).

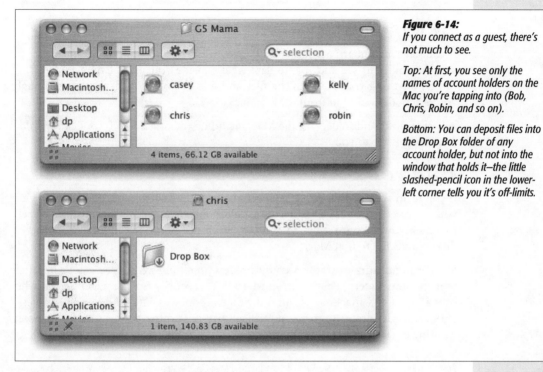

Figure 6-14:
If you connect as a guest, there's not much to see.

Top: At first, you see only the names of account holders on the Mac you're tapping into (Bob, Chris, Robin, and so on).

Bottom: You can deposit files into the Drop Box folder of any account holder, but not into the window that holds it—the little slashed-pencil icon in the lower-left corner tells you it's off-limits.

At this point, all you can do is this:

- **Put things into** anyone's drop box folder. (Open the account holder's folder to see the drop box folder.) You can copy files into a drop box, but you can't open it. Yes, Mac OS X is very secure, but even a high-security prison has a mailbox.

- **Open** anything that people have in their Public folders. Figure 6-15 illustrates the details.

Figure 6-15:
Suppose Chris put three files in her Public folder. (Every person's Home folder contains a Public folder.) When you connect to her Mac, you'll see whatever she put there, plus her Drop Box. You can't put anything in Chris's window (except in the Drop Box), but you can open the three files she's left there for you to see.

The rest of the Mac is invisible and off-limits to you.

Tip: Want to turn off Guest access on your Mac? Highlight the Public folder in each user's account, choose File → Get Info, and then change Everybody access to None. Page 135 has more on setting permissions.

If you're a Standard account holder

If you have a Standard account, you'll enjoy drop-box access, Public-folder access, *and* the ability to see and manipulate what's inside your own Home folder. You can do anything you like with the files and folders you find there, just as though you're actually seated in front of that Mac.

All other disks and folders on the Mac, including the System and Application folders, are invisible to you.

If you're an administrator

If you're an administrator, you get everything a Standard account holder gets, plus you get to see icons for all the account-holder folders as well as the hard drive itself to which you're connecting. In fact, you even get to see the names of any other disks connected to that Mac.

Standard and Administrator account holders aren't allowed to see what's in other users' Home folders. That's part of Mac OS X's security feature. Each person who uses a Mac OS X machine has an individual account to which he alone has access. (Even though administrators can seize control over other people's stuff in person by using the Get Info command, they can't do so from across the network.)

Note: There's actually one more kind of account on a Mac OS X system—the *root user.* Whoever holds this account has complete freedom to move or delete *any file or folder anywhere,* including critical system files that could disable your Mac. The root user is the beginning of all user-dom in Mac OS X and is all-powerful.

Getting Around from an OS 9 Mac

Apple gives you two different ways to connect *from* an OS 9 Mac to any of the other Macs on your network.

Using the Chooser

1. **Choose the Mac you want to connect to from your Chooser.**

   Go to → Chooser, and then click the AppleShare icon on the left side of the Chooser window. A list of available Macs appears in the right side of the window beneath the heading "Select a file server."

2. **Click the name of the Mac to which you want to connect. Then click OK.**

   A dialog box appears asking whether you want to connect as a guest or as a registered user.

3. **Select whether you want to connect as a guest or as a registered user.**

If you choose to connect as a guest, you don't need a password, but you get only limited access to the Mac to which you're connecting. If you log in as a registered user, you need to enter the account name and a password of the account you're using. You get whatever privileges come with the account you're using.

Note: In the Chooser, you can also click the Server 'IP Address button and type the IP address of the Mac OS X machine. Then click the Connect button.

---

4. **Click Connect.**

The folders or disk icons to which you've been granted access appear on your desktop. You're in!

Using the Network Browser

Mac OS 9 also lets you connect to another Mac using a feature that's a little like the new Sidebar in Mac OS X 10.3 and later. Called the Network Browser, this utility allows you to locate Macs on your network that might be sharing files (Figure 6-16).

Figure 6-16:
To use the Network Browser, go to → Network Browser. Once your Mac scans the network to determine what's available, it displays this information in a window similar to the one at the left. Connect to a shared folder by expanding the selections until you find the desired folder. Double-click the preferred folder. You might be asked to provide a user name and password for the resource. Make sure to use a file sharing file name if the target folder exists on a Mac OS 9 computer.

1. **Open the Network Browser.**

Go to → Network Browser and then click Local Network. The Macs on your network appear in a list in the Local Network window.

2. **Select the Mac you want to connect to.**

3. **Double-click the name of the Mac you want to connect to.**

A dialog box appears asking whether you want to connect as a guest or as a registered user. Follow steps 3 and 4 in the "Using the Chooser" list above.

Disconnecting Yourself

When you're finished using a shared disk or folder, you should disconnect yourself. The easiest way in Mac OS X 10.3 or later is to click the Eject button next to the disk or folder's name in the Sidebar. You can also drag its icon to the Trash (whose icon changes to an Eject button as you drag), highlight its icon and choose File → Eject, or Control-click its icon and choose Eject from the contextual menu. You also disconnect from a shared folder or disk when you shut down your Mac, or if it's a laptop, when you put it to sleep.

If you're using Mac OS 9, drag the shared volume to the trash to disconnect the volume. Don't worry—you won't delete anything by doing this.

Disconnecting Others

In Mac OS X, there's no visual clue to alert you that other people on the network are accessing *your* Mac.

Maybe that's because there's nothing to worry about. You certainly have nothing to fear from a security standpoint, since, as you'll recall, people from across the network are allowed to access only their own folders. Nor will you experience much computer slowdown as you work (another traditional drawback of having people access your hard drive from across the network), thanks to Mac OS X's prodigious multitasking features.

Still, if you're feeling particularly antisocial, you can slam shut the door to your Mac just by turning off the File Sharing feature. (Click System Preferences on the Dock, click the Sharing icon, and turn off the Personal File Sharing or Windows Sharing checkbox.)

If anybody is, in fact, connected to your Mac at the time (*from* a Mac), you'll see the dialog box shown in Figure 6-17. If not, your Mac instantly becomes an island once again.

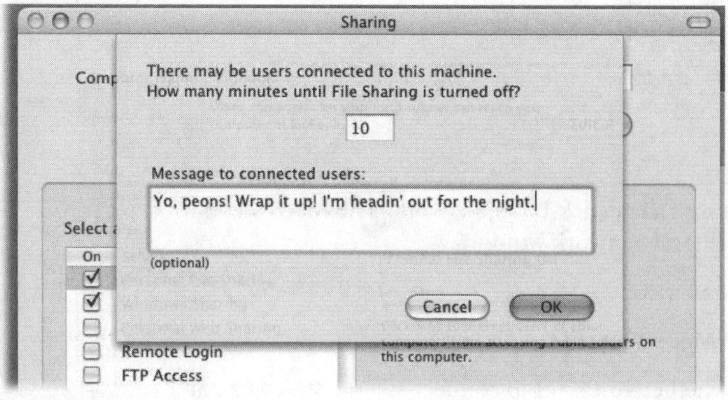

Figure 6-17:
This dialog box asks you how much notice you want to give your relatives that they're about to be disconnected—10 minutes to finish up what they're doing, for example. If you're feeling rushed or rude, type a zero. Doing so disconnects that person instantly, without warning. Then click OK. (When you disconnect people by closing your laptop lid, having a system crash, or unplugging the network wires, your relatives get no notice at all. A message appears on their screens that says, "The server has unexpectedly shut down.")

Mac OS 9 has Mac OS X beat in the activity-monitoring department. When people connect to your Mac OS 9 machine from other computers, the Mac OS 9 system keeps track of who they are and what's being shared. In fact, if you have the Owner account on a Mac OS 9 computer, you can quickly boot people off your computer and even change their access permissions *while they are still connected!* Figure 6-18 shows you how.

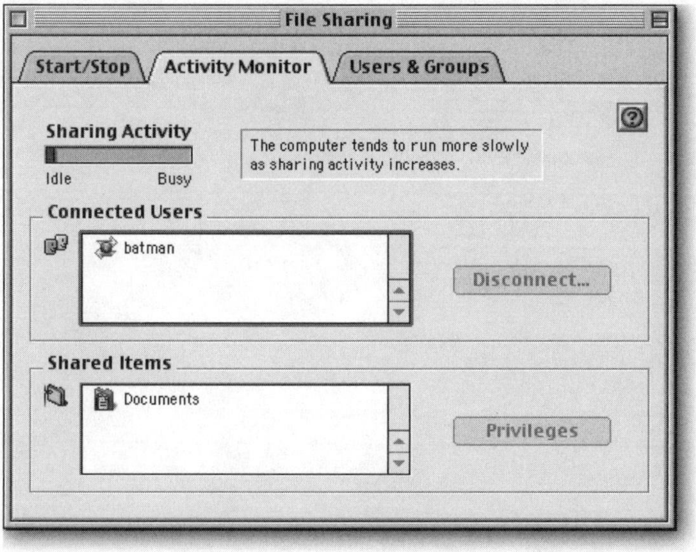

Figure 6-18:
To kick someone off your Mac, find their File Sharing user name in the Connected Users box and click Disconnect. At the bottom of the window, in the Shared Items box, is a list of everything you're sharing on the Mac. You can stop sharing an item, or change the access permissions, by clicking the Privileges button.

Mixing Macintosh and Windows Computers

Family relations aren't always easy, especially if you've got political divisions percolating inside your house. For example, maybe the computers on your network are a mixture of Windows and Macintosh machines, all linked in an uneasy, fragile alliance? Fortunately, thanks to the efforts of both Apple and Microsoft, all your hardware (if not your humans) now stand a much better chance of getting along.

Starting with Mac OS X 10.3, Apple began a new chapter in Mac–Windows relations: with the newest versions of the Mac OS, Macs, and Windows PCs can see each other on the network, with no special software (or talent) required. Now, instead of operating-system isolationism, your computers can find common ground and speak the same language.

Note: If you've got Mac OS X 10.2 or earlier, you'll still be able to communicate with Windows PCs, but just not in quite as many ways. See the note on page 159 about using the Connect to Server tool.

If you've got Mac OS 9, your Mac isn't quite advanced enough to talk to Windows without a translator, but you've got one in your good friend, DAVE. DAVE is software designed to bridge the communications gap between Mac OS 9 and Windows, and you'll read more about it later in this chapter.

Windows is no slouch in the works-and-plays-well-with-other-operating-systems department either: since the days of Windows 95, Windows PCs have been able to get along quite well with their Mac brothers and sisters.

As you'll see in this chapter, you can go in either direction: your Mac can see shared folders and use printers connected to Windows PCs, and a Windows PC can do the same with its Mac brethren—love is all around!

Connecting from Mac OS X to Windows

Even though you may be a hard-core Apple fan, the files and folders on that Windows XP computer sitting on your network might be holding some valuable goodies. In ages past, you might have scampered back and forth between machines with a floppy disk. But now the floppy's dead and even emailing files from one computer to another is a pain. Fortunately, Mac OS X makes it easy to connect to just about any Windows computer.

Suppose you have a Windows XP machine on the network (although the following steps work with Windows 95, 98, ME, and Windows 2000). Here's how you get the Mac and PC chatting:

1. **On your Windows PC, share the folders you want to make available.**

   Chapter 5 tells you all about how to share files on all different flavors of Windows machines. Here's a quick recap for Windows XP owners: right-click a folder, choose Properties from the shortcut menu, click the Sharing tab, and turn on "Share this folder on the network" (Figure 7-1, top). In the "Share name" box, type a name for the folder as it will appear on the network (no spaces are allowed).

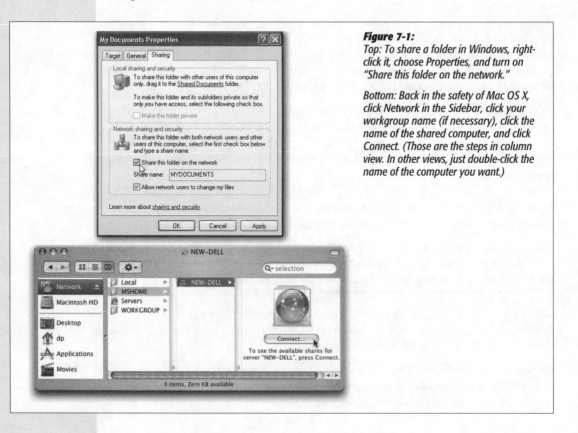

Figure 7-1:
Top: To share a folder in Windows, right-click it, choose Properties, and turn on "Share this folder on the network."

Bottom: Back in the safety of Mac OS X, click Network in the Sidebar, click your workgroup name (if necessary), click the name of the shared computer, and click Connect. (Those are the steps in column view. In other views, just double-click the name of the computer you want.)

2. **On the Mac, open up any Finder window. Click Network in the Sidebar.**

   The shared PCs may appear as individual computers or you may see only the icon of their *workgroup* (network cluster). Unless you (or a network administrator) changed it, the workgroup name is probably WORKGROUP or MSHOME.

Tip: You can also access the shared PC via the Connect To Server command (Go → Connect to Server), as described on page 147. If your Mac is running Mac OS X 10.2 or earlier, you'll need to use this method.

---

3. **If necessary, click LOCAL or the Windows workgroup name.**

   Now the names of the individual PCs on the network appear on the right side of the window (Figure 7-1, bottom).

4. **Double-click the computer you want.**

   The Authentication dialog box appears, as shown at top in Figure 7-2.

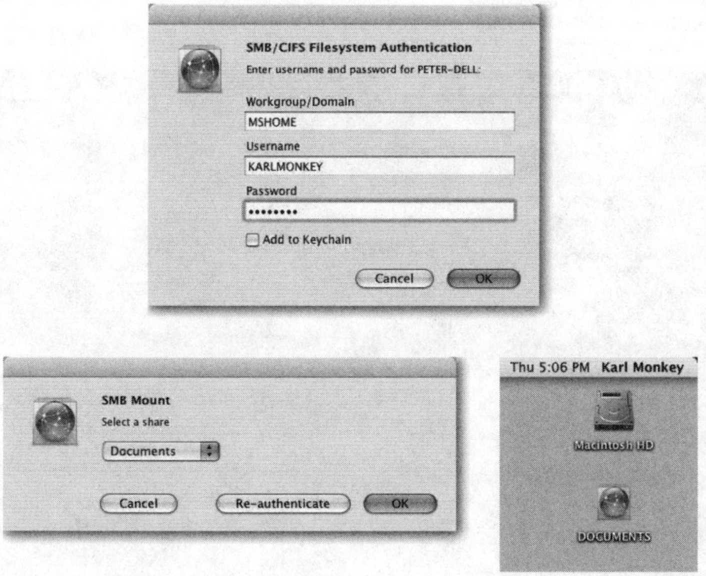

Figure 7-2:
Top: The PC wants to make sure that you're authorized to visit it. If the terminology here seems a bit geeky by Apple standards, don't worry—this is Microsoft Windows' lingo you're seeing, not Apple's.

Bottom left: Here, you see a list of shared folders on the PC. Choose the one you want to connect to, and then click OK.

Bottom right: Like magic, the Windows folder shows up on your Mac screen, ready to use.

5. **Type your name and password, if necessary, and then click OK.**

   If you have an account on the Windows PC, great—use that name and password. (Page 82 tells you all about how to set up an account on a Windows machine.) If the PC isn't part of a corporation where somebody administers access to each machine, you may be able to leave the password field blank.

   The SMB Mount dialog box now appears (Figure 7-2, bottom). Its pop-up menu lists the *shares* (that is, shared folders and disks) on the selected PC.

---

6. **From the pop-up menu, choose the name of the shared folder that you want to bring to your desktop. Click OK.**

At long last, the contents of the shared folder on the Windows machine appear in your Finder window, just as though you'd tapped into another Mac. From here, it's a simple matter to drag files between the machines, open Word documents on the PC using Word for the Mac, and so on, exactly as though you're hooked into another Mac.

Connecting from Mac OS 9 to Windows

Are you running Mac OS 9 (or even earlier)? Do you want to reach across the network and see what's doing on the Windows PCs on your home network? Then say hello to DAVE, a program that goes beyond even what your Mac OS X pals get when it comes to file sharing with the other side.

DAVE (available at *www.thursby.com*) gives your Mac OS 9 computer the ability to fully communicate with Windows in both directions—your Mac gets access to Windows machines, and vice versa.

FREQUENTLY ASKED QUESTION

DAVE vs. Mac OS X

I've got Mac OS X 10.3 on my Mac. Is there any reason I should get DAVE?

Even though the latest versions of the Mac OS include excellent file-sharing skills and are capable of easily connecting to Windows computers, they do have some drawbacks. For example, if you ever run Mac OS X 10.3 on a new corporate Windows network, the person responsible for that network might have to lower the security of the *entire* network just to allow your Mac to talk to the servers. In today's security-conscious world, that's not always going to happen.

Furthermore, on large networks, Mac OS X 10.3 will likely choke when it tries to show you a list of everything that's been shared on the Windows network. The reason? Mac OS X 10.3

has a technical shortcoming that doesn't really lend itself to being able to see the contents of everything on very large networks.

Fortunately, you can use DAVE to overcome both these problems.

Do you really need DAVE for your home network? If you're running Mac OS X, then the answer is no. Security isn't as important at home as in the workplace and—unless you have a 500-workstation computer lab in your house—your home network is small enough for Mac OS X to handle. If you're using a Mac OS X system on a large corporate network, talk to your technology manager about whether or not you might need DAVE.

Configuring DAVE for Your Network

Since you get a nicely written manual when you buy DAVE, this book won't waste space on how to install the program. After you install the program, make sure you restart your computer. Once you've done that, the DAVE setup assistant automatically starts and helps you configure DAVE. The following steps walk you through the setup process:

1. **Enter your license code.**

   In the License text box, enter the license code you received by email (if you down-loaded the program) or on the registration form (if you bought the boxed version).

2. **Select a NetBIOS name for your Mac.**

   Windows computers use NetBIOS names as a way of identifying one another on a network. In order for your Mac to join in this conversation, it too needs a NetBIOS name. This doesn't have to be the same name that you've given your Mac for file sharing with other Macs (page 143). You can use any letter or number in the name, but the name can't be longer than 15 characters.

3. **Pick your network type, if the setup assistant asks you to do so.**

   The setup assistant may ask if you have a Windows NT Server on your net-work. Unless your network is part of an office, the answer is probably no.

4. **Identify the workgroup you want your Mac to be a part of.**

   Workgroups in Windows are Microsoft's way of breaking computers down into smaller, more manageable groups. For home networks, you should make sure all of your Windows computers use the same workgroup name. (Page 80 tells you how to set up a workgroup name for your Windows PCs.) Most PCs at home use either WORKGROUP or MSHOME as their workgroup names. Enter your work-group name in the Workgroup text box, or select a name from the drop-down list.

5. **Enter a description for your Mac.**

   This is the name that the Windows folks on your network will see when they're looking for your computer.

6. **Decide whether to activate automatic network logon.**

   When you connect to a Windows computer from your Mac, you need to specify a Windows user and associated password to gain access to the Windows machine. (Page 82 tells you all about setting up Windows user accounts.) If you want DAVE to automatically log you on to the network, turn on the "I want to log onto the network at startup" checkbox.

7. **Activate file sharing.**

   DAVE gives you the ability to share files in both directions. That is, Windows computers can be given access to the files on your Mac, and your Mac OS 9 computer can view files on Windows computers. To enable this two-way access, turn on the "I want to set up DAVE to share my local files" checkbox.

   The next few steps explain what you need to do if you want to give the Win-dows PCs on your network access to your Mac's files. If you only want to view and retrieve files that are on a Windows machine, then skip ahead to step 12.

8. **Select a folder you want to share on your Mac.**

Launch DAVE by choosing $\bullet$ → DAVE. Then select File → DAVE Sharing. The DAVE Sharing control panel appears (Figure 7-3), which lets you pick which folders your Mac will share.

Figure 7-3:
To share a folder, click the New Share button. A dialog box appears that lets you navigate to the folder you want to share. Once you've selected the folder (by highlighting its name), click the Choose button. You can also drag folders directly onto the Shared Items list box.

9. **Assign a name to the folder you're sharing and select the access restrictions.**

The name you enter in the Share Name box is the folder name that Windows visitors from across the network will see. You then need to tell DAVE what these visitors can do with your files (view only, or view and change), as explained in Figure 7-4.

Figure 7-4:
If your choices in this dialog box remind you of the ones you learned about in Chapter 6 (page 137), that's because they're the same settings: DAVE simply gives you a different way of assigning access restrictions. Turn on the "Enable Read/Write Access" checkbox if you want your visitors to be able to view and change your files. Turn on the "Enable Read Only Access" checkbox if you want them to be able to only view the files. For either setting, you can also assign a password.

10. **Select any other folders you want to share.**

For any additional folders you select, repeat steps 8 through 10.

11. **Start file sharing.**

Click the Start button at the bottom of the DAVE Sharing dialog box (Figure 7-3) to start sharing the specified folders with the Windows computers on your network (Figure 7-5).

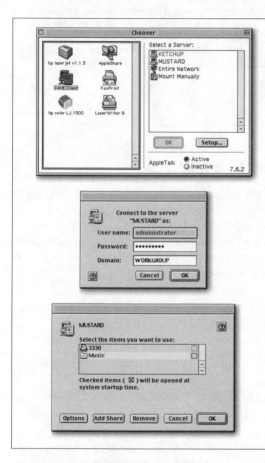

Figure 7-5:
Top: Here's a list of computers available to this Mac OS 9 computer. "Ketchup" is a Mac OS X Panther computer and "mustard" is a Windows 2000 computer. You'd connect to any of these computers by double-clicking an entry on the list.

Middle: Type a Windows user name and password to gain access to the Windows computer. If you need to create a Windows user account, see page 82 for instructions.

Bottom: Select the folder to which you'd like to connect. In this example, the only folder available is called Music.

12. **Connect to a Windows computer.**

Go to → Chooser and click DAVE Client. The Windows computers on your network appear in the "Select a Server" box. Figure 7-5 shows how to complete the connection. You can also open → DAVE to browse the Windows network as shown in Figure 7-6.

The ability to use your Mac to gain access to files shared by Windows computers is a huge reason that a lot of people install home networks, but it's not a one-way street: your Windows computers can see your Macs, too.

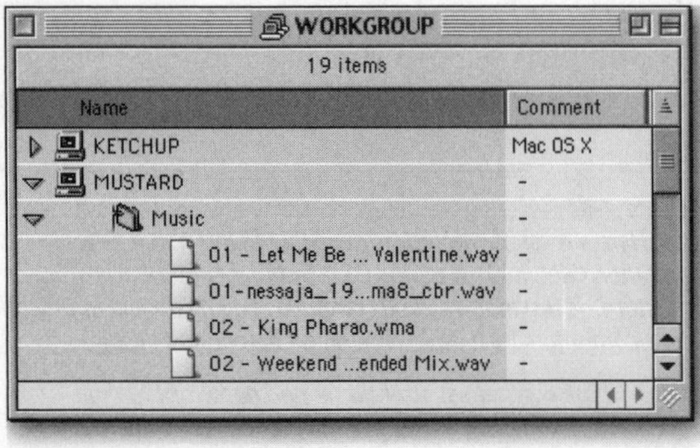

Figure 7-6:
The network browser included with DAVE is an excellent choice if you're having trouble finding Windows computers with the Chooser. The DAVE browser lets you scan the entire Windows network in a single window, whereas the browser in the Chooser method can be a little more cumbersome if you need to browse through multiple workgroups.

Connecting from Windows to a Mac

Suppose you're on the *other* side of the fence. You know, the one where roughly 95 percent of the computer-using world sits? Windows PCs are eager and willing to let you reach across the network and poke around inside a Mac. First, you need to make sure the Mac is ready for your arrival. And then you need to fire up one of your Windows network viewing tools (like My Network Places or Network Neighborhood [page 114]). Both steps are covered below.

Note: The first step here is for Mac OS X computers only. Mac OS 9 people should pick things up at step 2.

1. **On the Mac, open System Preferences. Click the Sharing icon. Turn on Windows File Sharing (Figure 7-7, top).**

   If you haven't created an account for whoever will be tapping into your Mac (page 122), this is your opportunity to do so. Otherwise, your Mac is ready for invasion. Quit System Preferences, if you like.

Note: If you've got Mac OS X 10.2, you also need to turn on the "Allow user to log in from Windows" checkbox, which you can find on the user's Account page (reachable from the System Preferences window).

2. **On the Windows machine, open My Network Places or click the Network Neighborhood icon.**

Note: "My Network Places" is used in newer versions of Windows (Windows ME and Windows XP), while that "Network Neighborhood" business is part of Windows 95, 98, and 2000.

The goal here is to find the Mac's icon. If it shows up by itself (this may take a minute or two), terrific; you must have sacrificed the proper animals to the Windows gods.

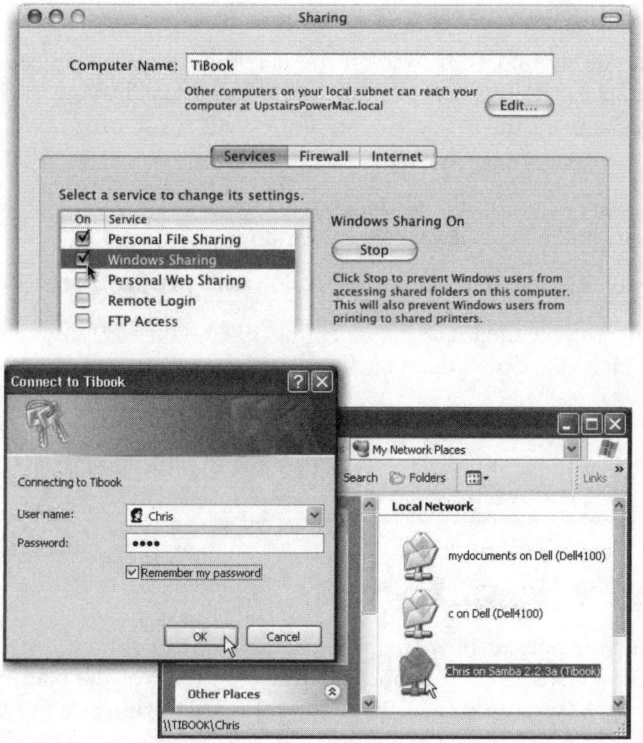

Figure 7-7:
Top: This magic checkbox in System Preferences makes it all possible. It's a system-wide On switch for invasion from Windows.

Lower left: Sign in, using whatever name and password the Mac's owner has given you.

Lower right: Here's the Mac's icon—in Windows! Open it up, and you'll see the Mac's Home folder.

If it doesn't appear, try each of these three approaches, in order of increasing desperation:

First resort: Click "Microsoft Windows Network" in the task pane.

Second resort: Click "View workgroup computers" instead.

Note: The *task pane* is the blue panel at the left side of every Windows XP desktop window. If you don't see it, try widening the window. If you still don't see it, choose Tools → Folder Options and turn on "Show common tasks in folders."

Last resort: If the Mac *still* doesn't show up, you'll have to add it the hard way. Click "Add a network place" in the task pane. On successive screens, click Next, click "Choose another network location," and then click Next. In the "Internet or network address" box, type *192.168.1.24\\chris* (substitute the Mac's IP address and the short account name you've been given), taking care to use *back-slashes*, not normal / slashes. Chapter 6 tells you all about setting up user accounts in Mac-land.

Tip: To find out the IP address of a Mac that's running OS X, on the Mac, go to System Preferences →
Sharing and click on the Services tab. In Mac OS 9, go to → Control Panels → TCP/IP.

Finally, click Next, type a name for your Mac on the network, click Next again, and click Finish.

In any case, when you *do* find your Mac on the network, its icon may bear a name like "Samba 2.2.3a (Robins-computer)." No, Microsoft isn't trying to give you dance lessons. Samba is the Mac's version of the SMB file-sharing protocol that Windows uses.

In the future, you won't have to do all this burrowing, because your Mac will appear automatically in the My Network Places window.

3. **Double-click the icon's name, sign in (Figure 7-7, bottom left), and go to town.**

In the final window, you see the Mac's actual Home folder—on a Windows PC! You're ready to open its files, copy them back and forth, or whatever.

Note: For you Mac OS 9/DAVE people, you'll only have to provide the read-only or read/write password (when connecting from the Windows PC) that you (or someone else) assigned to the share to gain access to that share.

Printing across the Network

In Chapters 5 and 6, you learned how to share printers among computers that used the same operating system. What happens if you want to cross the platform divide and, say, print *from* your Windows PC *to* the color laser printer connected to your wife's Mac?

The good news is that it's pretty easy to do. The first step is something you've already learned: set up the printer so it's ready to be shared. Chapter 5 (page 108) has all the details if you've got a printer attached to a Windows PC; Chapter 6 (page 142) shows you what to do for Mac-connected computers. The next steps depend on which operating system you're printing *from*.

Printing from Windows to a Mac Printer

Before you connect from a Windows PC to a printer shared by a Mac, make sure you've installed the driver software (page 108) your Windows machine needs to make the printer work. Often, Windows can figure out what kind of printer you're trying to use and install the appropriate software, but just as often, Windows throws up its hands and asks you for help in determining the make and model for the printer. And don't worry that the printer is Mac-only and won't have Windows software. It's a Windows world out there, and pretty much every printer made in the past few years comes with drivers for both Windows and Macintosh systems.

Note: If you don't have the original software that came with your printer, visit the manufacturer's Web site and download the software that matches your printer's model.

When you connect from Windows to a Mac computer running Mac OS X 10.3 or later (or DAVE) you see a list of everything shared by that Mac, including any printers the Mac is sharing. To use a shared printer, right-click the printer in the list and choose Connect. From that point, Windows will walk you through all the steps necessary so you can use the printer.

TROUBLESHOOTING MOMENT

When Your PC Can't See the Mac

If the Mac doesn't show up in the My Network Places (or Network Neighborhood) window of the PC, you may have to knock it into submission.

If this is your first attempt at Mac–PC communication, try restarting the PC. The My Network Places window updates itself only once per session.

If that doesn't work, on the PC, click the "View workgroup computers" link in the left-side task pane. In the next window, click the "Microsoft Windows Network" link.

Finally, you arrive at the Microsoft Windows Network window, which contains icons for the various workgroups on the network. Double-click the icons until you find your Mac. Log in as described in Figure 7-7; thereafter, the Mac's Home folder shows up like any other folder in the My Network Places window, saving you the trouble of going through all this again.

If your PC sees the Mac but doesn't let you sign in, on the other hand, the troubleshooting tactic is slightly different.

On Mac OS X: Go to the Mac and open System Preferences. Open the My Account panel and change your password to something else. Click OK—and then change the password back again, if you like. The point is that changing your password (even if you change it right back) shocks the Mac into re-memorizing it.

Mac OS 9 with DAVE: Make sure you followed step 4 in the DAVE configuration instructions (page 161). If you need to change the Windows workgroup to which you assigned your Mac, open the DAVE Sharing control panel (→ Control Panels → NetBIOS), and then change the Workgroup entry to match that of your Windows computers.

Now when you sign in from the PC, the Mac should recognize you—and let you in.

Printing from Mac OS X to a Windows Printer

Once you've enabled sharing on a printer connected to a Windows machine (page 108), printing from a Mac OS X computer is pretty easy. Just follow these steps:

1. **Open the Mac's Print & Fax control panel.**

   Go to → System Preferences → Print & Fax.

2. **Click the "Set Up Printers" button.**

3. **From the Printer List window, click the Add button.**

4. **Find the computer that's sharing the printer.**

   To connect to a printer, you need to locate the computer that's sharing the printer. Figure 7-8 shows this detail.

CHAPTER 7: MIXING MACINTOSH AND WINDOWS COMPUTERS

5. **Double-click the name of the Windows computer sharing the printer.**

In Figure 7-8, the Windows computer sharing a printer is Mustard. You might need to provide a user name and password when you try to connect to the Windows computer. (Chapter 5 tells you all about how to get a user account on a Windows computer.)

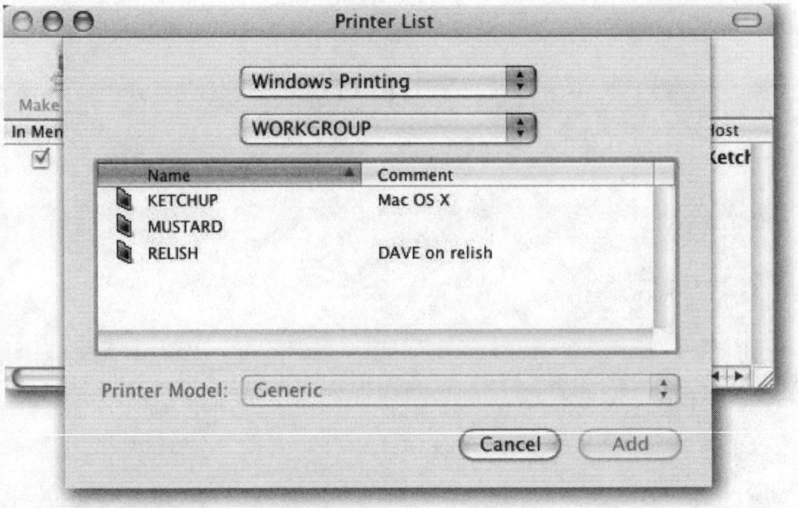

Figure 7-8:
The two drop-down menus at the top of this window help you find the right printer. First, make sure you're using the Windows Printing option in the top box. The second drop-down menu should have the name of the workgroup to which the Windows host computer belongs.

6. **Select the printer you want to use.**

Once you're connected to the Windows computer, your Mac shows you a list of the printers shared by that computer (Figure 7-9). You can get specific and select the manufacturer and particular model of the printer that's being shared by the PC.

7. **Click the Add button.**

8. **Print!**

To make it easier to print in the future, when you connect to the Windows computer that hosts the printer, save your user name and password to your Keychain (see Appendix A), so you don't have to provide it each time you want to print.

Printing from Mac OS 9 to a Windows Printer

Even older versions of the Macintosh operating system can print to a printer shared on a Windows computer, as long as the Mac is running DAVE. By now, you can probably tell that DAVE is an excellent investment if you're still running Mac OS 9. To connect to a Windows printer from a DAVE-equipped Mac OS 9 computer, follow these steps:

1. **Open the Chooser (** → Chooser).

2. **In the left-side Chooser window pane, click "DAVE Client."**

   Selecting DAVE Client tells the Chooser to explore the network for any Windows computers sharing files or printers.

3. **In the Select a Server window, double-click the name of the PC to which the printer's attached.**

4. **Provide a user name and password, if you need to, to connect to the Windows computer.**

   Chapter 5 tells you all about how to get a user account on a Windows computer.

5. **Select the printer you want to use.**

   In Figure 7-5, bottom, notice that the list of items shared by the Windows computer includes a printer named 3330. To connect to the printer, select the printer's name in the share list and click OK.

6. **Create the printer.**

Once you tell DAVE that you want to use the selected printer, the software asks you if you want to create this desktop printer. Click the Continue button to complete the sharing process and to create a printer icon on your Mac's desktop that points to this Windows printer.

You can now use the newly created printer just like any other printer connected directly to your Mac.

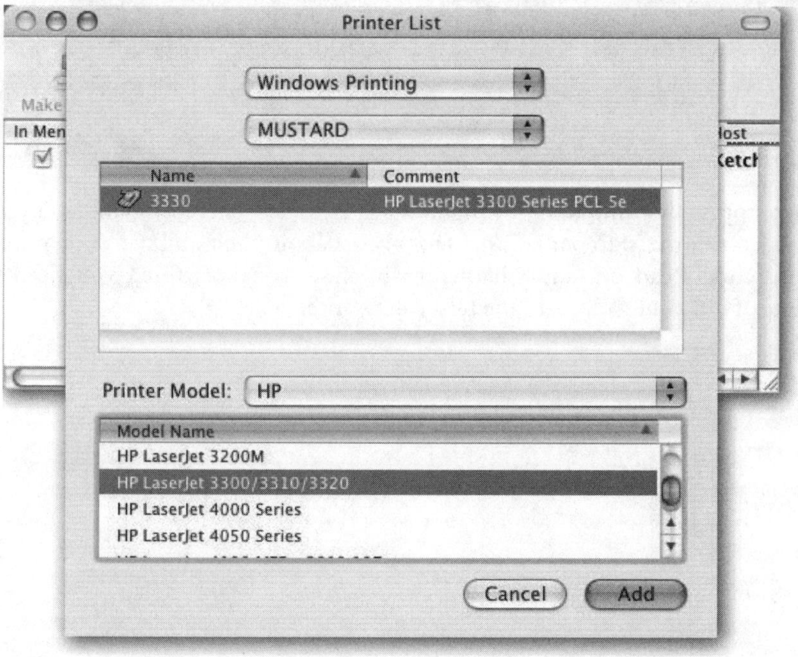

Figure 7-9:
Once you click the printer you want to use, you're allowed to select its make and model. In this example, the printer is an HP LaserJet 3330, so the printer model is HP and the model name is HP LaserJet 3300/3310/3320. The 3330 is not specifically listed, but the 3300/3310/ 3320 software works fine.

This chapter explored the nifty file and printer sharing capabilities that exist between computers with different operating systems. Your new home network is a kind of equalizer on which any computer is just as good as any other computer when it comes to sharing.

POWER USERS' CLINIC

More Mac–Windows Connections

The methods described in this chapter are the easiest and quickest ways to share files, but they're not the only ways. Here are a few more possibilities that are sometimes useful, but not very common in home networks.

- **Web serving.** Mac OS X's Apache software turns your Mac into a living Web site. And the beauty of the Web, of course, is that it doesn't care what kind of computer you're using. The contents of the Web site are dished up exactly the same way to Macs, Windows machines, Unix machines, and so on. All of this provides a great way to distribute files to other people on the network. You can simply list files for distribution on a simple Web page, to which other people on the network can connect. The point to note here is that other people on your office network can access your Mac in exactly the same way, just by typing *http://192.168.1.5/~shortname/* (that is, your IP address followed by ~ and your short account name (page 125) into the address bar of their Web browsers.

- **Via FTP.** Think of an *FTP server* as something like a Web site designed specifically as a holding tank for files that you want to distribute or accept. Here again, though, it's worth remembering that you can use the Mac OS X built-in FTP server to distribute and accept files on your local network, not just over the Internet. A person on a Windows PC, using only a Web browser, will be able to download any files in the folder that you've set up for such transactions. (And using an *FTP client* program, that person can copy files to *and* from the folder.)

- **Via Bluetooth.** If your Mac and a PC each have Bluetooth adapters, you can share files between them as though there's no language barrier at all. The Mac's Bluetooth adapter comes with a nondenominational file-exchange program called Bluetooth File Exchange; not all Windows Bluetooth adapters come with such a program. But if yours does (3Com's adapters do, for example), you should be able to shoot files between the machines with the greatest of ease—and no setup whatsoever.

But why stop with computers? So many devices today—stereos, game consoles, digital video recorders, to name just a few—boast about their ability to hop onto a home network. Read on, and Chapter 8 will show you everything you need to invite lots of different gadgets to the home networking party.

Fun and Games with Your Network

Sure, your home network lets you share your Internet connection, exchange files back and forth, and print to your heart's content. But you can do all *that* at the office. Welcome, at last, to the fun part of home networking—the gadgets, add-ons, and recreational options that you've probably heard about or seen if you've spent more than 10 minutes in an electronics superstore recently.

Now that your network is up and running, what you can do with it is pretty amazing:

- **Play your PC's music on your stereo.** Instead of listening to your music collection on your tinny, tiny computer speakers, you can find a product that lets you blast those audio tracks through your home network and out the speakers of your state-of-the-art home theater system.

- **Display digital photos on your television.** You can use your network as an escape tunnel and free your digital photo collection from the cramped confines of your computer's monitor and project them in all their glory on your television screen.

- **Add storage space that all your network PCs can use.** Music and pictures are fun, but they chew up a lot of hard-drive space. Your home network can ride to the rescue here, too, by giving you an easy outlet to quickly and easily add storage space that *any* computer on your network can use.

- **Play video games across the network.** A home network brings your gaming experience to an extreme, supreme level. Most game consoles sold today, like the Microsoft Xbox and Sony PlayStation 2, are network-ready and just waiting for you to connect them to your home network. Once connected, you can play games on your network or even with other people from around the Internet.

Any way you slice it, you can do *a lot* with your home network, but to do so, you'll need to buy some hardware helpers here and there, like a network adapter for your old PlayStation 2, an extra hard-drive, or maybe even a TiVo. To help explain how these gadgets work, this chapter takes you through several specific products, but keep in mind that these examples aren't official Missing Manual endorsements, nor are they your only option.

For almost every product covered, plenty of different manufacturers offer similar devices that work pretty much the same way. Throughout the chapter you'll see brief mentions regarding a variety of alternative products. Once you understand how to accomplish a particular task—playing digital music on your stereo, for example—you can pick and choose which device is right for you.

Playing a PC's Music on a Stereo

Even if you've gone and splurged on a decent set of speakers for your computer, you're still stuck having to sit in front of your PC when you want to listen to your tunes. But what if you could just forget about *where* your music is stored and instead play it out through your stereo? You could, of course, string an audio cable between your PC and your stereo, but there's an even better way: use your home network. All you need is a device—usually called something like a *digital media adapter* or a *wireless music player*—that connects to your stereo and pulls in the music files stored on your computer. Apple's AirPort Express, first covered back on page 35 in Chapter 3, offers one easy-to-use solution.

Note: If you've recently purchased a TiVo, you've got everything you need to stream music between your PC and stereo—plus you can display digital pictures on your TV. That's all covered starting on page 178.

Using an Apple AirPort Express

Apple surprised the world in 2002 by making a product designed to work with Windows: the iPod. And it did so again in 2004 with the introduction of the Mac- and Windows-friendly AirPort Express, which sells for around $120.

For something so small (Figure 8-1), the AirPort Express certainly packs a punch, as it can be used as a wireless router (page 39), a wireless network extender (so your WiFi network covers more area), a wireless print server (page 108), and most importantly here, a wireless music adapter. The music feature of the AirPort Express is called *AirTunes,* which lets the tiny device stream music from any of your network PCs to your stereo (or any other set of powered speakers).

Apple has churned through lots of engineers' brain cells making sure that setting up the AirPort Express is easy, regardless of what role you want it to play. The Express's setup assistant program provides step-by-step instructions for virtually all the usage scenarios (more on how to use this setup program in a moment). But since you've spent most of this book learning how to set up a home network, and this chapter is about fun ways to *use* that network, this section focuses on using the AirPort Express as a wireless music adapter in conjunction with an existing WiFi network.

Note: The AirPort Express is not without some flaws. While it's an innovative, easily hidden device, it lacks such features as a basic remote control. This means that if you don't like a particular song, you have to trot back to your computer to move to the next track. You can, however, buy an add-on remote control from at least one company: try Keyspan's Express Remote (*www.keyspan.com*).

Figure 8-1:
The AirPort Express comes with three ports, any (or all) of which you may use, depending on how you want to use the Express. The Ethernet jack on the left lets you connect your AirPort Express to your DSL or cable modem if you want to use the device as a wireless router. The USB port in the middle lets you connect any compatible USB printer, thereby making the printer available to anyone on your network. The audio mini-jack lets you connect the AirPort Express to your stereo. Rather than having to futz with an external power adapter, the AirPort Express just plugs right into the wall.

Here's what you need to get started: a working WiFi network (Chapter 3 shows you how to set one up), one AirPort Express, an audio cable to connect the Express to your stereo (details on your cable choices below), and at least one WiFi-ready, fairly modern computer, running Mac OS X 10.3 or later, or Windows 2000 or Windows XP.

Installation breaks down into two main steps, each of which you'll learn about in the following sections. First, you plug in the Express and connect the cables. Then, you install the AirPort software on one of your network's computers so that you can configure the AirPort Express.

Connecting the AirPort Express

To connect the AirPort Express, follow these steps:

1. **Plug the AirPort Express into an electrical outlet that's close to your stereo.**

   After a little time spent searching for your network's WiFi signal, the Express displays a small green light on its backside. If the light is flashing red, make sure your AirPort Express is within range of your WiFi router.

2. **Connect the AirPort Express to your stereo with an analog or optical digital audio cable.**

   You've got two choices here (either of which you need to buy separately, since Apple ships the Express without cables). First, you can use a standard Y-shaped audio cable with red and black connectors at the v-shaped end of the cable. Called a "mini stereo to dual RCA cable," this cable can be hooked to just about any stereo made in the last 20 years. If you've got a late model stereo, you can get slightly better sound by using a mini-to-optical digital audio cable. Apple sells both cables on its Web site, or you can pick them up online or at a local electronics store.

Installing iTunes and the AirPort Express software

Before you can unleash your music, you need to install two pieces of software:

- **iTunes.** Apple's digital music jukebox program and online store is friendly with both Macs and PCs. You'll need to have a copy of iTunes running on every network computer whose music you want to play on your stereo.

- **AirPort Admin Utility.** This slightly scary looking program looks like a dialog box on steroids: it's got about 10 tabs, each of which let you configure various settings on your AirPort Express. You only need to have this program installed on *one* of the computers (Windows or Macintosh) on your network. And the good news, as you'll learn in a moment, is that if everything works smoothly with the AirPort setup assistant, you never actually have to open this program.

WORKAROUND WORKSHOP

The Latest and Greatest Software

If you have any trouble connecting your AirPort Express to your existing WiFi network, make sure you've got the latest copy of the AirPort installation software (sometimes you'll get a CD that's been sitting in a warehouse, during which time Apple has updated the installation software).

To see whether your CD's fresh, first check the version number of the AirPort Admin Utility that the AirPort Express CD installed on your computer. In Windows, go to Start → All Programs → AirPort → AirPort Admin Utility. When the program launches, choose Help → About AirPort Admin Utility,

and you'll see the version number. On a Mac, go to Applications → Utilities → AirPort Admin Utility. Once the program opens, choose AirPort Admin Utility → About AirPort Admin Utility to see the version number.

Once you've got the version number, head on over to Apple's AirPort Express Web site at *www.apple.com/ airportexpress* and look in the AirPort Express Updates box on the top-right corner of the Web page. If there's a higher version number available, download it and repeat the installation steps.

Both iTunes and the AirPort Admin Utility come on the AirPort Express CD that comes with AirPort Express. Bring that CD over to any computer that's got a WiFi connection to your network and then follow these steps:

Note: The AirPort setup assistant, which handles all the configuration dirty work for you, doesn't work on Windows 2000 computers. If your house is a 2000-only shop, then follow the steps below (to get the AirPort Admin Utility onto your PC) and then move on to "Manually configuring the AirPort Express" on page 176.

---

1. **Insert the AirPort Express CD into your computer.**

   If you've got a Windows PC, the installation wizard launches right away. On a Mac, double-click the CD's AirPort icon on your desktop, and then double-click "Install AirPort and iTunes."

2. **Follow the steps provided by the installer.**

The installer asks you a handful of questions, including whether you accept the license agreement and on which hard drive you want to install the software. Follow the instructions for connecting your AirPort Express to an existing wireless network.

If you run into any problems during the installation, make sure you've got the latest version of the AirPort installer (see the box "The Latest and Greatest Software").

3. **If you've installed the software on a Mac, restart your computer.**

Now you're ready to start using the powerful pipes on your stereo to play your music. Just launch iTunes from any computer on the network (you'll need to make sure that all the computers on your network have at least version 4.6 of iTunes; go to *www.apple.com/itunes/* to download the latest version). And then, in the lower-right corner of iTunes, select the name of the stereo or powered speakers that you created during the setup (Figure 8-2).

Figure 8-2:
Once you get your AirPort Express up, running, and happily configured, the iTunes window has a new option that wasn't there before—a pop-up menu to select a set of speakers. This particular computer has two options: play the music on the computer speakers, or use the speakers in the entertainment center.

Manually configuring the AirPort Express

Like many networkable gadgets, the AirPort Express sometimes requires a bit of configuration before you can use it. The AirPort Admin Utility is your configuration control center. Whether you're here because your computer's running Windows 2000 (and Apple's given you no choice) or you're just curious about what you can do with this powerful command center, read on.

Note: Your existing wireless router must support *Wireless Distribution System* (WDS) in order to allow the AirPort Express to connect to your network. WDS is a tongue-jamming acronym for a pretty straightforward feature. Think of it this way: your wireless router is your main signal transmitter on your home network. When you use WDS, you force your AirPort Express to use your existing wireless network's configuration instead of its own.

To configure an AirPort Express using the AirPort Admin Utility:

1. **Start the AirPort Admin Utility.**

   In Windows XP: go to Start → All Programs → AirPort → AirPort Admin Utility. In Windows 2000: go to Start → Programs → AirPort → AirPort Admin Utility. In Mac OS X: go to Applications → Utilities → AirPort Admin Utility.

   A window appears that lists your AirPort Express (as well as any other wireless routers on your network that are made by Apple, like other AirPort Express devices or an Apple Extreme Base Station).

2. **Select your AirPort Express from the list.**

   The AirPort Express is probably named something like "Apple Network ######," where the # signs make up the unique ID assigned to your AirPort Express at the factory. Select your AirPort Express and then click Configure.

3. **Click the AirPort tab (Windows only).**

   The Windows version of the utility opens up to an information page. Mac owners don't have to deal with a tab, as the Macintosh version of the software gets right down to business.

4. **Rename your AirPort Express.**

   This step isn't mandatory, but it's a nice way of getting rid of the name Apple assigned the AirPort Express at the factory. It's also very useful if you have more than one AirPort Express device on your network and each one is connected to a different set of speakers. Enter the new name in the Name text box.

5. **Create an AirPort Express password.**

   Especially if you live in a populated area, make sure to assign a good password to your AirPort Express to prevent others from reconfiguring your network accidentally (or intentionally!).

   Click the Change Password button on the AirPort configuration page and type a new password for your AirPort Express.

6. **Join the AirPort Express to your existing network (Figure 8-3).**

In the drop-down list next to Wireless Mode, choose "Join an Existing Wireless Network (Wireless Client)."

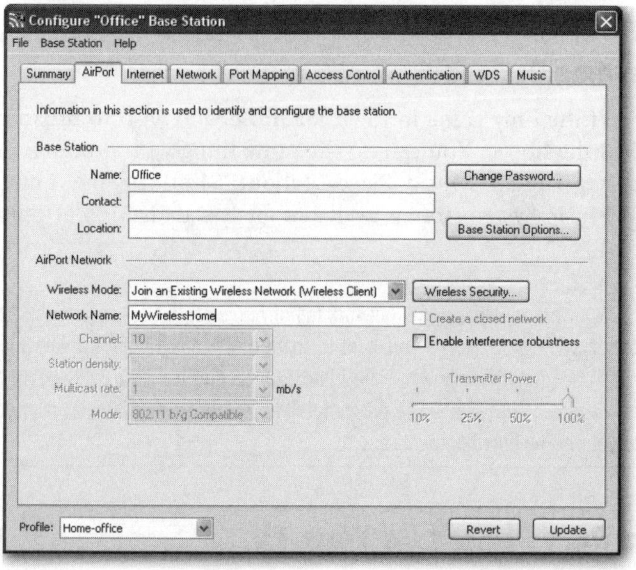

Figure 8-3:
From the Wireless Mode drop-down list choose "Join an Existing Wireless Network." In the Network Name box, type the name (or SSID) of the existing wireless network. For more information about SSID, see page 53 If you've got a Mac, you can also click the drop-down arrow and select the name of the wireless network from a list.

7. **In the Network Name text box, enter the name of the WiFi network you're joining.**

This is where you enter your WiFi network's SSID (page 53) or Network Name (if you've got an Apple Base Station).

8. **Select your wireless security settings (page 59) if the network you're joining is password protected.**

You'll need to activate wireless security if the network you're joining is using some kind of security. On the Windows Admin utility, click Wireless Security. On the Mac, click Security Options. Then, select from the available options (off, WEP, or WPA) and then enter a password.

9. **Enable AirTunes.**

Click the Music tab and then turn on the "Enable AirTunes on this base station" checkbox.

10. **Pick a name for your stereo or powered speakers.**

Enter the name in the iTunes Speaker Name box. You can also set up a password here if you want to limit access to the AirPort Express to those to whom you've given the password.

11. **Click the Update button.**

This saves your changes to the AirPort Express and restarts the unit.

Your AirPort Express is now joined to your existing network, and you're ready to start playing your computer's music on your stereo. See step 3 on page 175 for instructions on how to use iTunes to actually start playing music.

Other Music-Streaming Options

The AirPort Express isn't the only game in town for those who wish to broadcast their PC's music around the house. You can do the same thing with products like Netgear's MP101Wireless Digital Music Player (about $130) or the Linksys WMLS11B Wireless-B Music System (often available for less than $100 at online shops like Amazon.com).

Tip: If you're a proud Mac OS X warrior with a home network full of Apple products, consider the $200 EyeHome from Elgato Systems (*www.elgato.com*) if you want to share more media than just your music over AirTunes. The EyeHome works quite happily with the AirPort Express and lets you easily beam the digital photos, music, and movies from your Mac's iLife programs (iPhoto, iTunes, and iMovie) over your wireless network and right to your home entertainment center.

Displaying Your PC's Photos on Your TV

Apple has its loyal fans, but in a relatively short time, TiVo (*www.tivo.com*) has attracted devoted fanatics who trust the humble little box to record all the television shows they like—and all the ones TiVo *thinks* they might like, too. The TiVo digital video recorder (DVR) has transformed living rooms across the country into digital recording havens capable of storing anywhere from 40 to 120 hours of TV programming.

In addition to its television-recording software, the current Series2 versions of TiVo can join your home network and, by using optional software, put your own pictures on the TV and play your music through the TV's speakers. TiVo makes all this music-listening and photo-watching a snap by giving you a familiar, TiVo-like menu on your TV to navigate through your music and photo collections.

Using a TiVo Series2

Making all these features work requires a bit of effort and a little additional hardware. From the factory, the TiVo doesn't have the hardware you need to connect to your home network. Further, to allow a TiVo to tap into the music and picture files on your computer, you need to install and configure some software on your computer.

Note: Before you get started on your journey to network your TiVo, make sure the thing actually works. You can't use TiVo's home networking capabilities until you've completed the initial configuration and the unit has made that first phone call to TiVo central command to download updates and the first programming schedule.

Once your TiVo is happy and humming along nicely, you can unplug the phone line and dig into the networking challenge. Use the instructions included with your TiVo to get setup work done before forging ahead.

TiVo network hardware requirements

TiVo needs its own special network adapter (page 5) to make it work on your home network. Unlike your PC, not just any network adapter will do. You have to use one of the adapters that TiVo lists on its Web site (*www.tivo.com/adapters*) that are known to work with the Series2.

To save you the hassle of visiting the site and trying to figure out what the heck to buy, here are some adapters that *definitely* work with all Series2 TiVo units:

- (Wireless) Linksys WUSB11 (version 2.6 or version 2.8)
- (Wireless) D-Link DWL-120 V.E (not DWL120+)
- (Wired) Linksys 100TX
- (Wired) Linksys USB200M

POWER USERS' CLINIC

TiVo Network Speed

If you use a wireless adapter on your TiVo and listen to really high-quality MP3 music files stored on your computer, you *might* notice some skipping. This is because the supported wireless adapters use the 802.11b standard (page 36) which sports a maximum theoretical speed of 11 Mbps. (Real-life speeds of 5 to 6 Mbps are more common, though.)

With high-quality audio and enough interference, your TiVo simply can't keep up. If you notice this happening, you can try

a supported *wired* network adapter (page 179 lists a few options). Since wired networks don't suffer from the same interference problems that plague wireless networks, your data (that is, your music files) will move more quickly across your home network. Unfortunately, there's a limit (12 Mbps) to the speed that even wired adapters can achieve. Why 12 Mbps? That's the maximum speed of the USB 1.1 ports on the TiVo. The Series2 TiVo does not currently support USB 2.0, which would provide speeds of up to 100 Mbps.

Installing a TiVo network adapter

After you've purchased an adapter, you need to install it so your TiVo can start talking to your home network:

1. **Plug your network adapter into one of the USB ports on the back of the TiVo.**

   You'll need a USB cable to connect the network adapter to your TiVo. It doesn't matter which USB port you use on the TiVo. If you're using a wired network adapter, you also need to connect an Ethernet cable from the network adapter to your router.

---

2. **Navigate to TiVo's onscreen Phone & Network Settings screen.**

   Press the TiVo button on your remote control. From the TiVo Central menu, choose Read New Messages & Setup → Settings → Phone & Network → Edit phone or network settings.

3. **Configure Tivo's wireless settings (wireless only).**

   Like any other wireless device, your TiVo needs to know what wireless network it lives on and whether or not the network is secured with WEP (page 55). From the Phone & Network Settings menu, select Wireless Settings (Figure 8-4).

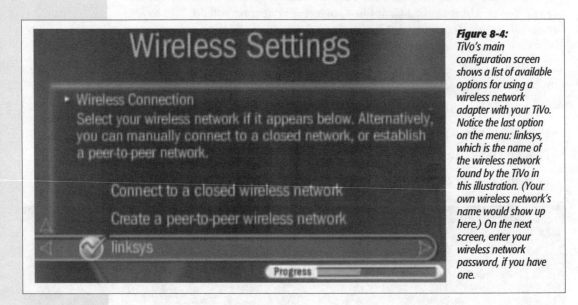

Figure 8-4:
TiVo's main configuration screen shows a list of available options for using a wireless network adapter with your TiVo. Notice the last option on the menu: linksys, which is the name of the wireless network found by the TiVo in this illustration. (Your own wireless network's name would show up here.) On the next screen, enter your wireless network password, if you have one.

4. **Configure the IP address.**

   Just like any other computer or device on your network, your TiVo needs an IP address to do its job. To configure your TiVo, choose TCP/IP Settings from the Phone & Network Settings screen. If you're using DHCP, or automatic IP addressing (page 25), choose "Obtain an IP address automatically."

   If you have a static IP address, choose "Specify static IP address" instead. To complete this step, make sure you have your IP address, subnet mask, default gateway/router address, and the IP addresses of your ISP's DNS servers (page 28). Walk through the steps as TiVo shows you how to enter these addresses.

   For both address types, TiVo also asks you to provide a DHCP client ID. Unless your ISP specifically requires this information (almost none do), you can skip this part.

5. **Get ready to enjoy your TiVo!**

   Now that your TiVo can talk to your network, you can make use of the cool features provided by the device, as soon as you take care of some software business.

Using the TiVo desktop software

For your TiVo to use its advanced home-networking features, you need to install some software on each computer on your network whose music and photos you want to share. The program is called the TiVo Desktop, which your TiVo uses to talk to your computer so it knows which music files and pictures are available to use.

The TiVo Desktop software is available for free download from *www.tivo.com/desktop*. The latest version, TiVo Desktop 2.0, works only with Windows 2000 and XP machines. This doesn't mean people with older versions of Windows or Macintosh computers can't use TiVo Desktop—it just means that you can't use the absolute latest version of the program. There are older versions of TiVo Desktop that work just fine with the Macintosh operating system and older editions of Windows, and the site tells you which ones.

Note: The Mac version of TiVo Desktop uses the music and pictures stored in your iTunes and iPhoto libraries. TiVo cannot, unfortunately, play music files encoded in the AAC format, including those you paid good money for at the iTunes Music Store.

Click the Download link next to the version of TiVo Desktop that works with your particular computer. Once the program downloads from the site, double-click the installer file to add TiVo Desktop to your computer. The installer guides you along the way, and gives you the chance to "publish" your music and picture folders during the installation (Figure 8-5). If you don't add your pictures and music here, you can go back and do it after the installation has finished.

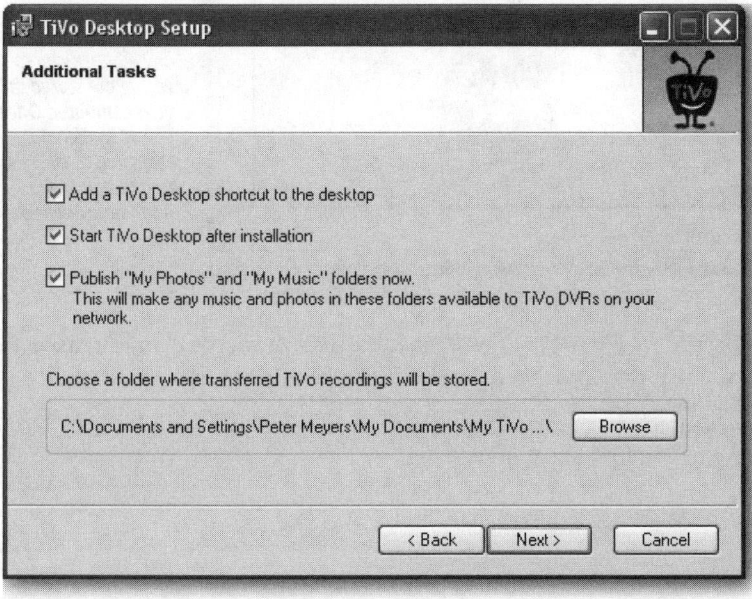

Figure 8-5:
If you want to save a step after the TiVo Desktop software installation is complete, turn on the checkbox to "publish" your My Photos and My Music folders—which means you're making all the files in both those folders available to all the TiVos connected to your home network.

The TiVo Desktop installer goes through a few more steps, including checking your network settings. When the installation is done, you'll have the TiVo software in your Programs menu (Windows) or Applications folder (Mac). If you didn't make your music and photo files available to TiVo during the TiVo desktop software installation, you can do so now by opening the TiVo Publisher program.

• In Windows, go to Start → All Programs → TiVo Desktop → TiVo Publisher.

• On the Mac, go to → System Preferences. Under "Other," select TiVo Desktop.

The next step for Windows owners, as shown in Figure 8-6, is to identify which music files and pictures you want to make available to TiVo.

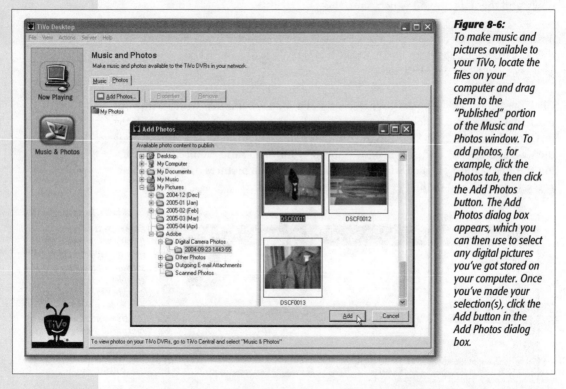

Figure 8-6:
To make music and pictures available to your TiVo, locate the files on your computer and drag them to the "Published" portion of the Music and Photos window. To add photos, for example, click the Photos tab, then click the Add Photos button. The Add Photos dialog box appears, which you can then use to select any digital pictures you've got stored on your computer. Once you've made your selection(s), click the Add button in the Add Photos dialog box.

If you've got a Mac, Figure 8-7 makes it clear that you have it much easier than your Windows counterparts. No muss, no fuss…just a few quick options!

Once you've shared your music and pictures, you're ready to use TiVo to actually start listening to and looking at everything.

Note: TiVo Desktop 2.0 for Windows 2000 and later includes the TiVoToGo feature that lets you copy recorded shows from your TiVo's hard drive to your computer or laptop's drive over your home network. It's not exactly a blazing fast transfer (transfers can sometimes take hours), but it does let you watch the last three episodes of *America's Top Supermodel Idol* on the plane instead of that chopped-up B-picture.

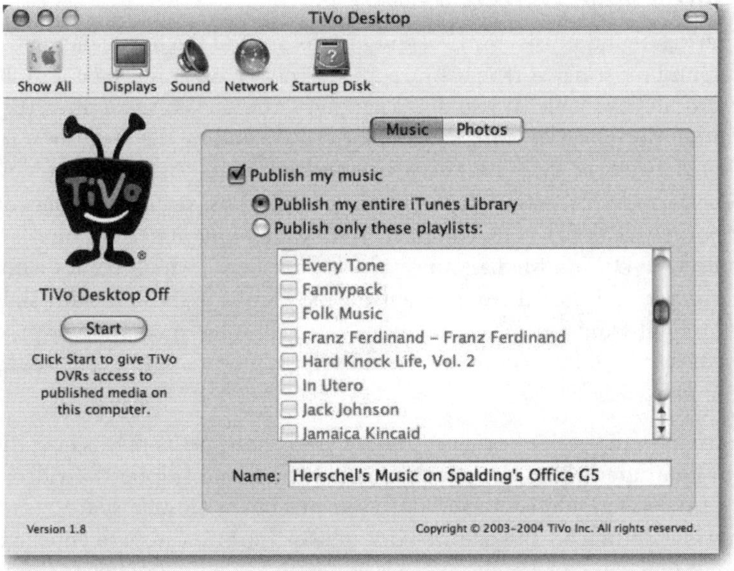

Figure 8-7:
The Macintosh version of the TiVo Desktop integrates right into iTunes and iPhoto. Even better, it uses any music playlists you've already created in iTunes so you don't have to do any music-mixing work twice. To start the TiVo Desktop, choose the button marked Start.

Playing music and viewing pictures with a TiVo

Now it's time to put TiVo's music and picture-sharing powers to work. Head on over to your TV, press the TiVo button on the remote control, and then choose Music & Photos from the TiVo Central menu. A list of computers running the TiVo desktop pops up (Figure 8-8).

Figure 8-8:
This TiVo menu shows a link to the music collection of someone named Cookie Monster, whose tunes are stored on a Mac that's named Ketchup.

Once you select a computer, use your TiVo's remote control to navigate to the photo album or playlist you want to use. The TiVo menus give you basic controls over how the photos or music is played. For example, you can rotate photos or play slideshows on the TV screen by selecting the appropriate option on the TiVo screen. TiVo's music player lets you shuffle and repeat playlists as well.

Other Network Photo-Viewing Options

The idea of sharing digital music, movies, and photos around the house has proven to be a winner, and most network-hardware makers now have some sort of multi-media server product available. If you don't happen to be a TiVo subscriber, there are plenty of other options that work in a similar way, including the Netgear Wireless Digital Media Player MP115 (*www.netgear.com*) and ADS Technology's Media-Link (*www.adstech.com*). These types of devices sit on your home network and serve as go-betweens for your computer and your home entertainment system. There's also the D-Link MediaLounge (*www.dlink.com*), which comes with a built-in DVD player and a card reader right on the front for those instant slide-shows pulled straight from a camera's memory card. All these media server products use the 802.11g standard (page 36), work with Windows, and cost between $250 and $350.

One thing you may realize once you start sharing your multimedia files is how easy it is to fill your computer's hard drive with music, photos, and snippets of video. If there comes a time when you've maxed out your machine's storage space, it may be time to consider adding an annex onto your network so you can park your massive collection of files. The next section shows you how to set up a network storage device that everyone can use.

Adding Storage to Your Network

Have you ever gotten to a point where you need to dump files and programs from your hard drive because it was getting full? Have you ever found yourself needing to grab a document from another computer, but you can't get to it because the computer it lives on is turned off? There's an easy answer to storage dilemmas like these: add more of it, and make the space available to everyone, all the time, from every PC on your network.

In this section, you'll learn how to add storage to your home network by connecting additional USB hard drives to your router. Using the Linksys Network Storage Link, you can connect USB-based hard drives directly to your network. You just need a Network Storage Link (which sells for less than $100), a spare USB external hard drive or two, and some USB and Ethernet cables. You connect the Storage Link to your router, then connect your USB disks to the Network Storage Link. After you configure the Storage Link, those USB drives show up as shared drives on your network, which everyone can use. And best of all the Storage Link supports both Macintosh and Windows computers.

Note: Network-based storage drives are not completely without drawbacks. The primary problem plaguing network-attached hard drives is performance, or rather, speed. Even though you use the same type of hard drives you'd attach to your computer, you're not able to transfer data to and fro quite as fast as you would if the hard drive was attached directly to a computer. That's because rather than enjoying the speedy 480 Mbps channel you get when you plug a USB drive directly into your computer, your data has to travel *from* the USB drive *to* the Network Storage Link *across* the network and, finally, *to* your computer. Makes sense, right?

The Linksys Network Storage Link

Setting up the Network Storage Link is pretty easy and makes your files accessible from any computer—Windows or Macintosh—on the network. Here's a basic outline of the steps you need to take when setting up the Storage Link:

1. Connect the Storage Link to your network's router (wired or wireless) using Ethernet cables. Plug the hard drive(s) into the Storage Link.

2. Use one of your computers to make the Storage Link visible on your network.

3. Install the Storage Link software on one of your computers so you can configure the Storage Link to store and use the hard drive's files.

Before you get *too* excited about the Storage Link, make sure you understand the implications of what happens in step 3, particularly if you're planning to connect external hard drives you already own and use. During the installation process, your hard drives are *erased* (that is, reformatted) and *cannot* be connected directly back to your Windows or Macintosh computer without completely erasing them again.

The two key points to keep in mind here: first, before you get started, back up anything that's currently stored on a USB drive you plan on using with the Storage Link. If you like, you can return the backed up data to the USB drive (over the network) once you've got the Storage Link up and running. Second, don't plan on sidling up with your laptop and plugging directly into a Storage Link–attached USB drive. The only way you can access that drive will be over the network.

Connecting the Network Storage Link to your network

To get started, the first thing you need to do is plug in all your gear. The following steps guide you through the process of connecting your Network Storage Link and the external hard drives it's using to your network:

1. Connect the Network Storage Link to your router.

   The Storage Link includes an Ethernet cable that you can use to connect the device to one of the wired ports on your router. If you have no available Ethernet ports on your router, you'll need to either get a new router with more ports or add a switch (page 17) to your router, which will give you more ports.

Note: If you're really dedicated to the wireless life, your other option is to add a special wireless network adapter—called an *Ethernet-to-wireless bridge*—to your Network Storage Link. That will give you a wireless link between your router and the Storage Link, which means you can then move the Storage Link (and its attached drives) anywhere on your WiFi network that you like.

2. **Connect your hard drive (or drives) to the Storage Link.**

   Make sure the Storage Link is *off* before you start connecting devices to it.

   You need a USB cable to connect your hard drives to the Storage Link. If you have only one drive, be sure to connect it to the "Disk 1" port on the Storage Link. If you have two drives, connect one drive to each port on the device. Turn on the drive(s).

3. **Plug the Storage Link into an electrical outlet.**

   Use the included power cord and give the Link some juice.

4. **Turn the Storage Link on.**

   The power button is located on the bottom front of the Storage Link. After you turn it on, the powering-up process takes a few seconds and you might hear the unit beep. Make sure the appropriate lights come on; for example, if you have a single disk connected to the unit, the Disk 1 light will brighten right up. If you have a disk connected to the unit and you aren't getting a light, check your connections and make sure the external hard drive is actually turned on as well.

That takes care of the first part of the installation. Next up is getting one of your computers on the network to communicate with the Storage Link so the Storage Link can share its newly acquired storage space with everyone else on the network.

Configuring your computer to use the Network Storage Link

The Network Storage Link doesn't automatically pop up on your network and invite people to store files on it. To get the Storage Link talking to your network's computers, you need to configure the device to play nice with your network's router.

If you happen to have a Linksys router, this router-to-Storage Link communication works automatically, because Linksys makes sure all of its network gear fits together like peas in a pod. (Technically speaking, the first three sets of numbers in each device's IP address match, which means they can communicate seamlessly.) So if you've got a Linksys router running your network, you can save yourself some reading by skipping this entire section and going right to page 190.

If you have a non-Linksys router, on the other hand, you'll probably need to make some temporary configuration changes to the computer you're using to set up the Storage Link. You need to do this because routers from different companies have different IP addresses built into their equipment, and the IP address on, say, a D-Link router won't automatically communicate with the Linksys Network Storage Drive.

So if you don't have a Linksys router running your network, you can temporarily trick your PC into thinking it's on a Linksys network just long enough to tap into the Storage Link and get it configured. This little workaround will temporarily knock you off the Internet, but don't worry. Once you finish configuring the Storage Link, you'll learn how to revert your PC to its original settings so that your Internet connection will be good as new.

Changing the IP address in Windows XP . If you're setting up the Storage Link from a Windows XP computer, follow these steps:

1. **Go to Start → Control Panel → Network Connections.**

   As explained above, you're going to *temporarily* change your PC's IP address so that it's compatible with the Network Storage Link.

2. **Select your current network connection from the list.**

   If you have only a single network adapter in your computer, you'll probably see only one choice. If, however, you have more than one network adapter, select the one you're actually using; it's the one listed as Connected in the Status column. Double-click the selection. The Network Adapter Status window opens.

3. **Click the Properties button.**

   The configuration box for the network adapter opens.

4. **Double-click "Internet Protocol (TCP/IP)."**

   Since you're temporarily changing the IP address of the computer, you'll need this configuration window.

5. **Change your TCP/IP settings.**

   Figure 8-9 shows you what to do.

6. **Click OK twice.**

   Pressing OK the first time saves your network configuration while the second tap exits the network configuration screen.

   At this point, your computer won't be able to get on the Internet, but you don't need Internet access to complete the configuration of your Storage Link.

7. **Configure the settings for your Storage Link.**

   The next section ("Configuring the Network Storage Link," page 190) provides all the details you'll need to get your Storage Link up and running. Skip ahead to complete the installation of your unit, and then return to step 8 to readjust your PC's IP address settings.

8. **Put your computer's network connection settings back the way you found them.**

Once you finish up the installation of your Network Storage Link, change your IP address information back to the original settings. Follow steps 1 to 6 in this list, but for step 5, either turn on "Obtain an IP address automatically," or put it back to the IP address it had if it was originally set to "Use the following IP address."

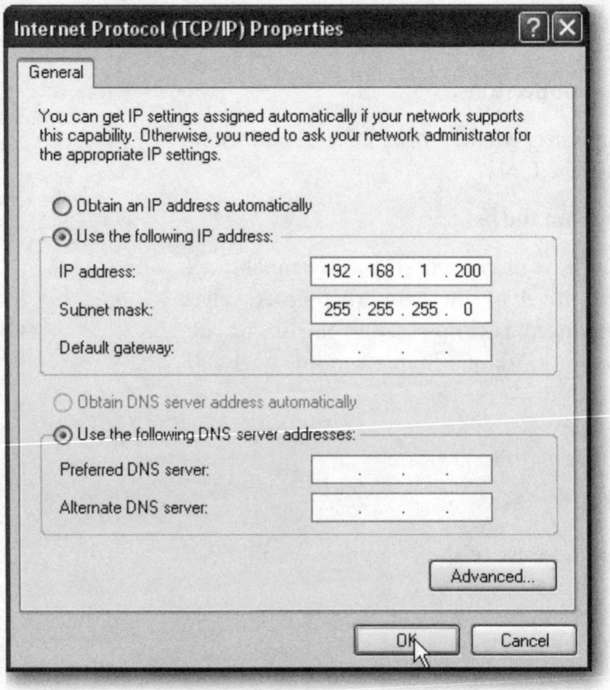

Figure 8-9:
Most computers use DHCP (page 25), in which case the "Obtain an IP address automatically" button is turned on. If, however, your computer is set to "Use the following IP address," write down the numbers listed here before changing them, since you'll need them later on to reset your computer's networking configuration.

Next, turn on the "Use the following IP address button (if it's not already on) and type the IP address and subnet mask shown in this figure. The IP address is 192.168.1.200 and the subnet mask is 255.255.255.0. You can leave the DNS server address spaces alone.

Changing the IP address in Mac OS X. If you've got a Mac OS X computer and a non-Linksys router, follow these steps so that you can configure the Network Storage Link:

1. **Go to → System Preferences → Network.**

The goal in this series of steps is to temporarily change your Mac's IP address so that it's compatible with that of the Storage Link. This step just opens up the Network system preference panel.

2. **Select your network connection from the list.**

If, as is probably the case, you have more than one network adapter, like an AirPort Extreme wireless card, a 56K dial-up modem, and an Ethernet jack, select the one you're using at the moment—it'll have a green dot next to it. (If you see more than two green dots, pick the one you're using to connect to the Storage Link.)

3. **Click the Configure button.**

The configuration window for the network adapter opens.

4. **Select TCP/IP.**

Since you're temporarily changing the IP address of the computer, you'll need this configuration window.

5. **Change your TCP/IP settings.**

Figure 8-10 shows you what to do.

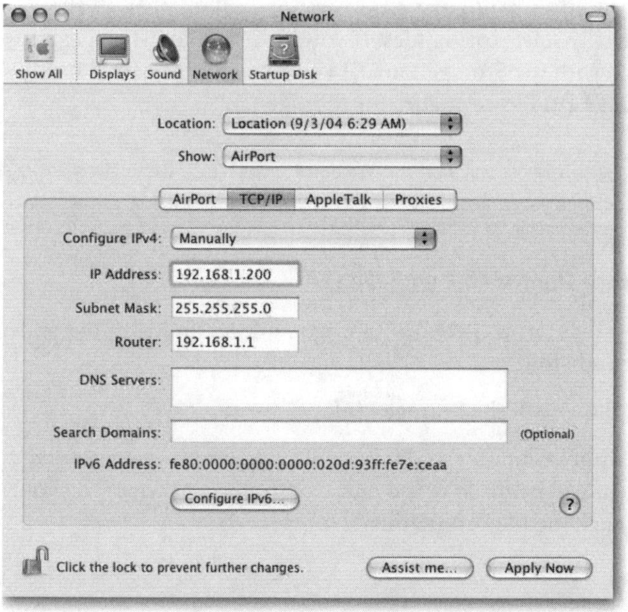

Figure 8-10:
Most computers use DHCP (page 25), so you'll probably see "Using DHCP" in the Configure IPv4 drop-down menu. If, however, your computer is already set to "Manually," write down the information before changing it, since you'll need it later on to reset your computer's networking configuration.

To get your Mac to chat with the storage link, change the Configure IPv4 setting to "Manually" and type the IP address and subnet mask shown in this figure. The IP address is 192.168.1.200 and the subnet mask is 255.255.255.0, with a router address of 192.168.1.1. You can leave the DNS server address spaces alone.

6. **Click Apply Now.**

Your computer immediately saves your network settings.

At this point, your computer might not be able to get to the Internet, but you don't need Internet access to complete the configuration of your Storage Link.

7. **Configure your Storage Link.**

"Using a Web browser to configure the Network Storage Link" on page 191 shows you how to get your Network Storage Link up and running without using the software provided by Linksys (which is a Windows-only deal). Skip ahead to complete the installation of your unit, and then return to step 8 to readjust your Mac's IP address settings.

8. **After you finish with the last configuration step on page 191 or 193, put your computer back the way you found it.**

Once you finish up the installation of your Storage Link, change your Mac's IP address settings back to their original settings. Follow steps 1 to 6 here, but for step 5, in the Configure IPv4 drop-down list, select "DHCP," (if that's what your Mac was originally set to) or enter the IP address it had if it was originally set to "Manually."

Configuring the Network Storage Link

Now that you've got your computer talking to the Network Storage Link, you still need to spend a few minutes configuring the Storage Link so that all the PCs on your network can actually start storing files. If you have Windows, you can use the setup CD that shipped with the Storage Link. If you're on a Mac, you'll need to use your Web browser (page 191) to configure the Storage Link.

Note: The steps for Macintosh owners will work for Windows people, too. These steps are useful if you've lost, damaged, or destroyed your CD.

Configuring the Network Storage Link with the CD

You've just got a few steps left to get your Storage Link up and running and your attached hard drives ready to use:

1. **Grab the CD that came with the Storage Link.**

   Pop the disc into your computer's CD drive. The setup program should automatically launch, but if it doesn't, use My Computer to browse to your CD drive and double-click the file SetupUtility.exe.

2. **Choose Setup.**

   On the Setup utility's main menu, located in the lower-left corner of the screen, select the Setup option.

3. **Select your Storage Link and click Yes.**

   This is really the first screen of the configuration program. The utility snoops around your network in search of new Storage Link devices. Once it finds one, the program displays the serial number of the unit along with some significant information, like the unit's IP address and the date and time.

4. **Enter the configuration password.**

   Before the configuration utility lets you start messing around with a Storage Link device, it prompts you for a password. If you supply the right password, you get to keep going. The factory-set password for your Storage Link is "admin". (Skip the quotes, though.)

5. **Configure your Network Storage Link's IP address.**

The factory-assigned IP address of your Storage Link is 192.168.1.77. If you're using a Linksys router, this address works just fine for moving through the setup steps. If you're using a different kind of router, you have to change this address to something that works on your network. You can either opt to use DHCP to automatically assign a compatible address to your Network Storage Link (which is what most people are going to want to do), or, if you're brave, go ahead and provide a static IP address. The first three sets of numbers in the IP address have to match your router's IP address. To check your router's IP address see the box "DNAS -611 Error" on page 204. For an easier life, use DHCP.

6. **Set the date and time.**

Your Storage Link is basically another server sitting out on your network. Because of that fact, if you want the date and time for files you save on the attached hard drives to be correct, the Storage Link itself needs to know the current date and time.

7. **Confirm your configuration.**

If everything on this screen looks correct, click Save. Otherwise, click Back and correct any typos.

8. **Prepare the attached hard drive(s).**

After the Storage Link unit saves the settings, the configuration program is ready to erase the contents of the external hard drive connected to the Storage Link. Just before your data is wiped away, the configuration program warns you that all data on the disk(s) will be lost if you proceed. If you're sure you don't need the data, click OK. If you're having second thoughts, click the Cancel button. Now's your chance to go reconnect the drive to your computer, burn all the data to a CD or DVD, and come back to the Storage Link.

The disk preparation process takes a few minutes and will take a little longer for bigger hard drives. When it's done, you have one last step—getting the computers on your network to go ahead and use the newly prepared hard drives that are connected to the Storage Link.

Note: If you had to change your computer's IP address to configure the Network Storage Link, change it back now by following step 8 on page 190.

Using a Web browser to configure the Network Storage Link

As most long-time Mac fans know, it's often not a friendly world out there when it comes to software compatibility. (But then again, you never had to deal with a computer that came installed with Microsoft Bob.) In these modern times, a Web browser is a great mediator and can often help you configure networkable devices. Fortunately, that's the case with the Network Storage Link.

Tip: If you've lost or damaged your CD, and need to make configuration changes to your Storage Link from your Windows PC, you can also use this Web-based configuration scheme.

To configure your Storage Link using nothing but your bare hands and a Web browser, follow these instructions:

1. **Open your Web browser.**

   Fire up Safari, Internet Explorer, Firefox, Mozilla, Opera, or any Web browser you like.

2. **Browse to your Storage Link.**

   Your Network Storage Link's IP address is 192.168.1.77. To get to it, type *http:// 192.168.1.77* in your browser's address bar.

3. **Click on the Administration option.**

   Everything you need to do takes place on the Administration tab. When you select it, a window pops up asking for your user name and password. For this mission, the device uses a factory user name of "admin" with a password of "admin". (Skip the quotes, though.)

4. **Type in an IP address for the Storage Link.**

   Linksys recommends that the Storage Link be assigned a fixed IP address, but these can be a pain in the neck to keep track of unless you have a photographic memory. For a home network, it won't make much of a difference which option, DHCP or fixed IP address, you choose for your Storage Link. That said, if you're comfortable assigning the unit a fixed IP address, do so (see Figure 8-11 for details).

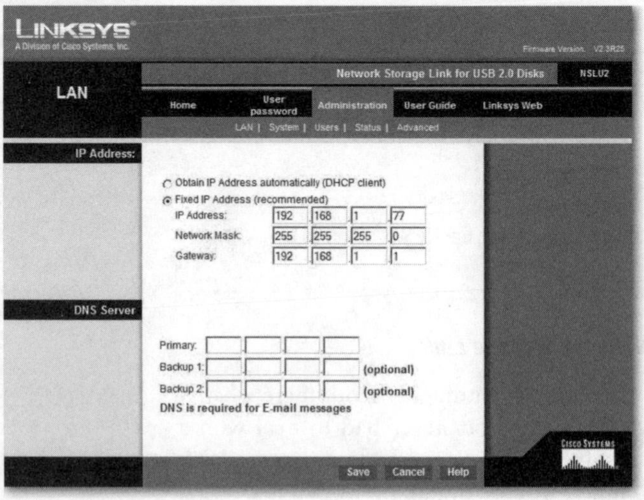

Figure 8-11:
The factory-assigned IP address of your Storage Link device is 192.168.1.77. If you're using a Linksys router, this address works just fine. If, on the other hand, you're using a different kind of router and want to use a fixed address, you have to change this address to something that works with your own router. If you're uncomfortable trying to make the thing work with a static IP address, just use DHCP to automatically assign a compatible address to your Storage Link.

5. **Give the Storage Link a name.**

   Linksys ships the Storage Link with a ridiculous name that's pretty hard to remember: its serial number. Give the device a good, network-y name (like "Storage" or "Larry") that's easy to remember. (Instructions for this bit are in the box "Name or Serial Number?" on page 195.)

6. **Prepare your connected disk (or disks) for use.**

   Your device has an address. It has a good name. Now you just need to prepare the disks for use with the Storage Link by *erasing them completely*, as shown in Figure 8-12.

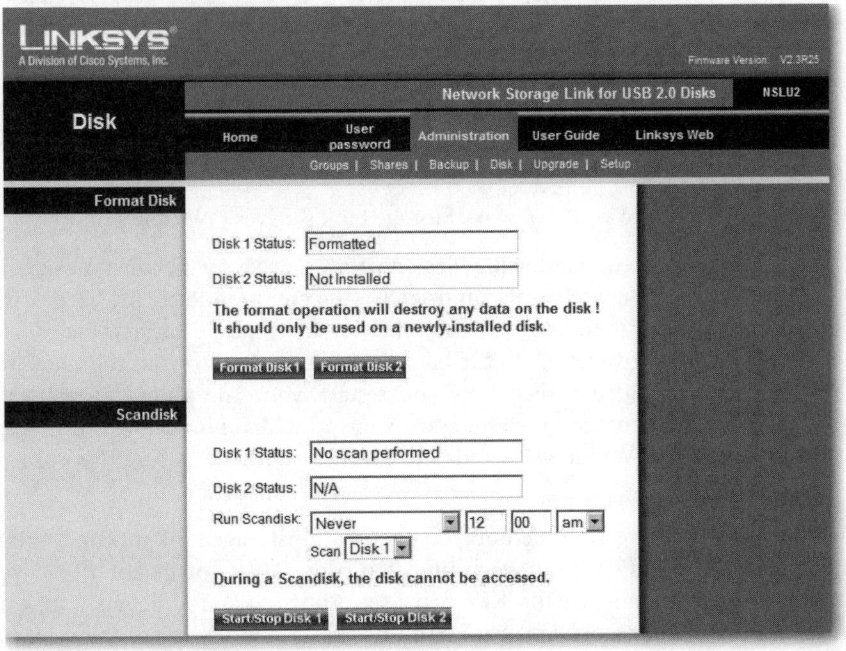

Figure 8-12:
To get started, click the Advanced option. Then, click the Disk option that appears. For disks that are not Storage Link–ready, the caption next to the status will read "Not Formatted." In this figure, there is one disk that's already been formatted. Disk preparation took place by clicking the "Format Disk 1" button, a process that takes about 10 minutes to complete. Once done, the disk is completely empty and is usable by the Storage Link. You'd repeat the process for Disk 2 if you had a second disk you want to use for data.

Remember, the Storage Link uses a format that Macs and PCs don't recognize, so if you want to unhitch the disk from the Storage Link and stick it back on your Mac, you'll have to reformat the poor disk again so the Mac will recognize it.

Note: If you had to change your computer's IP address to configure the Storage Link, change it back now by following step 8 on page 188 (Windows) or page 190 (Macintosh).

Your Storage Link is ready to store your music, videos, and massive family photo album. Now all you need to do is access the drives from any of your network's computers, which the next section shows you how to do.

Using the Network Storage Link on Your Network

You've got a bunch of different ways to get to the drives attached to your Network Storage Link:

- Use My Network Places (Windows XP and ME), Network Neighborhood (Windows 95, 98, and 2000), Finder (Mac OS X), or Go To Server (Mac OS X).

  Which method you use here depends on your operating system, but if you look around, you'll find a "server" with a name matching the serial number of your Network Storage Link (unless you changed the unit's name; see the box on page 195). When you open the server, you'll see shares named "disk 1" and "disk 2"—one for each hard drive you have connected to the Storage Link. Page 110 in Chapter 5 (Windows) and page 143 in Chapter 6 (Macintosh) detail the exact steps to take to use each connection method. Use the *Universal Naming Convention* (UNC) to connect to the drives (Windows only).

  Any version of Windows can use the UNC method, which is explained in detail on page 113. You can use UNC by either connecting to the Storage Link with its IP address or its name.

- *Map* a drive letter to your Network Storage Link's drives (Windows only).

  You're probably used to accessing files on your "C drive," which just means that the files you're using are stored on drive C:, the common letter for hard drives on Windows machines. You can use other letters, though. In fact, it's easy to assign your own drive letters to the hard drives connected to your Storage Link. When you map a drive, each time you restart, your computer automatically reattaches to the Storage Link and assigns the same drive letter each time. Page 115 in Chapter 5 (Windows) details the exact steps to take to use this connection method.

Regardless of the connection method you choose, the Storage Link prompts you to enter a user name and password each time you connect. (If you've got a Mac, you can add your login info to the Keychain; see Appendix A for details.) In your home, a high level of security probably isn't necessary, but if you use the device in your small business, you might want to limit access to specific people. The next section shows how you can restrict access to the Storage Link's drives.

Protecting Data on the Network Storage Link

The Network Storage Link includes some built-in features that handily overcome much of the security risks that come with having shared storage hard drives. First, Linksys lets you restrict who can do what to the data on the drives by controlling access to them. Second, the Storage Link lets you automatically back up the contents of one attached disk drive to the other attached disk drive. This process is called *mirroring* the data, and it works by saving the exact same data on both disks. It might seem wasteful at first, but as soon as one of your external hard drives croaks, you'll be *very* glad you decided to "waste" storage space on an automatic backup.

Restricting access to files and folders

Does your kid seem to know more than you do about manipulating files and folders on your computer? Your Storage Link can thwart the efforts of anyone in your house who wants to get unauthorized access to your stuff.

POWER USERS' CLINIC

Name or Serial Number?

Linksys assigns cryptic machine-generated names to its Network Storage Link devices, but the company also gives you the ability to *change* this license plate of a name to something that makes a little more sense on your own network. Especially if you plan on using the UNC method (page 113) to connect your network drives, having an easy-to-remember name can really help.

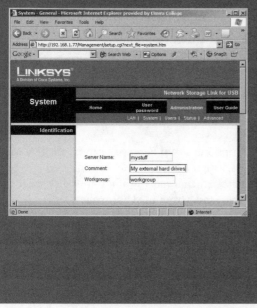

Follow these steps to change the name:

1. Connect to your Network Storage Link using a Web browser. Use the IP address you assigned to the unit earlier in this section (page 187 if you've got a Windows machine or page 188 if you're on a Mac). Browse to http://192.168.1.77 if you left the unit alone when you set it up.

2. Click on Administration to modify the Storage Link's configuration.

3. When prompted, enter an administrative user name and password. At the factory, Linksys provides a user name of "admin" with a password of "admin".

4. Click the System Link.

5. On the next screen, in the Server Name field, type the name you want for the unit as shown in this figure. Make it something easy to remember like "storage," "Netdisks," or "spock."

6. At the bottom of the window, click the Save button (not shown).

Now, rather than using a UNC name of \\F7VGH16237, you can use the easily remembered \\SPOCK or whatever you named your Storage Link.

Just like your Windows and Mac desktop computers, the Storage Link can be setup to restrict access based on *who* you are. The concept of user accounts discussed in Chapters 5 and 6 carries over to this device, but is implemented a little differently.

Note: If you need to refresh your memory about how to cre'ate users and groups, see page 82 (for Windows PCs) and page 122 (for Macs).

Before you learn about creating new personal accounts on your Storage Link, you should know that the device includes some accounts that are already included for you by Linksys. The main account, admin, can do *anything*, including create new files, delete files, and even erase a whole connected hard disk. This is the Grand Poobah of accounts on the device. In fact, having this account around is so important that you aren't allowed to delete it or change its access rights. It *always* has full privileges. The most you can do is change its password.

The second built-in account on the Storage Link is named "guest" and it's exactly what it sounds like. Guest isn't omnipotent like admin, and guest can only *use* the disks and their contents; the guest account can't make any configuration changes to the Storage Link itself. As with the admin account, you cannot delete the guest account.

The Storage Link's Web-based administration utility handles all these account-related chores. To get to this utility, follow these steps:

1. **Connect to your Storage Link using a Web browser.**

   Use the IP address you assigned to it earlier (page 187 if you've got a Windows machine or page 188 if you're on a Mac). Browse to *http://192.168.1.77* if you didn't make any changes when you set it up.

2. **Click on Administration to modify the Storage Link's configuration.**

3. **When prompted, enter an administrative user name and password.**

   Linksys supplies a user name of "admin" with a password of "admin".

4. **Click on Users.**

   The Users dialog box will open up, allowing you to manage all aspects of your user accounts.

The Users page includes a number of options. From here, you can create new users, delete existing users, change passwords, assign a *private folder* (a cloistered area for a particular user's files), or enforce a *quota*, which limits the amount of disk space that one user can hog. You can handle all these tasks from the Users page.

- **Creating a user.** On the User tab, in the Properties section (see Figure 8-13), type the user name and password of the new person in the proper fields. You can also enter a comment, such as "Fido's account" or something that helps you identify the user, but for very small networks, this usually isn't necessary.

- **Deleting a user.** This one is easy. Select the user's name from the list and click the Delete button.

While limiting access to data is a good way to protect it, nothing is better than actually copying the data so it resides in two places.

Backing up data on the Network Storage Link

You've probably heard the horror stories, like the time a friend of yours was almost done with a 600-page manuscript and his hard drive died. If you have important data that would be a disaster to lose, why not automatically store it in *two* places rather than one?

Your Storage Link can back you up with just a few clicks of the mouse. Of course, for this to work, you need two hard drives connected to your Storage Link and the disk connected to the "Disk 2" port has to be at least as large as Disk 1.

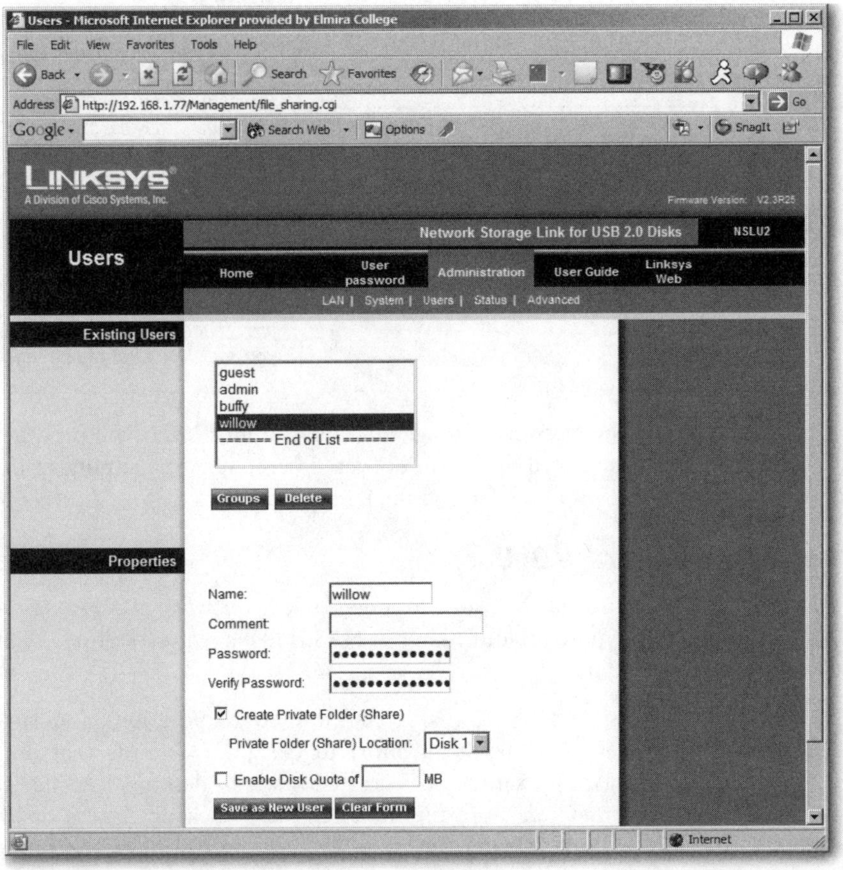

Figure 8-13:
If you want to give the person private space to store her files, turn on the checkbox "Create Private Folder (Share)" and also specify on which connected disk you want to have these files stored. When you connect to the Storage Link, you'll see a list of shares that includes a share named for the person (in this example, "willow") along with the rest of the shares.

1. **Connect to your Storage Link using a Web browser.**

   Use the IP address you assigned to the unit earlier in this section (page 187 if you've got a Windows machine or page 188 if you're on a Mac). Browse to *http://192.168.1.77* if you left the unit alone when you set it up.

2. **Click on Administration to modify the Storage Link's configuration.**

   When prompted, enter an administrative user name and password. At the factory, Linksys provides a user name of "admin" with a password of "admin".

3. **Click on Advanced.**

4. **Click on Backup.**

   The various options for backing up your configuration and data appear.

---

5. **Turn on the drive backup function.**

To automatically back up your data, follow the steps shown in Figure 8-14.

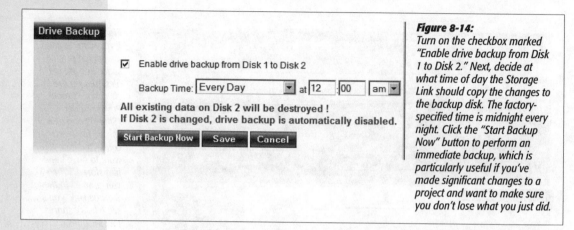

Figure 8-14:
Turn on the checkbox marked "Enable drive backup from Disk 1 to Disk 2." Next, decide at what time of day the Storage Link should copy the changes to the backup disk. The factory-specified time is midnight every night. Click the "Start Backup Now" button to perform an immediate backup, which is particularly useful if you've made significant changes to a project and want to make sure you don't lose what you just did.

For a device so small, the Network Storage Link does quite a lot. If you need help with something more advanced that wasn't covered here, open the administration tool using your Web browser and click on the User Guide link.

Other Network Storage Options

If you don't want to use the Network Storage Link, a *network-attached storage* (NAS) device might be more to your liking. A NAS is like a Network Storage Link with the hard drive built in.

Although these devices tend to be marketed more to corporations and small offices, some companies are making an effort to design NAS units that don't frighten civilians. Iomega, for example, has created a line of desktop NAS devices (*www.iomega.com/nas*) that can store files and remotely back up data from the computers on your network. Ximeta (*www.ximeta.com*) and Buffalo Technology (*www.buffalotech.com*) also offer NAS drives. They're not the cheapest things out there (prices start around $300 or so), but they do provide another storage option for your bustling home network.

Playing Video Games on Your Network

Even better than playing alone or with one other pal, many video game consoles let you connect them to your shiny new home network so you can play against the world by joining a *MMORPG* (which stands for Massively Multiplayer Online Role Playing Game). Rather than a few people in your house huddled around the TV, you get to join millions of other players around the globe in their gaming efforts.

Connecting your Xbox or PlayStation to your network isn't hard, but requires a little additional hardware, a dab of configuration, and the time to game.

The Microsoft Xbox

Microsoft's Xbox makes networking easy since it sports an Ethernet jack on its backside and has a number of network-enabled titles to its credit. Microsoft gives you two ways to connect your Xbox to your network: wired (you connect your Xbox to your router with an Ethernet cable) or wireless (you add a wireless network adapter (page 5) to your Xbox). Once you decide whether you want your Xbox tied (wired) or untied (wireless) you need do little configuring, as explained in the next few pages.

UP TO SPEED

Talking the Big Game

Online gamers live in a world separate from the one most mortals inhabit. As you play more and more games over the Internet, you may soon find yourself discovering new places to visit as well as a new vocabulary to express your feelings about it.

Here are some common gaming terms and what they mean:

- **Latency.** Latency is how long information takes to get from your home network to the servers running the game you're playing. In high-action gaming, short times (called *low latency*) are important because it allows players to respond more quickly to avoid losing. The lower the latency, the quicker the response. Players with very low latency figures (less than 100 milliseconds) are considered extremely fortunate. Latency is measured by using the *ping* command described next.

- **PING.** PING is an acronym that stands for Packet InterNetwork Groper; it was created a long time ago as a quick tool for network troubleshooting. PING has become both an adjective (the *ping* utility) and a verb ("Ping the server to see if it's still up"). The *ping* command provides you with numbers measuring how long it takes information to travel between your network and a specific computer on another network.

Ping results are always measured in milliseconds (ms), or one one-thousandth of a second. Sporting folk consider latency of 100 to 300 or so good for gaming. Ping is invoked from the command line available at Start → Programs → Command Prompt in older versions of Windows and at Start → All Programs → Accessories → Command Prompt in Windows XP. (Mac OS X people can ping away in living color with Applications → Network Utility → Ping.) Check with your game console maker for the URL to ping to determine your latency.

- **Lag.** As you might suspect, lag is a term that indicates that a game is running slowly or that there is high latency. A high lag time usually means that your multiplayer game will be short since someone with a lower latency will eventually *frag* you.

- **Frag.** Kill. To kill another player. Either way, someone's character is pushing up the cyberdaisies.

- **Player Killing (PKing).** The wholesale slaughtering of new player's characters to advance your own character. For obvious reasons, this practice is frowned upon and is sometimes not allowed by certain games.

- **Bots.** A "character" being controlled by another computer. Bot is short for *software robot*. These little automatic programs have been floating around the Internet for decades.

If you plan to use the online features of the Xbox (known as Xbox Live), you also need a subscription to the service. As of this writing, Microsoft boasts more than a million members on the Xbox Live service, so you'll probably find someone to play with.

There are a couple ways to get an Xbox Live subscription. First, you can drop by your local electronics superstore (or even your local Wal-Mart) and pick up a 12-month Xbox Live subscription package for around $50. If you'd rather test things out first, some Xbox Live–enabled games include a trial Xbox Live subscription code that provides two months of service. Once you've purchased an Xbox Live subscription, the next sections show you how to get your console ready to play games against the world.

Note: If you've got multiple Xboxes jacked into your network and just want to play against each other and skip the competition on the Internet, everyone doesn't need to cough up the cash for an Xbox Live package. You just need to pony up for one subscription and then everyone on your network can play against each other.

Connecting your Xbox to a wired network

One really nice thing about most wired network connections is that they're a snap to get configured. Your Xbox console is no different. To get the Xbox on your wired network, just plug one end of an Ethernet cable into the back of the console and the other end into your network's router or switch (page 6). The Xbox uses DHCP (page 25) to get the information it needs to network (Figure 8-15).

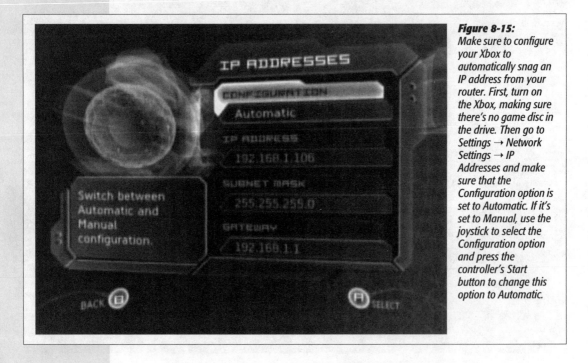

Figure 8-15:
Make sure to configure your Xbox to automatically snag an IP address from your router. First, turn on the Xbox, making sure there's no game disc in the drive. Then go to Settings → Network Settings → IP Addresses and make sure that the Configuration option is set to Automatic. If it's set to Manual, use the joystick to select the Configuration option and press the controller's Start button to change this option to Automatic.

Connecting your Xbox to a wireless network

Using a standard, fairly inexpensive device, you can convert your Xbox from its natural wired state and make it a part of your *wireless* network. Network wonks call this gadget an *Ethernet-to-wireless bridge.* A bridge is a device that seamlessly converts a signal between differing network types. In this case, the bridge enables the Xbox's wired Ethernet port to communicate with your wireless network.

Most home networking vendors, including Linksys, Netgear, and D-Link, sell Ethernet-to-wireless bridges. In the gaming world, many manufacturers refer to Ethernet-to-wireless bridges as *game adapters,* though, so be on the lookout for that name if you want to get your Xbox on a wireless network.

Note: Many people have reported good success with the Linksys WGA54G Game Adapter. It doesn't need special software to run, so it works with any game console. Since this is an 802.11g adapter, it will work with either your 802.11g or 802.11b home network. (Pop back to page 38 for a refresher on the difference between G and B.)

Making your Xbox work on your wireless network requires four things:

- An Xbox
- A configured and working wireless router (see Chapter 3 for details on how to set that up)
- An Ethernet-to-wireless bridge (a.k.a. a game adapter)
- In some cases, a Windows PC connected to the network

Needing a PC may seem like a mystery since you're working with an Xbox here, but you're not actually making configuration changes to your game console when you connect it to your wireless network. Instead, you're configuring the wireless bridge/game adapter; the management software included with most of these devices runs only on Windows.

The setup steps are pretty straightforward: use the software included with the wireless bridge/game adapter to set up the unit's SSID (page 53) and security configuration, such as WEP or WPA (page 54). Then use an Ethernet cable to connect the Xbox and the wireless bridge.

Finally, follow the steps in Figure 8-15 to make sure your Xbox shows up on your network. If it doesn't, make sure your cables are plugged in and verify the configuration of your game adapter to make sure it's set up properly, too.

Activating your Xbox Live subscription

You can, of course, use the Xbox all by yourself, but what's the fun in that when you've got a home network and a world full of gamers just a network connection away? In order to play head to head against other online Xbox buddies, you need to sign up for Microsoft's Xbox Live service.

To configure the Xbox Live subscription settings, follow these steps:

1. **Buy an Xbox Live subscription package.**

   Xbox Live subscription packages are available pretty much anywhere you can buy Xbox games, including places like Circuit City, Wal-Mart, and EB Games. The full package usually includes some sample games, the actual subscription (a code), and an *Xbox Communicator*—a set of headphones with a boom microphone that lets you talk to other players while you play games online.

2. **Get your Xbox on your network.**

   Follow the steps described in the previous two sections to make sure your Xbox is up and running on your home network.

3. **Connect the Xbox Communicator to your game controller (optional).**

   Since some games are easier to play when you're in contact with the other participants, consider using the Xbox Communicator to help thrash your opponents. The Xbox Communicator plugs into the top expansion slot on your Xbox controller.

4. **Insert an Xbox Live Online Enabled game into your Xbox console.**

   Make sure your game is built for online play, as only Xbox Live–enabled games can join the Xbox network.

5. **Select the Xbox Live option from the game's menu.**

   Exactly where you find this option changes depending on the game you're playing. In Figure 8-16, the Xbox Live option is right on the game's main menu.

Frag away! You're all set up with your Xbox Live subscription and can play games against millions worldwide!

The Sony PlayStation 2

Microsoft's Xbox is hardly the only entertainment in town. The Sony PlayStation 2 (PS2) has been around longer and has legions of devotees and a huge library of games. Even better, some of these games can be played online against other people, as long as you have the right hardware. (Good news for Xbox defectors: Sony doesn't charge you to play PS2 games online against other PS2 fans.)

Your PS2 console can connect to your home network in two different ways: wired (using an Ethernet cable to make the connection) or wirelessly (using WiFi signals in conjunction with a special adapter).

Note: Older versions of the PS2 didn't come with a built-in Ethernet port. If you've got an older PS2, fear not: page 205 tells you everything you need to do to make your console network-ready

Connecting your PlayStation 2 to a wired network

Joining your PS2 to a wired (Ethernet) network requires the following items:

- A PS2

- An Ethernet cable to connect the PS2 to your router

- The PS2 startup CD that came with your console (to help configure your network settings)

- An 8-megabyte memory card to store some of the network settings you configure

The configuration steps are pretty straightforward. Plug the memory card into the PS2 and then use the Ethernet cable to connect your PS2 to your router or a switch (page 6). Pop in the PS2 startup CD and then follow the instructions for creating and saving the network settings.

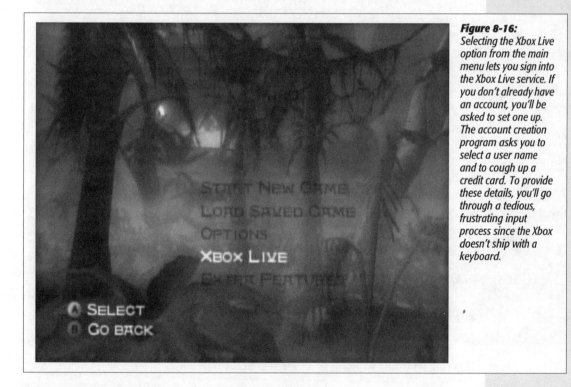

Figure 8-16:
Selecting the Xbox Live option from the main menu lets you sign into the Xbox Live service. If you don't already have an account, you'll be asked to set one up. The account creation program asks you to select a user name and to cough up a credit card. To provide these details, you'll go through a tedious, frustrating input process since the Xbox doesn't ship with a keyboard.

Connecting your PlayStation 2 to a wireless network

Like the Xbox, the PS2 doesn't come with built-in wireless capability. Fortunately, as with the Xbox, it's pretty easy to add a wireless adapter to the PS2 so it can hop on your wireless network. All you need is an *Ethernet-to-wireless bridge,* a device that seamlessly converts a signal between differing network types. In this case, the bridge enables the PS2's wired Ethernet port to communicate with your wireless network. (In the world of game consoles, these bridges are sometimes called *game adapters.*)

Most home networking vendors, including Linksys, Netgear, and D-Link, sell Ethernet-to-wireless bridges. Many people have reported success with the Linksys WGA54G Game Adapter. It doesn't need special software to run, so it works with any game console. Since this is an 802.11g adapter, it will work with either your 802.11g or 802.11b home network. (Pop back to page 38 for a refresher on the differences between G and B.).

TROUBLESHOOTING MOMENT

DNAS -611 Error

When you see this error, it usually results from some kind of problem related to automatic IP address assignment. For whatever reason, your PS2 console can't use its DHCP-assigned IP address to communicate with the Internet. (See page 25 for a recap of DHCP basics.)

The solution? You just need to assign a static (manual) IP address to your PS2, and you're on your way. Static IP address assignment isn't that hard. First, you need to pick an IP address that works.

One way to find a compatible IP address on your network is to have a look on one of your PCs and see what *it's* using. After all, if it's working, it must have a kosher IP address, right?

From a Windows XP computer, go to Start → Run, type *cmd* in the Open box, and press OK. At the resulting command prompt, type *ipconfig /all* and press Enter. The illustration shows the results of your search.

In the figure, the computer's IP address is 192.168.1.103. The first three parts of the IP address, (192.168.1) are what make an IP address work with your network. Choose an IP address that starts with these numbers (or whatever numbers your computer spits out). For the last digit, select a number between 2 and 100 or between 200 and 254.

The other information you'll need, the Subnet Mask, Default Gateway, and the DNS Servers' IP addresses, are also here. (Page 26 tells you what all these terms mean, if you're interested.) Write these down since your PS2 asks for this information as well. For these numbers, use them exactly as you see them on your screen.

To provide your PS2 with static IP addressing information, choose the Advanced setup option from the ISP Setup menu. Enter an IP address that you know will work on your network. Note that the netmask and default router entries are also required. The netmask field is the same as your computer's Subnet Mask field and is almost always 255.255.255.0 on a home network.

The next screen asks you for your DNS server IP addresses. Enter them as well and you should be all set up with a manual address and ready to test your connection again.

```
C:\ C:\WINDOWS\system32\cmd.exe                          _ □ ×

Ethernet adapter Wireless Network Connection:

        Connection-specific DNS Suffix  :
        Description . . . . . . . . . . . : Dell TrueMobile 1300 WLAN Mini-PCI
        Physical Address. . . . . . . . . : 00-90-4B-77-C4-8D
        Dhcp Enabled. . . . . . . . . . . : Yes
        Autoconfiguration Enabled . . . . : Yes
        IP Address. . . . . . . . . . . . : 192.168.1.103
        Subnet Mask . . . . . . . . . . . : 255.255.255.0
        Default Gateway . . . . . . . . . : 192.168.1.1
        DHCP Server . . . . . . . . . . . : 192.168.1.1
        DNS Servers . . . . . . . . . . . : 24.92.226.238
                                            24.92.226.98
        Lease Obtained. . . . . . . . . . : Sunday, November 11, 2004 2:43:35 PM
        Lease Expires . . . . . . . . . . : Tuesday, November 13, 2004 2:43:35 PM
C:\>
```

Making your PS2 work on your wireless network requires the following items:

- A PS2 with a network adapter (that's where you'll plug the bridge into)

- The PS2 startup CD that came with your console (to help configure your network settings)

- An 8-megabyte memory card to store some of the network settings you'll configure

- A configured and working wireless router (page 39 shows how to set that up)

- An Ethernet-to-wireless bridge plus an Ethernet cable

- In some cases, a Windows PC connected to the network

You may wonder why you need a PC since you're configuring the PS2. But you're not actually making changes to your game console when you connect it to your wireless network. Instead, you're configuring the wireless bridge; the management software included with most of these devices only runs on Windows.

The setup steps are pretty straightforward. Use the software included with the wireless bridge to set up the unit's SSID (page 53) and security configuration, such as WEP or WPA (page 54). Then use an Ethernet cable to connect the PS2 and the wireless bridge. Finally, insert the memory card and the CD into the PS2 and follow the network setup instructions that come with the CD.

Note: Although the PlayStation 2 console debuted before home networking really took off, Sony made sure to include wireless networking in its latest handheld entertainment device. The Sony PSP (short for PlayStation Portable), which can play movies, music, *and* games, comes ready for 802.11b action right out of the box.

Adding an Ethernet adapter (older PlayStation 2s only)

If you've got an older PS2 (generally any model sold before the fall of 2004), you'll first need to add a Sony-made network adapter to the PS2 before you can connect your console to a wired or wireless network. (Don't try using one of the generic network adapters you learned about in Part 1 of this book; you need to buy Sony's adapter for this to work.)

Note: The PS2 network adapter gives your console two ports. The first is a standard Ethernet port; the second is a telephone modem jack. This book discusses only the high-speed Ethernet connection.

To install the network adapter, follow these steps:

1. **Buy a network adapter, an 8-megabyte memory card, and an Ethernet cable (page 17).**

   The adapter is officially called the "Network Adaptor (Ethernet/modem)(for PlayStation2)." The memory card goes by an equally bureaucratic name: "Memory Card (8MB) for PlayStation2." You can pick up this gear at most big electronics stores like Circuit City, Wal-Mart, and EB Games.

2. **Turn off your PS2.**

   Make sure the console is off before upgrading it, or you could damage the components.

3. **Remove the expansion bay cover from the back of your PS2.**

   The expansion bay cover has a small indentation at the top; wedge in a small finger or a coin to pry the cover off. Once you have the cover partially removed, just pull it the rest of the way out with your fingers.

---

4. **Attach the network adapter to your PS2.**

Remove the plastic cover from the network adapter's console connector. Line up the console connector with the matching jack on the PS2. This will also align the connecting screws with the holes on the PS2's expansion slot.

5. **Fasten the connecting screws.**

Using a coin, tighten the connecting screws on the network adapter until snug.

6. **Insert your memory card.**

7. **Connect your PS2 to your network.**

Use the Ethernet cable to connect your PS2 to your router. If you want to connect your PS2 to a WiFi network, pop back up to page 203 and follow the instructions for buying and configuring the Ethernet-to-wireless bridge. Once you've got the bridge connected to your PS2, come back here and move on to step 8.

8. **Insert the network adapter startup CD into your PS2.**

This CD contains all of the software you need in order to update your PS2 console so that it can recognize the new network adapter.

9. **Select ISP Setup from the main menu.**

The ISP Setup option lets you specify the settings that let your PS2 console work on your home network.

10. **Accept the license agreement.**

Gaming consoles aren't immune to bossy end user license agreements(EULAs).

11. **Select Local Area Network (LAN).**

From the Connect to the Internet screen, select the Local Area Network (LAN) option.

12. **Select Automatic Configuration.**

For most people, Automatic Configuration using DHCP (page 25) is the easiest way to get the PS2 on your network. This option automatically gives the PS2 a network address so you can get to gaming.

If you're using static IP addresses (Sony calls them "manual" IP addresses) on your home network, select the Advanced Setup option instead and follow the instructions in the "DNAS -611 Error" box on page 204 to learn how to configure a static IP address.

13. **Choose the Test Settings option.**

Before saving your configuration, you need to test your settings to make sure everything works as it should. Choose the Test Settings option from the Connect Test screen to make sure your PlayStation 2 can communicate with the Internet.

If the test is successful, your PlayStation 2 will tell you so. If you get an error message, see the "DNAS -611 Error" box for some potential fixes.

14. **If your test was successful, choose Continue.**

Choosing Continue now saves your network configuration.

When you're done, your PS2 asks you to register your new network adapter. Wired or wireless, you can now join the great big massive multiplayer online role-playing game of your choice.

Note: Nintendo, the third big member in the Game Console Club, also has networking options for its GameCube machine that work in a similar manner to networked Xboxes and PlayStation 2 systems. You can find information on multiplayer network gaming for most of Nintendo's game machines, (including the Nintendo DS handheld console that comes with built-in wireless networking) at *www.nintendo.com/connectgcn.*

Using Your Network on the Road

Your home network doesn't have to be restricted to your home. Assuming you can tear yourself away from the networked fun you learned about in Chapter 8, the time may come when you're out of the house and want to hop back onto your home network. Perhaps you need a document, want to hear a favorite song, or just want to enjoy the pure geek thrill of creating a folder on your desktop PC from 3,000 miles away. Good news: using the Internet as the world's longest extension cord, you can tap into your networked computers using a variety of tools. Some of these methods are for hard-core computer lovers, but many new methods are now available that make this whole world of *remote access*—connecting long distance from one computer to another—pretty easy for the average civilian.

To help you keep the roles of the various computers involved in a remote access operation straight, the computer industry has done you the favor of introducing specialized terminology—and learning these terms now will help keep your brain from tying itself in knots:

- The *host computer* is the home-base computer—the one that's sitting there, waiting for you to connect to it. It could be your office computer (if you connect to it from home) or your home computer (if you connect to it from your laptop on the road).

- The *remote computer* is the one that will do the connecting: your laptop on the road, for example, or your home machine when you tap into the office network.

The remote access tools that are available and the ways in which they work differ depending on which operating system you're using. This chapter takes you through a variety of procedures and shows you how to use them all.

Connecting to Your Windows PCs

If you've got one or more Windows machines on your home network, you may come to treasure the different ways Windows gives you for connecting when you're on the road. Each of these systems requires a bit of setup and some scavenging through the technical underbrush, and each offers slightly different features. But when you're in Tulsa and a spreadsheet you need is on your PC in Tallahassee, you'll be grateful to have at least one of these systems in place.

Note: You can also use these tools to dial into your office PC, but you'll first need to check with your company's technology crew to make sure they allow such access.

The next few sections cover two different methods, but here's a quick summary:

- **Dialing direct.** You can dial directly from your laptop to a PC at home, modem to modem, and join your home network. At that point, you can access shared folders exactly as described in Chapter 5. The downside: your PC at home has to have its own phone line that only it answers. Otherwise, its modem will answer every incoming phone call, occasionally blasting the ears of hapless human callers.

- **GoToMyPC.** This Web-based service doesn't just connect your laptop to the network at home. It actually turns your laptop *into* the PC at home, filling your screen with its screen image. When you touch the trackpad on your laptop, you're actually moving the cursor on your screen at home. Plus, you're not limited to a clunky dial-up connection; GoToMyPC works from any Internet-connected computer (including a Mac).

Using Dialing Direct

To set up your home PC to make it ready for access from the road, you first must prepare it to answer calls. Then you need to set up the laptop to dial out.

Setting Up the Home PC

If your PC at home has its own private phone line—the lucky thing—here's how to prepare it for remote access.

1. **Choose Start → Control Panel. In the Control Panel window, double-click Network Connections.**

   You see the icons for the various network connections you've created.

2. **In the task pane at the left side of the window, click "Create a new connection."**

   As you might have predicted, something called the New Connection Wizard appears (Figure 9-1, top).

3. **Click Next. On the next screen, click "Set up an advanced connection," and then click Next.**

   Now the Advanced Connections Options screen appears.

4. **Ensure that the "Accept incoming connections" option is selected (Figure 9-1, middle). Then click Next.**

Now you're shown a list of the communication equipment your PC has—including its modem.

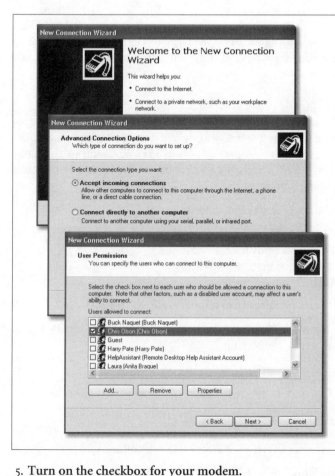

Figure 9-1:
The New Connection Wizard is the key to setting up direct dialing. To set it up, you answer its questions once on the home-base computer, and again on the laptop (or whatever machine you'll use to dial in).

Top: The welcome screen.

Middle: The all-important "Accept incoming connections" option on the Advanced Connection Options screen (which is what makes your PC answer the phone)

Bottom: The User Permissions screen, where you indicate which account holders are allowed to dial in.

5. **Turn on the checkbox for your modem.**

At this point, you could also click the Properties button and, in the resulting dialog box, turn on "Disconnect a call if idle for more than _ _ minutes." Doing so makes sure that your home PC won't tie up the line after your laptop in the hotel room is finished going about its business. Click OK.

6. **Click Next. Leave "Do not allow virtual private connections" selected, and then click Next.**

As shown in Figure 9-1 at bottom, you're now looking at a list of every account holder on your PC (see page 82 for more about setting up accounts).

7. **Turn on the checkboxes corresponding to the people who should be allowed to dial into this home PC.**

Don't turn on Guest because doing so creates a welcome mat for hackers.

If you highlight a name and then click Properties, you can turn on the *callback* feature—a security feature that, after you've dialed in, makes your home PC hang up and call you back at a number that you've previously specified. (This system rules out the possibility that some teenager in Germany is tapping into your network, having somehow figured out your name and password.) Click OK to close the dialog box.

8. **Click Next.**

You're shown a list of networking protocols that Windows XP will make available to you when you call in. In general, you should simply confirm that all the checkboxes are turned on. (The Properties button may be useful to the paranoid, however; it lets you limit a remote caller to just this particular PC, instead of having full access to the network.)

9. **Click Next again, and then click the Finish button.**

A new icon in your Network Connections window called Incoming Connections, is born. Your home-base PC is ready for connections.

Setting Up the Laptop

Now pick up your laptop and get it ready to phone home. Here's what to do:

1. **Choose Start → My Network Places. At the left side of the My Network Places window, click "Create a new connection."**

The New Connection Wizard appears.

2. **Click Next. Select "Connect to the network at my workplace," and then click Next.**

Now Windows wants to know if you'll be connecting via modem ("Dial-up connection") or via Internet ("Virtual Private Network connection").

3. **Click "Dial-up connection," and then click Next. Type a name for your connection (like "Phone home"), and then click Next. Type a phone number for the line your home PC is connected to, and then click Next again.**

You'll have an opportunity to specify area codes and dialing codes later.

4. **On the final screen, turn on "Add a shortcut to this connection to my desktop," and then click the Finish button.**

The stage is set. Book your flight, check in, and hook up the laptop to a phone jack.

Making the Call

Once you're prepared to phone home, follow these steps:

1. **Tell Windows where you are.**

   If your area code has changed, open the Phone and Modem Options icon in your control panel. Specify your current location, complete with whatever fancy dialing numbers are required by it. Click the current location and then click OK. Now Windows knows what area code and prefixes to use.

2. **Double-click the shortcut icon you created in the previous step 4.**

   If it isn't on your desktop, you'll also find it in your Network Connections window (which you can open from the control panel). The dialog box shown in Figure 9-2 appears.

Figure 9-2:
You're ready to phone home.

3. Type in a Windows user name and password, and double-check the phone number.

4. Click Dial.

   That's all there is to it. Windows dials into your home PC, makes the connection, and—if the phone number, name, and password are all correct—shows you a balloon on your taskbar (Figure 9-3, top).

You're free to open up any shared folders, even use shared printers, on your network back home. And although it may make your brain hurt to contemplate it, you can even surf the Internet if your home PC has, say, a cable modem. (Don't try to run any *programs* that reside on your home PC, however; you'll be old and gray by the time they even finish opening.)

When you're finished with your address lookup, document transfer, or whatever, right-click the little network icon in your notification area and choose Disconnect from the shortcut menu (Figure 9-3, bottom).

Note: If you're having trouble connecting, confirm that the name and password you're using are correct—that's the number-one source of problems. If the remote system still doesn't recognize you, click the Properties button in the dialog box shown in Figure 9-3. On the General tab, make sure that your laptop's dialing the right number; on the Networking tab, confirm that all the checkboxes are turned on.

Figure 9-3:
Top: Congratulations—you're in. (When two 56K modems connect, alas, they're limited to the top uploading speed of either—and that's about 33K.)

Bottom: Disconnect by right-clicking the notification-area icon. (The Xed-out network icon shown here, by the way, represents the office Ethernet cable that's currently disconnected from this laptop, which is in a hotel room somewhere.)

Using GoToMyPC

GoToMyPC (*www.gotomypc.com*) lets you remotely access one Windows computer from any other computer using nothing more than a standard Web browser. You can take the reins of any *Windows* computer using GoToMyPC. That's the good news. The bad news…it isn't free.

Using GoToMyPC, you can control a single PC from afar for $19.95 a month—or $179.40, if you prepay for a full year. Controlling additional PCs costs more, but not an additional $19.95 a month. GoToMyPC only charges you for each host PC you set up. You're free to access your host PC from as many different remote PCs that you like. (Pop back to page 209 for a quick refresher on the difference between host and remote PCs.)

Tip: If you're not sure that GoToMyPC is worth it, you can sign up for a 30-day trial that lets you test drive the service. There's a sneaky little catch to this "30-day" business, though: the total amount of time you can actually *use* the trial service is 60 minutes, and that 60 minutes runs out after just 30 days. It's not the most generous demo offer in the world, but at least you'll get an idea of what you can do with GoToMyPC.

Getting started with GoToMyPC involves a few steps, none of which are particularly complicated. First, you need to create an account at GoToMyPC.com. Then you need to download and install a special program on your host PC. Finally, from the remote computer, you need to download another program that lets you control the host PC. The next few sections explain everything in detail.

Tip: You might want to check out the Microsoft alternative, Remote Desktop Connection (*http://support. microsoft.com/?kbid=313292*). It's not Web-based (so you need to install the software on both the host and remote computers), but it's free, and the remote part works if you're stuck on a Mac. For more details, see: *http://www.microsoft.com/mac/otherproducts/otherproducts.aspx?pid=remotedesktopclient*.

FREQUENTLY ASKED QUESTION

On the Mac Track

Does GoToMyPC.com support Macintosh computers?

Yes and no.

GoToMyPC does not currently support Macs as *host* computers. That is, you can't remotely control a Macintosh computer from another machine via this service. However, you can use a Macintosh to *control* a Windows PC set up as a host computer.

This is not to say that the service will never let you control a Mac remotely. GoToMyPC says that support for Macintosh hosts may come sometime in the future.

Signing Up and Installing GoToMyPC

To start the sign-up process, visit *www.gotomypc.com* and click either the Try It Free button or the Buy Now button. The next screen asks for your name and email address and then, on the next screen, you create a password. You'll use your email address and password later on, when you want to connect from the remote computer. Finally, you need to enter your credit card information.

Note: You might wonder why you need to provide a credit card for a *free* trial. This question is so common that GoToMyPC puts the canned answer right at the top of the payment page: after your free trial is over, the company "renews" your membership at the $19.95 rate. It's obviously a little on the shady side to bill like this, but you can get out of this renewal clause by calling GoToMyPC customer service at (888) 259-3826.

Once GoToMyPC's servers have verified your good name and credit card information, your registration is complete and you're presented with a Web page reminding you that you should be at your host PC (that is, the one you want to access when you're away from home). On that Web page, click the Install GoToMyPC button and then follow the installation instructions below.

1. **Download the GoToMyPC program.**

   When you click the GoToMyPC button, one of two things will happen. If *Java* (a programming language used to write software that runs on many different computer platforms) is already installed and working on your PC, the download process is push-button quick.

A large gray box appears, asking you if it's okay to install the GoToMyPC software. Click Yes or Grant in this box (Citrix, which is the name you see on the security certificate you're looking at, is the company that runs the GoToMyPC service). Next, a progress -1bar appears letting you know that you're now "Downloading" the software on your host machine. Wait for the download to complete. The InstallShield Wizard appears, and you're ready to move on to step 2.

If for some reason Java isn't working on your system, you get a message saying "The automatic download has failed. Click here to download the software." Click the green underlined word "here" and you see another window with a Download button, which you should click. Once the file has arrived on your system, close your browser window and double-click the downloaded file to begin installing the software. The Install Program window appears.

2. **On the InstallShield Wizard window, press the Next button.**

   This starts the actual software installation on your computer.

3. **Choose "No, I will restart my computer later."**

   For the GoToMyPC software to support *Fast User Switching* (a Windows XP feature that lets you provide accounts to all members of your family and use them simultaneously), you *do* need to restart your computer. However, if you don't need to let another user log in for a while, don't restart now—you can do it manually later on instead.

4. **Click Finish.**

   Click the Finish button to complete the installation. The GoToMyPC software then automatically starts a program that verifies that a good connection can be made between your host PC and the GoToMyPC Web site. A dialog box appears asking you to enter your email address and the password you created.

5. **Type in your email address and password.**

   Use the same email address and password you used when you signed up at the GoToMyPC.com Web site. This part of the installation logs you into your GoToMyPC.com account.

6. **Enter a nickname and create an access code for this host computer.**

   The computer's nickname appears on the GoToMyPC.com site when you log in later on. The access code helps provide additional protection for your host PC, as explained in Figure 9-4.

7. **Restart your computer.**

   Your host computer is now ready to be controlled when you're away from home.

Controlling Your Host PC from Another Computer

You can wait until you go away to set up your remote PC. But, considering Murphy's Law, why not test out how the GoToMyPC service works while you're still at home? All you need is any computer that's not your host PC. Whenever you're ready to get connected, follow these steps:

1. **Fire up a Web browser and visit the GoToMyPC.com Web site. Enter your email address and password and click Log In.**

   The nickname of the host computer that you just finished setting up appears.

Figure 9-4:
The nickname is useful pretty much only if you've installed GoToMyPC on multiple PCs. The access code, however, is important. It prevents someone from unauthorized use of your computer, even if she manages to log into your GoToMyPC.com Web account. For the best protection, use a password that's different from the one you used when you initially created an account on GoToMyPC.com.

2. **Click the Connect button.**

   The GoToMyPC viewing software (called the Universal Viewer), which you'll use to remotely control your host computer, loads itself into the remote PC's Web browser. Once the Universal Viewer has gotten itself settled in—the process may take a minute or so, depending on the speed of your Internet connection—you see the desktop of your host PC inside the remote PC's browser (Figure 9-5).

Note: If you don't have Java installed on the remote PC, you'll need the host PC's access code (which you created back on page 216).

---

3. **Hello, host computer!**

   The desktop of your host PC appears in a window on your remote computer Transferring Files and Printing with GoToMyPC.

Now that you've got GoToMyPC up and running, here are a few ways you can put it to work.

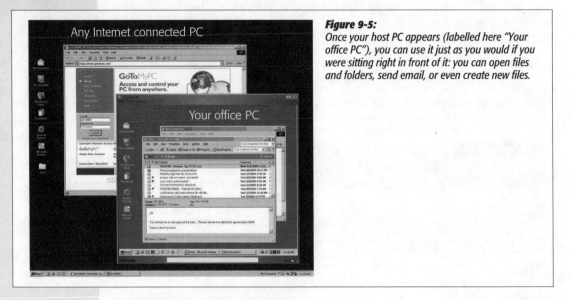

Figure 9-5:
Once your host PC appears (labelled here "Your office PC"), you can use it just as you would if you were sitting right in front of it: you can open files and folders, send email, or even create new files.

Transferring files with GoToMyPC

Having a GoToMyPC account is like having a full-time secretary waiting for you at home, when you're on the road. Here's how to use your virtual assistant to help transfer files *from* the host PC *to* the remote computer.

1. **Connect to the host computer.**

    Connect just as you did before, by following steps 1 and 2 in the previous list.

2. **From the GoToMyPC Universal Viewer menu, select Tools → Transfer Files.**

    The File Transfer window opens.

3. **Copy the file from the host PC to the remote computer.**

    The host PC's folders are listed on the left side of the File Transfer window, while the remote PC's are listed on the right. To navigate to different folders on either PC, click the pull-down menu on the right side of the folder you're currently in (see Figure 9-6, which also shows how to move a file from one PC to another).

Tip: The GoToMyPC file transfer tool can copy files between your host and your remote computer.

You can see from Figure 9-6 that you can perform a few more tricks than simply copying files. You can create, delete, and rename folders, too. To create a folder, click anywhere in the left or right pane, (depending on where you want to create the folder). Then click "Create a New Folder," and give the folder a name. After a couple seconds, the new folder appears in whatever window you selected.

To rename or delete folders, select the folder and choose the Rename or Delete options. Be especially careful when you're deleting folders. Having both computers showing on the screen at the same time can be confusing, and you don't want to delete the wrong folder by mistake.

You can even transfer the entire contents of a folder from one computer to the other. When you select a folder on one of your computers, in the Tasks box, the Transfer This File option automatically changes to Transfer This Folder. If you're transferring large files, be patient. Keep in mind that you're transferring files over Internet connections, which may not be as fast as you'd like.

Navigate to different folders

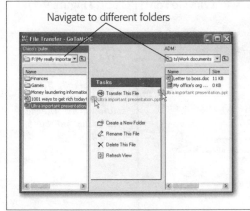

Figure 9-6:
Once you've selected the folder containing the file you want to copy, you can copy it in one of two ways: you can highlight the file and then click Transfer This File in the Tasks box, or you can drag the file, as shown here.

Printing with GoToMyPC

You've probably already figured out that printing can be something of a logistical challenge while you're using GoToMyPC. After all, wouldn't it make sense that anything you print on the host computer would appear on the printer *next to* the host computer (assuming of course there was a printer there)?

Luckily, the good people at GoToMyPC figured out this brain-bender early on and came up with a convenient solution. After you do a little configuring, anything you print while connected to the host computer will print to a printer connected to the remote computer.

This trick, of course, requires one important ingredient (aside from GoToMyPC): you need to have a printer already attached to the remote computer. If you've got that, then you're ready to follow these next steps:

1. **Start up a GoToMyPC connection from the remote computer (page 209).**

2. **From the GoToMyPC viewer menu, select Tools → Set Up Printer.**

   This opens the Printer Selection dialog box.

3. **Select the printer you want to use.**

   From the drop-down list, select a printer connected to the remote computer. The Windows Add Printer Wizard starts on the host computer. At this point, you need to install the correct printer-driver software on the *host* machine so it can print to your nearby printer.

4. **On the "Local or Network Printer" screen, select "Local printer attached to this computer."**

   Even though you're printing over the Internet, the GoToMyPC service will add software that makes the printer right next to you look just like it's directly connected to your host computer back home.On this same screen, make sure to turn off the checkbox next to "Automatically detect and install my Plug and Play printer."

5. **On the Select a Printer Port screen, select the GoToMyPC port (Figure 9-7).**

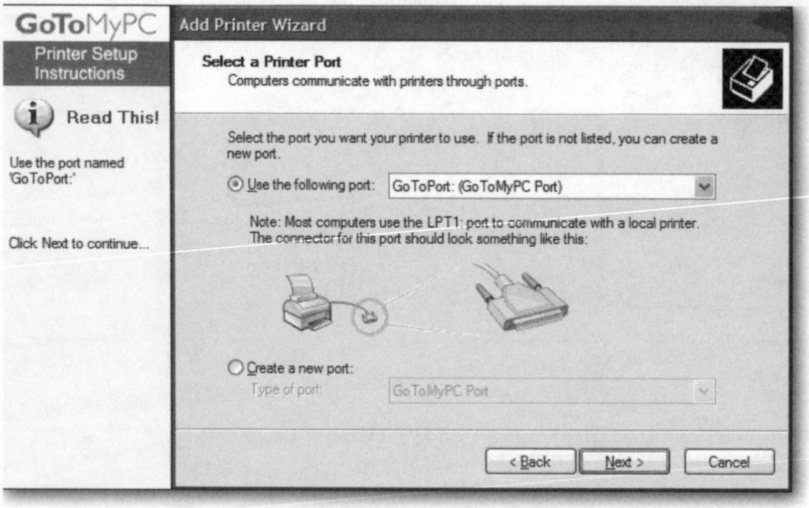

Figure 9-7:
The GoToMyPC port option should come up automatically. If it doesn't, click the down arrow in the "Use the following port" box to find it.

6. **On the Install Printer Software screen, find and select the make and model of your nearby printer.**

   This is definitely the hardest part of the installation, because your host computer might not have the driver software for the printer connected to you current computer. If this is the case, use the Web browser on the host computer to download the driver software (page 108) for the printer connected to the remote PC.

   For example, if the remote PC is currently connected to a Xerox Phaser 8400, use the Web browser on the host computer to visit *www.xerox.com*; once there, click the Support & Drivers link, find the Phaser 8400 in the list, and click the link to download the printer driver for your host PC.

Tip: If you can't find your printer in the list on the Install Printer Software screen, select the HP LaserJet Series II printer from the list instead. Many of today's printers still understand the language used by the old, reliable HP LaserJet Series II. You won't be able to use your newer printer's advanced features like duplex and color printing but you'll be able to print perfectly good basic text.

In the remaining steps in your printer installation adventure, you need to name your new printer (the wizard helpfully suggests a name starting with GoTo-MyPC to help you keep track of it later on) and decide whether to share this printer with other people.

After you've been off to see the wizard, the documents you print from your host computer should slide right into the paper holder on the printer next to you, wherever you and that printer happen to be. Just make sure, when you print, you select the GoToMyPC printer.

Connecting to Your Macs

Email and Web surfing may be the most popular Internet activities, but the world's most gigantic network can also help you stay in touch with your Macs back home when you're on the road. Mac OS X offers a few tools for manipulating your Macs, including remote access technologies like long-distance file sharing and SSH (a geeks-only program that you'll learn more about in a moment).

Note: These techniques are designed for full-time Internet connections (cable modem or DSL, for example). If you have a dial-up modem, these features work only when you're actually online. Still, they may occasionally be useful even when you're not. You could always call up a friend and say, "Check out my Web site right now–here's the current IP address" or call someone back home to say, "I have to grab a file off my hard drive. Could you make the Mac on my desk go online?"

Using the Mac's File Sharing Tool

You can tap into your Mac's regular File Sharing feature (Chapter 6) from over the Internet. This feature is a blessing to anyone who travels, whether with a laptop or to a branch office, because you'll never be up the creek without a paddle if you discover that you left an important file at home.

To connect over the Internet, make sure that you've set up the home-base Mac for file sharing, as explained in Chapter 6. Then, once you're on the road, go online and proceed like this:

1. **Choose Go → Connect To Server.**

   The Connect To Server dialog box appears, as shown in Figure 9-8.

2. **Type in the IP address (or domain name) of the Mac to which you want to connect, and then click Connect (or press Enter).**

   If you don't know the shared Mac's IP address, pick up the phone and call somebody who's at home. That person can find out the IP address by opening the Network pane (or Sharing pane) of System Preferences.

   And if you've signed up for a DNS naming service as described in the box "IP Addresses and You," you can type your Mac's domain name instead.

---

3. **Enter your name and password, and then click Connect.**

From here, it's just as though you were connecting to another computer on your office network, although it's a good bit slower. But when you're in Hong Kong and need a document from your Mac in Minneapolis, you may not care.

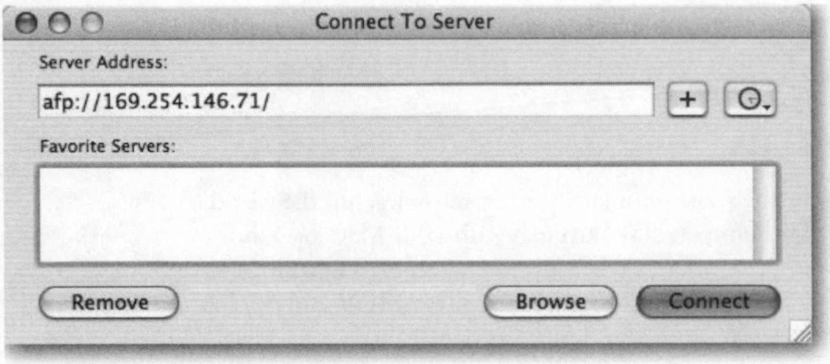

Figure 9-8:
The Connect To Server dialog box lets you type in the IP address for the shared Mac to which you want access.

Tip: Two other programs worth checking out if you're a Mac owner with some serious remote access needs: Timbuktu Pro (*www.netopia.com*) and VNC (*www.realvnc.com*), both of which also work with Windows.

Remote Access with SSH

Are you a geek? Take this simple test at home. Do you get excited about Mac OS X's ability to permit SSH access?

If you answered "What's SSH?" or "I'm *already* being quiet," then the following discussion of Unix remote control may not interest you. To be sure, SSH is not a program with a graphic user interface (icons and menus). You operate it from within a program like Terminal (the Mac's Unix-based control system) by typing commands.

If you're willing to overlook that little peccadillo, though, SSH (Secure Shell) is an extremely powerful tool. It lets you connect to your Mac from anywhere—from across the network or across the Internet. And once you're connected, you can take complete control of your machine, copying files, running commands, rearranging folders, or even shutting it down, all by remote control.

Getting In

Here's how you go about using SSH:

1. **Set up your Mac by opening the Sharing panel of System Preferences, and then turning on the Remote Login checkbox.**

You've just told the Mac it's OK for you (or other people with accounts on your machine) to connect from the road. Quit System Preferences.

2. **Go away.**

You can move to another machine on the network, or another computer on the Internet. Once you're online with that other machine, you can contact your home-base machine from within a program like Terminal.

UP TO SPEED

IP Addresses and You

Every computer connected to the Internet, even temporarily, has its own exclusive *IP address* (IP stands for Internet Protocol). What's yours? Open the Sharing pane of System Preferences to find out. As you'll see, an IP address is always made up of four numbers separated by periods.

Some Macs with broadband Internet connections have a permanent, unchanging address called a *static* IP address. Clearly, life is simpler if you have a static IP address, because other computers will always know where to find you.

Most other Macs get assigned a new address each time they connect (a *dynamic* IP address). That's virtually always the case, for example, when you connect using a dial-up modem. (If you can't figure out whether your Mac has a dynamic or fixed address, ask your Internet service provider.)

You might suppose that Mac fans with dynamic addresses can't use any of the remote-connection technologies described in this chapter. After all, your Mac's Web address *changes* every time you connect, making it impossible to provide a single, permanent address to your friends and co-workers.

The answer is a *dynamic DNS service* that gives your Mac a name, not a number. Whenever you're online, these free services automatically update the IP address associated with the name you've chosen (such as *haroldandmaude. dyndns.org*), so that your friends and colleagues can memorize a single address for your machine.

To sign up for one of these services, just go to their Web sites—*www.dyndns.org, www.dhs.org, www.dtdns.com, www.hn.org, www.no-ip.com,* and so on.

You'll also need to download and run a utility called an *update client,* which contacts your DNS service and keeps it up to date with your latest IP address, regularly and automatically. Check your DNS service's Web site for a list of compatible update clients.

Once you've got a fixed DNS name associated with your Mac, you'll be able to access it from elsewhere (provided it's online at the time) via File Sharing, or the SSH method described later in this chapter.

(If you have a fixed address, you can also pay a few dollars a year to register your own *domain name,* a bona fide address like *www.yournamehere.com.* To register one—or to find out if the name you want is taken—visit a site like *www.networksolutions.com.*)

Tip: It doesn't have to be Terminal, and it doesn't have to be a Mac. You can get SSH client programs for almost any kind of computer, including Windows and Mac OS 9. To find SSH programs, visit *www. versiontracker.com,* click the appropriate operating system tab, and search for SSH.

---

3. **At the $ prompt, type** *ssh -l chris 111.222.3.44.* **Press Enter.**

Instead of *chris,* substitute your short account name (as you're known on the Mac you're tapping into), and replace the phony IP address shown here with your real one. (If your Mac back home has a domain name unto itself, such as macmania.com, you can type that instead of the IP address.)

If all goes well, the *ssh* command acknowledges your first successful connection by displaying a message like this: "The authenticity of host '74.120.15.36 (74.120.15.36)' can't be established. RSA key fingerprint is d9:f4:11:b0:27:1a: f1: 14:c3:cd:25:85:2b:78:4d:e7. Are you sure you want to continue connecting (yes/ no)?" (This message won't appear on subsequent connections.) You're seeing SSH's security features at work.

4. **Type *yes* and press Enter.**

Now you see one more note: "Warning: Permanently added '74.120.15.36' (RSA) to the list of known hosts." You're then asked for your account password.

5. **Type your account password and press Enter.**

You're in. Issue whatever commands you want. You can now conduct a full Unix Terminal session—but by remote control.

Tip: For a list of options you can use in SSH, type *ssh* at the prompt (nothing more) and press Enter.

FREQUENTLY ASKED QUESTION

Connecting Through a Router

I want to connect to my home network from the road. Trouble is, I have a router that shares my broadband modem with a bunch of Macs. How do I get into one specific Mac? It doesn't really have a "real" IP address, because the router is sharing the cable modem's signal!

It's possible—just complicated.

Most home broadband routers offer a feature called port forwarding, in which signals intended for a specific port on the router (port 22 for SSH, for example) get passed on to whichever computer on the network you've designated to receive it. (You specify this using the router's management

software.) You can specify a different machine for different ports: all port-80 communications go to one machine doing Web serving, for example; all 548 goes to another machine doing file sharing, and so on.

Even if you're enough of a technical mastermind to set up this port-forwarding business, however, you still won't be able to access two different machines using the same port. For some services, including SSH, you can work around this limitation by logging into the machine specified for port forwarding, and then from that machine, log into the others on the rest of the network.

Remote Control Program Killing

One of the most common uses of SSH is quitting a stuck program. Maybe it's a program that doesn't respond to the usual Force Quit commands—maybe even the Finder or Terminal. Or maybe, having just arrived in Accounting on the fifth floor, you realize that you accidentally left your Web browser, open to Dilbert.com, up on your screen in clear view of passersby.

In any case, you'd fire up Terminal and proceed like this (what you type is shown in bold; responses are in normal type):

```
home-mac:~ chris$ ssh 172.24.30.182

The authenticity of host '172.24.30.182 (172.24.30.182)' can't
be established. RSA key fingerprint is d9:f4:11:b0:27:1a:f1:14:
c3:cd:25:85:2b:78:4d:e7.

Are you sure you want to continue connecting (yes/no)? yes

Warning: Permanently added '172.24.30.182' (RSA) to the list of
known hosts.

chris@172.24.30.189's password: fisheggs

Last login: Thu Nov 13 17:23:38 2003

Welcome to Darwin!

office-mac:~ chris$ top
```

The *top* command displays a list of running programs. After a block of memory statistics, you might see a list like this:

```
294 top        6.5%  0:01.10  1   16   26   276K    416K   652K   27.1M

293 bash       0.0%  0:00.03  1   12   15   168K    856K   768K   18.2M

292 login      0.0%  0:00.01  1   13   37   140K    408K   492K   26.9M

291 Terminal   0.0%  0:05.50  3   60  115   2.99M   5.41M  6.59M  149M

287 HotKey     0.0%  0:00.34  4  151   78   760K    2.24M  2.67M  96.5M

283 Finder     0.0%  0:02.04  2   89  162   3.95M   17.1M  15.5M  165M

282 SystemUISe 0.9%  0:01.51  2  241  327   3.03M   7.85M  8.54M  158M

281 Dock       0.0%  0:00.24  2   77  132   780K    10.7M  2.80M  139M
```

As you can see, the Finder is process number 283. If that's the stuck program, then, you could quit it like so:

```
office-mac:~ chris$ kill 283
```

Or if you're sure of the program's exact name, just use the *killall* command with the program's name instead of its process ID. To handle a stuck Finder, you would type this:

```
office-mac:~ chris$ killall Finder
```

Either way, the Finder promptly quits (and relaunches in a healthier incarnation, you hope). You could also, at this point, type *sudo shutdown -h now* to make your Mac, elsewhere on the network, shut down. Then type in your administrator's password when Terminal prompts you. Note that this command ends, for the time being at least, your ability to control the host Mac, since once the host Mac is shut down you can't start it remotely.

If you ended your SSH session by shutting down the other Mac, you can just close the Terminal window now. Otherwise, type *exit* to complete your SSH session.

Tip: If you're intrigued by the notion of accessing your Mac from across the Net, try out Memora Server. It lets you—or selected family and friends—listen to music, open photos, or watch movies stored on your Mac OS X machine, from any Web browser on any machine. A three-week trial is available at *www.memora.com*.

FREQUENTLY ASKED QUESTION

Where Did Telnet Go?

How do I telnet into my Mac OS X machine?

telnet and *ssh* are very similar in concept. But the problem with *telnet* is that it's more susceptible to hackers. For one thing, *telnet* sends passwords without encrypting them.

The *ssh* networking program, on the other hand, is extremely secure, immune to all kinds of the hacker attacks

you may have read about: IP spoofing, IP source writing, DNS spoofing, and so on. That's why Apple replaced its *telnet* feature with *ssh* beginning in Mac OS X 10.1.

Apple also hopes that Unix-savvy Mac fans will recognize *ssh* to be a superior replacement for such remote control Unix programs as *rlogin, rsh,* and *rcp* (via *scp*), for that matter.

The Macintosh Keychain

With a topic as wide and complex as Macintosh networking, it's hard to cover every morsel of information. This Appendix zeroes in on a feature that's not quite central to networking, but can be awfully helpful if you spend a lot of time logging in and out of various user accounts: the Macintosh Keychain.

Stringing Your Passwords on the Keychain

Apple has done the world a mighty favor by inventing the *Keychain* as part of its Macintosh operation system. The concept is brilliant: whenever you log into Mac OS X and type in your password, you've typed the master code that tells the computer, "It's really me. I'm at my computer now." The Mac responds by *automatically* filling in every password blank you encounter in your networking adventures (and in your Web-surfing exploits, too, if you use a Keychain-smart browser like Safari or OmniWeb).

You can safely forget all of the passwords required for accessing the various other Macs on your network. (Of course, it's a good idea to write them down somewhere for protection and posterity, in case your hard drive dies and takes your Keychain with it or you want to buy a book on Amazon.com from your PC at work.)

Note: The Keychain feature is also included in Mac OS 9.

Because the Keychain is on all the time and memorizes most passwords automatically, it winds up being invisible for many people. (You do have to go through one step: the first time you enter a password into a dialog box, you need to turn on the checkbox asking if you want Keychain to remember this password.) Then you just go about your business, tapping into other computers on the network (Chapters 6 and 7), connecting to your iDisk (the cool chunk of online data storage space you get when you sign up for a .Mac account with Apple), and so on. Behind the scenes, the Mac quietly and courteously collects the various passwords so that you don't need to enter them again.

Tip: In Mac OS X 10.3, and later, the Keychain Access program described below has a toolbar, just like so many other Mac OS X programs. It features a white, oval toolbar *button* in the upper-right corner. Each time you ⌘-click it, you change the look of the toolbar: with or without text labels, with or without icons, large or small, and so on.

Locking and Unlocking the Keychain

When your Keychain is unlocked, you can open your password-protected FTP sites, iDisk, network servers, and so on, without ever having to tap in a password. Technically, you're supposed to enter a name and master password to "unlock" the Keychain every time you sit down and log into your Mac, thereby turning on this automatic-password feature. But Apple figured: "Hey, you've *already* entered a name and master password just by logging into the Mac, and that's good enough for us." If you work alone and are the only one to use the computer, the Keychain therefore becomes automatic, invisible, and generally wonderful.

But if you work in an office where someone else might sit down at your Mac while you're off getting an Almond Joy, you might want to *lock* either your whole Mac or the Keychain itself when you wander away to the vending machine. (Locking the Keychain doesn't require a password.) Mac OS X won't automatically fill in your passwords until you return to your desk and *unlock* the Keychain again.

You can lock the Keychain in any of several ways, each of which involves the Keychain Access program (Mac OS X: in your Applications → Utilities folder; Mac OS 9: → Control Panels → Keychain Access):

- **Lock the Keychain manually.** Click the Lock button in the toolbar of the Keychain Access window (see Figure A-1).

- **Lock the Keychain manually using the Apple menulet.** Open Keychain Access and then choose View → Show Status in Menu Bar. This gives you an always visible Keychain menu icon at the top of your screen, including a Lock Keychain command, as well as some other useful commands (like Lock Screen). Once this menu is in place you won't need to use Keychain Access again when you need to lock and unlock the Keychain.

- **Lock the Keychain automatically.** In the Keychain Access program, choose Edit → Change Settings for Keychain [your name]. The resulting dialog box lets you set up the Keychain to lock itself, say, after your Mac has been inactive for five minutes, or whenever the Mac goes to sleep. When you return to the Mac, you'll be asked to reenter your account password to unlock the Keychain, restoring your automatic-password feature.

Note: You unlock your Keychain using the same password you used to log into Mac OS X, but that's just a convenience. If you're really worried about security, you can choose Edit → Change Password for Keychain [your name], thereby establishing a *different* password for your Keychain, so that it no longer matches your login password. Of course, doing so also turns off the automatic-Keychain-unlocking-when-you-log-in feature.

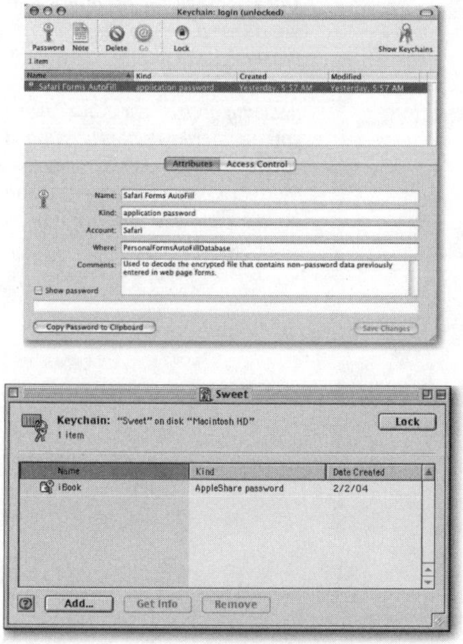

Figure A-1:
Top: You can use the Keychain Access program to see the passwords stored in the Keychain. Click any row that's listed to see more information about that entry in the Attributes window.

Bottom: The Mac OS 9 version of the Keychain manager. To get more information about a Keychain entry, click it and press the Get Info button. From there, you can view the password.

Managing Keychains

To take a look at your Keychain, open the Keychain Access program as described in the previous section. When you click one of the password rows, you get to see its *attributes*—the name, the kind, the account, and so on (Figure A-1). At this point, if you're running Mac OS X, you can turn on "Show password" to see the actual password that's stored safely here in the Keychain. In Mac OS 9, select the name of the Keychain item and press the Get Info button. Then, from the dialog box, click View Password.

Getting OS X Keychain Information

You can also click the Access Control tab, which gives you even more control over the security settings (see Figure A-2).

Tip: The primary purpose of the Keychain is, of course, to type in passwords for you automatically. However, it's also an excellent place to record all kinds of private information just for your own reference: credit card numbers, ATM numbers, and so on. Just click the Access Control tab, then click the Add button.

No, the Mac won't type them in for you automatically anywhere, but it does maintain them in one central location that is, itself, password protected.

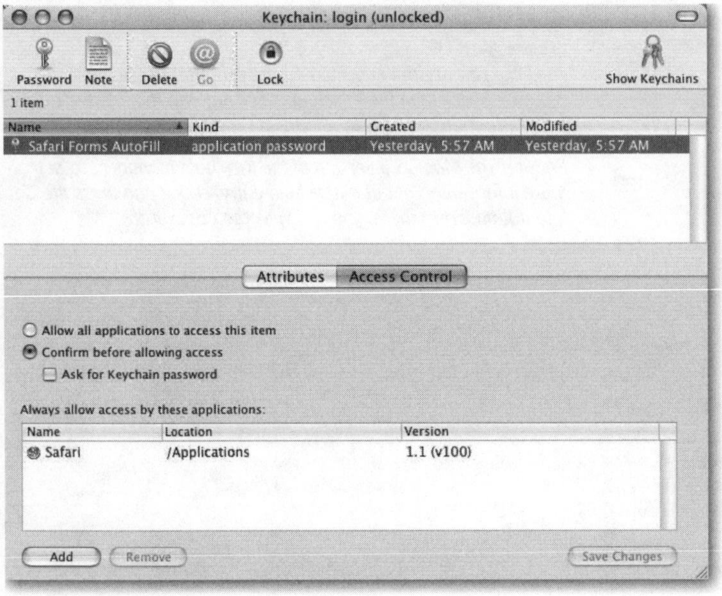

Figure A-2:
This panel lists the programs that are allowed to "see" this password—yet another degree of security. The "Confirm before allowing access" checkbox gives you another layer of protection. If you turn on the checkbox here, Mac OS X asks you for permission before filling in a password for you automatically.

Using Multiple Keychains

By choosing File → New → New Keychain (or File → New Keychain in Mac OS 9), you can create more than one Keychain, each with its own master password. On one hand, this might defeat the Zen-like simplicity of the Keychain. On the *other* hand, it's possible that you might want to encrypt all of your business documents with one master password and all of your personal stuff with another, for instance.

Tip: If you do have more than one Keychain, click the Keychain's toolbar icon to make a "drawer," which lists all Keychains on the Mac and displays them on a sliding panel on the side of the main window. Double-click the Keychain names to switch among them.

Finding Your Keychain Files

Keychains are represented by separate files in your Home folder → Library → Keychains folder. Knowing where the Keychains hang out can be handy in several circumstances:

- **Deleting a Keychain.** You can delete a Keychain easily enough—just drag a Keychain file out of this folder and into the Trash.

- **Copying a Keychain.** You can copy one of your Keychain files into the corresponding location on another computer, such as your laptop. It carries with it all the password information for the networks and Web sites of your life.

Multiple User Accounts in Mac OS 9

Mac OS 9 was the first version of the Mac OS to support Multiple User accounts: the tidy and secure system in which every account holder who logs onto a computer gets his own distinct version of files, folders, settings, and so on.

Unlike the File Sharing accounts you learned about back in Chapter 6, Multiple User accounts don't have any influence over what happens when visitors tap into a Mac from across the network. Multiple User accounts only control what happens when different people log on, in person, to the same computer. (Geeks call that *local access,* versus the *remote access* that takes place when you log on from across the network.) Still, these Multiple User accounts are useful to know about, and this Appendix will give you a quick introduction to these kinds of accounts in Mac OS 9.

Note: In Mac OS X, Multiple User accounts and File Sharing accounts were (thankfully) merged. In Mac OS X, your user account takes care of both your local access and your remote access needs.

Creating a New Multiple User Account

Mac OS 9 doesn't automatically start you out with Multiple User accounts. You've first got to flip a virtual switch on your computer to activate the account system. To do so open → Control Panels → Multiple Users and click the On button at the bottom of the dialog box (Figure B-1).

To create a new account, click the New User button. Up pops an Edit "New User" dialog box (Figure B-2) which asks you for the following information.

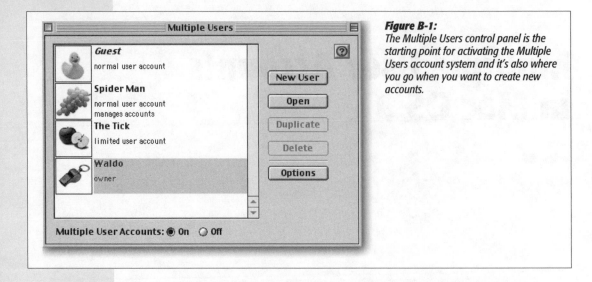

Figure B-2:
The New User dialog box. The Applications and Privileges tabs are enabled only if you select the Limited or Panels account types.

- **User Name.** Mac OS 9 uses the user name, which can be up to 31 characters long, to identify each account.

- **Password.** If the Mac you're using is in your house and you trust your family, or you're in a small company, keep things simple by assigning either no password or something pretty easy to remember. Of course, if you're in a large company where you don't know who else might use the Mac, use something a little harder to figure out.

- **Kind of User Account.** Mac OS 9 lets you assign one of three user account types.

Note: There is a fourth account type known as the *Owner* account. There can be only one Owner and it's always the first account you set up on your Mac. The Owner account is all-seeing and all-knowing, and no one is allowed to mess with it..

A **Normal user** can do pretty much anything except mess around with the Owner's account and with other people's stuff. At its inception, a Normal user can access the Finder and all applications on the startup disk. If you opt to grant a Normal user the "Can manage user account" privilege (see below), the newly created user has the power to do just that. They can create, delete, and modify all user accounts (except the Owner's account).

A **Limited user** can view the contents of the hard disk, but can't run any programs unless the Owner or a Normal user with the appropriate privileges has granted her permission to do so. Furthermore, a Limited user can save files only to her own Documents folder unless you, the all-powerful Owner, grant her rights to other folders.

Finally, the lowliest of the account types—**Panels**—provides one-click access to only those items (files, folders, and programs) that you, the Owner, provide to them. These users can save files only in their Documents folder. These accounts are good for really young children or anyone else whose choices you want to restrict in a big way.

- **User Info options.** The options here give you additional control over what the new user can and can't do on your Mac. You can change the profile picture for the new user by using the up and down arrows next to the User Picture.

Tip: If you're not seeing the bottom half of the Edit "New User" dialog box, click the flippy triangle in the lower-left corner that says Show Setup Details.

Below that, you see four other options. Turn on the **User can change password** checkbox to let the account holder change his own password.

If you're mad at your wife and decide you don't want to let her use your Mac anymore, you can prevent her from logging in by turning off the **Can log in** checkbox. Once you make up, come back here and turn this option back on.

Depending on the account type you select, the next option—**Can manage user accounts**—may or may not be grayed out. This option is available only to the Owner and to Normal account holders. If you've opted to create a Limited or Panels account, you don't even get the chance to grant this privilege. Users with the "Can manage user accounts" checkbox turned on are allowed to completely manage all other user accounts (except for the Owner account).

Finally, if you want to create a hard barrier between each of your users, *don't* turn on the **Access by others to user's documents** checkbox. When turned off, only the Owner and the new user have the ability to access this account holder's work. If you *do* want others to be able to access this person's stuff, you have three access options: "Read only," "Write only," and "Read & Write." "Read only" lets others just *look* at the user's work. If they want to *change* anything, they need to copy it to their own workspace. "Write only" lets people put new files into this user's folder but doesn't let them see what's already there. Lastly, "Read & Write" grants full access by all other users to this account holder's files.

- **The Applications tab.** If you've created a Limited or Panels account, the Applications tab becomes active. Keep in mind that unless you actually go to this tab and choose one or more programs, the new user won't be able to run anything! On this tab is a list of every program on the computer with checkboxes next to each entry. If you'd like to let an account holder use an application, turn on the checkbox next to the program's name.

- **The Privileges tab.** Again, only the lowly Limited and Panels users have this tab enabled. At the top of this window is a big box labeled "Allow access to." Inside the box, you see a series of checkboxes with such tantalizing options as CD/DVD-ROMs, the Shared Folder, Control Panels, and so on. Here's what you can do on this tab:

Turn off the **CD/DVD-ROMs** checkbox to prevent the user from inserting a CD or DVD into the Mac and playing it. Likewise, if you have a Zip drive or other type of drive, turn off the **Other removable media** checkbox if you don't want the account holder to use those, either. Want to disable the account holder's access to the **Shared Folder**? Turn off the Shared Folder checkbox. If you're concerned about an account holder accessing other computers on the network, turn off the **Chooser and Network Browser** checkbox. If you're worried about the user messing around with the local Mac's settings, shut down access to the **Control Panels**. To prevent the user from using programs listed in the Apple menu, turn off the **Other Apple Menu Items.**

Finally, if you don't want the user to print, turn off the **User Can Print** checkbox. If you'd like her to print but want her to print to a specific printer, leave the User Can Print checkbox turned on and just select the appropriate printer from the **Allowed Printer** drop-down menu.

- **Alternate Password.** This option is for users who want to speak a phrase rather than type in a password. To enable this option, first go to the main Multiple Users dialog box (→ Control Panels → Multiple Users), click the Options button, and then turn on the Allow Alternate Password checkbox. Next, return to the user's account and click the Alternate Password tab. Turn on the "This user will use the alternate password" checkbox, click the Create Voiceprint button, and then follow the instructions to set up a speakable password.

Logging In Using a Multiple User Account

To log into your Mac after taking care of all this account creation business, click the correct user name from the list that appears when you start your computer (Figure B-3, top). Then click the Log In button. If you have a password associated with the user, the password dialog box (Figure B-3, bottom) pops up. If you type the wrong password, the box shudders and you'll need to try again.

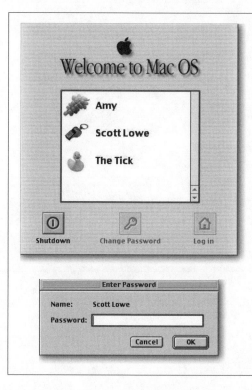

Figure B-3:
Top: Once the Multiple Users option is turned on and you have more than a single user, the login window appears each time you start up your Mac or when you log out (Special → Logout).

Bottom: For password-protected accounts, Mac OS 9 pops up a little box and cheerfully asks you to enter your password. If you enter the wrong password, the window shudders and lets you try again.

Index

Colophon

Jamie Peppard was production editor and proofreader for *Home Networking: The Missing Manual*. Linley Dolby was the copy editor. Marlowe Shaeffer and Claire Cloutier provided quality control. Johnna VanHoose Dinse wrote the index.

Ellie Volckhausen designed the cover of this book, based on a series design by David Freedman. Karen Montgomery produced the cover layout with Adobe InDesign CS using Adobe's Minion and Gill Sans fonts.

David Futato designed the interior layout, based on a series design by Phil Simpson. This book was converted by Andrew Savikas from Microsoft Word to FrameMaker 5.5.6. The text font is Adobe Minion; the heading font is Adobe Formata Condensed; and the code font is LucasFont's TheSans Mono Condensed. The illustrations that appear in the book were produced by Robert Romano, Jessamyn Read, and Lesley Borash using Macromedia FreeHand MX and Adobe Photoshop CS.

Better than e-books

Buy *Home Networking: The Missing Manual*
and access the digital edition FREE on
Safari for 45 days.

Go to www.oreilly.com/go/safarienabled
and type in coupon code BHGM-NVWI-Z1HQ-D2ID-HRCE

Search
over 2000 top
tech books

Download
whole chapters

Cut and Paste
code examples

Find
answers fast

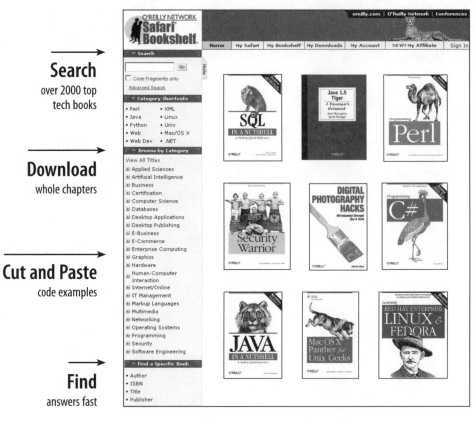

Search Safari! The premier electronic reference
library for programmers and IT professionals